Elder Wisdom Circle
Volume I

Elder Wisdom Circle
Volume I

❖

Letters, Guidance and Advice from America's Elders

Blanche Anderson

Writers Club Press

San Jose New York Lincoln Shanghai

Elder Wisdom Circle Volume I
Letters, Guidance and Advice from America's Elders

Writers Club Press
an imprint of iUniverse, Inc.

For information address:
iUniverse, Inc.
5220 S. 16th St., Suite 200
Lincoln, NE 68512
www.iuniverse.com

ISBN: 0-595-24909-4

Printed in the United States of America

Dedicated to the Elders of EWC

On behalf of those who have requested advice, wisdom and consideration from the Elders of **Elder Wisdom Circle**, thank you for your time, compassion and energy. Each letter is a unique snapshot of American life and experience. From teenage angst to starting new midlife careers, from relationship issues to orchid care, the people who come to EWC for help are gratified by the care, attention and love in each response.

Please visit us at **www.ElderWisdomCircle.org**.

Contents

List of Contributors

Elders
Dispensing Advice, Compassion and Consideration Across the United States
The Elders are volunteer senior citizens who offer their lifelong learning, wisdom and compassion through the Elder Wisdom Circle to anyone with a question. Their insight, experiences and reflection on the issues and concerns facing people of all ages provide an extraordinary opportunity for anyone to learn and grow through these online interactions.

Sharon L. Morrison
Progress Administrator, Elder Wisdom Circle
Married for over forty years, we have three children, one granddaughter, two cats, and live happily in a Philadelphia suburb. Although I've lived in this area since I was 18, I consider myself a Southerner and a true Virginian. My pleasures in life include my family, friends, and home, reading, writing, gardening, cooking, volunteering, interior design, small silver collecting, studying and learning. My involvement with the Elder Wisdom Circle is very rewarding to me.

Chelsea Wind
Project Designer, Elder Wisdom Circle
I have lived in San Francisco, CA for two years. I am a freelance copy-editor and work at the University of San Francisco. I am very involved with my three brothers and three sisters and consider my family to be my best friends and closest allies. I am motivated and moved by the goals and values of Elder Wisdom Circle, especially in terms of creating community using new technologies. I would like to dedicate my involvement in this project to my Bubbe, Minnie Goldrath, who

taught me to listen to my elders and to commit myself to meaningful work within my community.

Foreword

By Doug Meckelson, Founder
Elder Wisdom Circle

Founded in October 2001, *Elder Wisdom Circle* accepts any request on any subject (but of course refrains from offering specific legal, tax, investment or medical advice). Why waste money on psychic hotlines or other unreliable sources? We advise with our experience and knowledge. Most cultures around the world seek the advice of their elders above all others, now we all can too!

At *Elder Wisdom Circle* our mission is to share elder know-how and accumulated wisdom. Our goal for the advice-seeker is that the experience be similar to getting advice e-mail from a trusted family member.

We operate as a membership not-for-profit organization and invite you to enjoy our service.

Just go to **www.ElderWisdomCircle.org**

Preface

By Blanche Anderson
Editor-In-Chief, Elder Wisdom Circle
Blanche is a fictional representative of the EWC Elders and serves as the volunteer Cyber-Editor-In-Chief. Blanche is the voice of the Elder Wisdom Circle. She acts as our Virtual Editor and as an icon to our online community.

As volunteer Editor-In-Chief of the Elder Wisdom Circle, I welcome you to the EWC as a reader and future participant. As a widow with two adult children and five grandchildren, the simple pleasures of daily life are the most satisfying moments to me. Elder Wisdom Circle fulfills my lifelong dream of combining unity, cooperation, technology and writing with creating an arena for people to take advantage of the wisdom of elders in our society.

In order to continue to implement the mission of Elder Wisdom Circle (EWC), I am pleased to bring you *Elder Wisdom Circle: Volume I.* EWC is an online community made up of elders from all across the United States answering requests for advice, help and support. Queries arrive in our email queue from folks of all ages and walks of life, and are responded to by the community of elders that make up the EWC.

I hope you find this selection of the best of EWC as moving and insightful as I do. The broad range of subjects addressed, as well as some of the true connections made between questioner and elder, make the letters compelling reading to all of us here at EWC. It's been my privilege to read and share these nuggets of wisdom from my peers, and I have faith that you will enjoy them too. Please visit us at

www.elderwisdomcircle.org

to become a part of the Elder Wisdom Circle by joining our online community, asking a question or simply looking at the Circle's offerings.

Best regards,

Blanche

> *Where no counsel is, the people fall;*
> *but in the multitude of counselors there is safety.*
>
> —— Proverbs 11:14

Introduction

Welcome to Elder Wisdom Circle: The Book. *Yes, we know that there are some misspellings and errors!* All letters appear exactly as written and answered, in order to retain the flavor, attitude, and interaction just as they occurred online. Therefore, all typos, errors and biting advice are included just as they were written.

Here is how it works...

The request e-mail is routed to our database and a Senior Citizen who has a relevant or appropriate life experience will reply. The Elder's response will arrive **exactly** as written by the Elder. Each Elder is a unique person who responds to each request as he or she sees best. Subsequent e-mails will be replied to by the best-matched Elder (no one is assigned one specific Elder). If anyone wishes a second opinion they may feel free to resubmit their question.

Anyone may request advice on a personal issue, marriage, relationship, children, home, garden, career or even health/home remedies, really anything. All writers remain anonymous to the Elder so each writer may feel free to ask any questions, as they like. A personalized response arrives via e-mail within 10 days.

To seek advice simply log onto:

www.ElderWisdomCircle.org

...then from the "seek advice" page click on "seek advice" near the top of the page.

1

Work and Career

Stick With The Job

Dear Elders,

I work for a technology company that has gone through some hard times, and my personal life has been a real struggle over the past year. I don't like my job and frequently have fantasies where I quit, never to return. I am, however, the main salary in our household, and need to stick with it, at least for another 6 months to a year.

I have thought frequently during my struggles to keep focused and attempts at being content of how past generations didn't have any choice either when it came to careers—the job was what brought food to your table, and not necessarily the most compelling part of your life. I see this as a compromise, but am realistic enough to know that it's as necessary a one for me as it was for past generations.

I am 11 years out of college, and have worked for a total of 5 companies (longest tenure was 4 years). My peers (especially those in technology) have all had this amount of movement in their careers. We're used to being able to move on when things go the wrong way or when the company hits a rough patch. If things were different in the economy and in my personal life, I would most certainly look to change jobs now.

I would like to have an understanding of how office workers in the past stayed with one company for 20 or more years. How did that work? How did you motivate yourself? There must have been ups and downs over the course of that many years—how did you manage the 'downs'?

Thank you.

Elder Response

Hi, thanks for writing. I disagree that previous generations who had no choice of careers "compromised" by staying in jobs that were not compelling, JUST to bring food to the table. This is an incredible diminution of what those generations believed to be a holy responsibility—supporting their own families, not taking from others; doing the best with what they could get and keep trying; being a burden to no one as long as they could work.

Strangely enough, what kept most of us at work on a job that carried sparce financial gratification was something called "work ethic," that used to be common. It is doing the best one can in whatever job we find ourselves, because our time on that job belongs to our employer, who pays us to do that job. It was a matter of personal pride that we were appreciated in our devotion and our clear goal of doing well. That mattered just as much as earning a living for those who could find a measure of contentment in the job.

Today the measure of contentment appears to be money—sometime how much you can get by giving as little as you must to an employer. I understand some of the reasons this is true today, but I don't understand why any job is not a source of gratification to the person doing it.

What you will learn is that you will have to adjust to life as it is today, whether you like it or not, whether you had it better a few years ago, or whether it will get worse. In any case, you will have to adjust. Whether you are happy or contented in doing so is entirely up to you; you will decide whether to be happy or disgruntled, sullen and angry. You might find you have to compromise, and then you will have to decide whether you can see that as necessary for survival, or something to regret and fret about all your life. This is always your choice.

Good luck.

Arianne

Eager To Make My Stamp On The World

Dear Elders,

Hello. I'm lost. I'm 22 years old and have great hopes and ambitions for doing something great in/for this world—but I have no idea what. So many people tell me one might never know what he/she wants to do, but I cannot accept that. I believe everyone has a passion; there's a distinct characteristic in all individuals that makes them exceptional. Whether you recognize that trait in yourself or not will determine your path in life, and I am wandering aimlessly. I would like to know how to find my passion. I have acquired many hobbies trying, but still haven't found that certain something that I love to do. I don't want to waste any more time! Thank you for your time in advising me!

Elder Response

Hello,

How about sitting quietly with yourself and asking yourself this questions:

1. If money were no object, what would you like to be doing in the next 20 years? Listen quietly for the answer, the voice may be small, but it's there.

2. What special gift/talent do you have that no one else has in exactly the same way you do? That little voice, when answered humbly and honestly, can direct you to a path in your life.

If the answers don't come right away, ask them again and again and they will come when you're ready to hear them, I believe. Instead of rushing around trying out more and more hobbies, the key is getting yourself in a quiet place and asking your...heart

Best regards,

Cindy

Regaining Focus At Work

Dear Elders,

I've been under a lot of personal stress recently. My daughter has a serious illness and I've been having conflicts with my husband. In addition, there has been a lot of turmoil at work with constantly shifting priorities. The stress at home and the fear that my work priorities will keep changing is making it difficult for me to stay focused at work. I've been getting very little accomplished recently. Any suggestions on how I can regain some focus while I'm at work?

Elder Response

Hello,

Staying focused at work is difficult when we have other problems vying for our attention. How about writing down a few sentences before you leave for work that remind you that work is what you'll focus on for the next 8 hours or so. This is a gentle reminder that all things have their place in our lives and it may help you to remain focused. When at work and a stressful idea or thought appears, take one minute and do deep breaths ten times—this clears the mind/spirit and helps to refocus you. At lunchtime, don't think about anything (not work, not family)…just relax, take a bit of fresh air, walk slowly for 5 minutes. These also help reduce stress.

Best regards,

Jack

Parents & My Employment Search

Dear Elders,

In these times I'm sure that there have been numerous requests for advice on career and job finding issues...

However I think my situation is a little different, and having an outsider's view on it might give a little perspective.

I was a medical student at Cornell Medical School until August of last year (2001). For a year previous to that I was on medical leave of absence due to Clinical Depression.

My wife, a wonderful person, felt that New York City was too stressful of a location for me. Through her law firm, she found a position here in Austin, and arranged for us to move down. It worked wonders and now I'm ready to rejoin real life again...

The problem is this: I seem to be either overqualified or underqualified for every position that I apply for!! This is starting to drive me to distraction. My parents, constantly hound me about getting a job until I can reapply to a medical program. And Honestly I am trying...

I've applied to a full range of positions...and the problem with the lower end ones, such as a local bookstore, is that they don't seem to believe my educational background...or feel that I'd only be there short term, which is true.

I don't qualify for workforstudents.com jobs.

I don't have an MD...and what is worse, I have a period of illness that may cause employers not to consider me.

I'm stuck in employment limbo.

Any advice or encouragement or perspective would be great.

Thanks for your time.

Elder Response

Hello,

How great to hear that the move to Texas, among other things, helped with your depression! I'm not sure how many years of Med school you have, but you're in almost the same position as many young people who (I assume) majored in the sciences a few years ago and entered the job market, while you chose med school.

From my experiences as a college professor, this suggests that you might be able to land a job with a drug manufacturing company, a research company or similar work that looks for recently graduated science majors. Have you also considred a job in the health field working for a non-profit? There are many positions in medical and health-related fields that require a B.S. degree but not an M.D.—technical, administrative, human resources, research, etc.

Also, have you considered teaching science for a year or so? Science teachers are in great demands in most parts of the country and I'm sure you could find a private school where having an education degree is not required. I'd check into that option too.

Finally, why your parents are badgering you about a job is beyond me. You are an adult, have had a tough medical crisis, are married, etc. and they seem to be treating you like a child! Hope you don't spend too much letting this bother you. You have come through a difficult time and need all the support you can get. Being unemployed isn't easy in the best of circumstances, so…take it easy, keep healing, and good luck with your job search…

Best regards,

Cindy

Help Starting a Business

Dear Elders,

I am starting a business and don't know the first thing about buying wholesale to sell retail. I am creating cards, invitations, key chains, calendars, little books, montages, etc. using customer's photos. I need to buy stock paper, key chains, ink, lamination supplies etc. Where do I go to do this? I live in CT, so how do I go about taxing people? I've applied for my business license with the Revenue board so I'll be eligible to sell. HELP...

Elder Response

Are you familiar with SCORE [Service Corps of Retired Executives] a volunteer organization sponsored by the SBA [Small Business Administration]

I suggest that you run the concept past a SCORE counselor. You can find a local chapter by calling 800-634-0245. They will also be able to direct you to an e-mail site, should you care to go that route.

The price of the service is right! It's FREE!!

Best wishes,

Frank

Military Service?

Dear Elders,

Hello. I am considering military service as a way of repaying a portion of what I owe to those who have worked so hard to make this country what it is. My only reservation is the separation from my son. He is 18 months old. I have a strong desire to do more than go to work and add to my employers bottom line and bring home a paycheck. I also have great reservations about leaving my son fatherless for the duration of my service. A boy in his teens I could explain to why I have to do what I have to do. I believe a young man can understand that. A three year commitment would leave my son without a father for the greater part of his life until he's nearly school aged. I'm not exactly the youngest of men to be considering service. I'm 25. If I delay entry into national service I fear I might be disqualified based on my age. Is there anyone who has been in my sons position, with a father mostly away from home than at home? How has this effected you? I do know that serving my country will serve my son. I just fear for the future of my child…in particular the effect my being away will have on him.

Elder Response

Well, hard to answer these kinds of letters because there are some questions to ask and I can't ask them. So I have to try to answer for each contingency.

First, where's his mother? Are you all still together? If not, don't go into the military. Today's military requires you to give up custody to someone else. Every case I've seen, I served 26 years, was not good. There are other ways to serve, through volunteer organizations, that are every bit as important as the military.

If you and your wife are together, and are planning on this, then what is it that makes you feel like you'll be out of his life? The military is not as bad as the media makes it out to be, depending on the service. Don't go Navy or Marines. Go Army or Air Force. I recommend Army of course. The Air Force it is much harder to make rank, and there for money. The Army is big enough to need a lot of people at a lot of ranks. Faster moving up.

If you join the Army then it depends on the job that you select. That also depends on your overall outlook on the military. If your only going to stay for the first hitch, then get a job that will train you in a skill that will be marketable when you get out. Electronics has traditionally been the best. Nowadays computers is even better.

If you are thinking about it as a career then go into Armor or Infantry. These are the fastest jobs to move up in rank.

Regardless of what job you pick, you'll go off to basic training and advance individual training. During this time you're not allowed to bring your family. It generally only lasts a few months, but depends on the job that you pick. Some require extensive training and can be as long as a year.

After this you will be sent to your first assignment. Generally there is a high chance that this will be overseas. Normally Germany or Korea. If it's Germany, you're in great luck. Can take the family, Army will pay their expenses, etc. and a chance to travel in Europe. If it's Korea then chances are you won't be able to take the family at Army expense, but I've gone twice and paid for my family's way and had a great time both times.

If you are one of the few who gets a stateside assignment for your first assignment, then the Army will move your family from where they are to where you'll be.

Normally, you are home every day except for field exercises and deployments. Field exercises last from a week to six weeks and deployments can be a month to a year. On those, of course, your family doesn't go. However, in a 26 year career, I've spent only about two years in areas where my family couldn't go. Add in field exercises and deployments out of the whole 26 years I've been away around 5 years. Not as bad as it may seem to outsiders.

Again, bottom line, if you're married and your wife and son will be moving around with you, then don't worry so much about being away. Yes, there will be times, and some may be long, but he is young and long before it's an impact you'll be back. I had six kids, and they've all turned out fine.

If you're single and have to give up your son, I don't recommend it. In that case then yes, you'll be away from him for at least 3 years and by the time you're back he'll have a hard time remembering you. Serve your country by help others in your local community.

Hope this helps.

Tom

23 & Totally Lost!

Dear Elders,

I left my first post-college job in November b/c of issues with my new boss (a heinous, manipulative monster). I can't use her as a reference. My bills are due, I'm not getting job offers, and am becoming increasingly depressed. Help! I don't want my $100,000 education (liberal arts) to go down the drain!

Elder Response

Thanks for writing. My first boss once said to me, "NEVER leave a job badly, because sooner or later it will hurt you."

You have discovered that is very true. A boss is a boss, and if you can't get along with that boss, it's past time you look for another. You hurt only yourself if you try a power struggle.

I suppose you'll have to mention that there was a serious personality conflict with your former boss and hope that prospective employers will accept that it sometimes happens. Then, when you do get a job, be very, very certain that this doesn't happen again.

Is there no chance that you can get a reference from someone else in the company, or that your former boss absolutely won't give you one? You might try both again and see if you can get one.

Don't try to hide this episode, but be brief, clear, free of rancor or blame, and short about it. In time, you will find another job because you have the education and probably the motivation to go forward.

Best wishes and good luck,

Julia

No Job, No Money, No Self-Esteem

Dear Elders,

At 43 with no degree except a High School diploma. It seems very hard for me to find a job. I started back to school to gain confidence in my abilities except my Algebra class has defeated that purpose. There are no more tears to shed, I have no vision or goals to give me the encouragement I need.

Elder Response

Hello,

Good for you that you started back to school! Algebra is a rough one for most of us…it defeated me, but in most schools you can try to substitute another course. If not, you can still continue your education and leave that class to later on when you can get some tutoring. I'm not sure if you're in a college or technical institute but regardless, you seem to have lost your confidence. This is the real barrier to getting ahead, and like any other problem in life, it's important to not let setbacks stop us cold. As the saying goes, when that horse throws us, we brush ourselves off and get back on. Sure, it isn't easy, but we can do it! Set some goal for yourself…make it small, do-able and attain it, then set another small goal and do that. It's really important to also get support from folks close to you so find those with a positive attitude and hang with them. If you don't have them in your life, that's another goal.

We all have something we do that we're good at…find that thing, and make it your vision…see yourself as getting better at something you're already good at.

best of luck and let us know how things are going.

David

Entering New Phase In Life

Dear Elders,

I just turned 30 and am facing a bit of a dilemma regarding the next phase of my life. I am currently finishing a part-time research and writing job and am closing down an internet company I started 2 1/2 years ago, which failed to make money but was a success in many other ways. I would desperately like to have children and settle down (I am happily married) and have decided to take the summer off from all work to relax and try to get pregnant. I am worried, however, that it might take some time, and if so, I should have been working on my career skills rather than volunteering/spending time with family and friends. My husband is very supportive and thinks it's great that I take some time off (I won't work when we have kids), but I am nervous about 'wasting my time' if it takes a year or more to become pregnant and i should be contributing to our bank account. What should I do? Am I being over anxious? I just want to feel good about this decision so I can enjoy my summer off from work.

Thank you for 'listening.'

Elder Response

Hello,

Thanks for writing. It sounds like you have a bit of anxiety/guilt about this next stage of life, but it could also be the most wonderful thing for you to do for yourself and your future family! You've given lots to your career and you can maintain/enhance those skills by volunteering too. I've learned as much from volunteering as I have from my professional associations for sure.

If money is a concern, you can freelance/work part-time. If you just feel guilty, maybe you can work on letting go of this guilt by recognizing that you have been doing the homemaking job as well as your career! Take this sabbatical for yourself, this summer, relax, do something different from your usual routine, and give back something to your community. You'll be doing just fine by the end of the summer, methinks, if you let go of the guilt and fear.

best of luck,

Linda

What Is Honor?

Dear Elders,

I left my job last week after 5+ years. It was a hard decision given these economic times but my marriage was suffering and I was burnt out. Still I wanted to leave with honor, to hold my head high and know I had given it all I could.

My company has taken a different stand and has been less than honorable when it comes to the way I've been treated since I left. This is eating at me because of all the extra hours I put in and the good things I did. Can't anyone look beyond him or herself and just be happy for another person. I don't know why in this day and age it's no longer about the job you did but what someone else didn't do. I see it all the time, no one takes responsibility, I see walls of incompetence being build and I see people getting hurt.

Part of me says this is a self-confidence thing but it's more than that. My generation is so unwilling to admit that they made a mistake and if you don't make mistakes you don't learn. I'd just like to not have walls built up I've worked my entire life bring understanding but in the end ego gets in the way and this makes me sad.

I going to take the summer off and learn to Exhale but when I go back to the work place I wonder will it be the same? Is there honor or should I stop dreaming.

Thank you for your time.

Elder Response

I hate to burst your bubble, but that is the reality in the business world today. There is no such thing as honor. It is all about the short run and the bottom line. People are a resource and nothing more. When I first entered the working world, I was taught that if you worked hard and were loyal to a company, the company would take care of you. That is long gone. Nevertheless, I survived in this atmosphere for more years than I want to remember. I have to admit that I am much happier in retirement. My suggestion to you is to find fulfillment outside of the workplace. The job is only a means to an end in today's business climate. If you keep trying to find honor in the business world, you are headed for disappointment.

Best regards,

John

Betty is Inspiring...

Dear Elders,

I read the article on the "featured elder" and was inspired. I am a second year elementary school teacher and would like to know how Betty did it? I am teaching second grade and am having a hard time balancing my work and social life. I seem to be spending so much time working that I don't have time for much of anything else. My poor husband...we have only been married for a little over a year...has told me that I give all of my time and patience to my students. What do you think?

Elder Response

Hi there. You are living your life, but not managing it. Unfortunately, you're in the majority in this country, and most are unhappy about the proportions of work and relaxation.

You have the ability to change your life and get more social time back, but it requires a tremendous amount of wanting to do so, and it's not easy. I definitely think your marriage deserves more attention, if your husband feels you give all your time—and patience—to your students. They will grow up and go away, but I hope your husband will be with you forever.

I worked for many years in demanding jobs but still found time for my husband, my children, my huge house, my social activities, my civic works, my volunteer work and free time pleasure. This was in the days when women were still fighting for equal rights, and it was very difficult for those of us who were in the front lines.

Absolutely it takes an enormous amount of planning and desire to do so much, but I felt the only life I was sure of living was well worth it. You are making, every minute, the decision to live as you do. I in no way am trivializing your job and career; I know it is very important to you, as it was for me, and should be.

Now that I have the time to ponder my life, I find that the most important and happy times have been in my relationships with my family, friends and other people, without exception. All that I accomplished makes me proud, but people make me happy. It is a shame today that so many women think they have to sacrifice their personal life to have a career. It just isn't so, and you're cheating yourself, your husband, your friends and your possible future children unless you come to some arrangement with yourself that allows a full life.

As an example, I once told an executive who complained to me that he never had time to do what he wanted to do at the office because people kept interrupting him. I guaranteed him an hour a day without interruptions so he could do what he wanted. For one day he did it, then announced it simply wouldn't work because he had to be available all the time. He had the free hour, no one suffered, no more work appeared, nothing bad happened because he wasn't available for an hour. But he couldn't accept that he was not so important that he couldn't take an hour out of his day for what he wanted to do.

There is always time available if we make it so, until we run out of time at the end of our life.

I think not having patience with others because of the lifestyle we choose is a very dangerous act; our loved ones certainly deserve our patience. I hope you can change your situation before you lose much more of your life being overwhelmed. Best of luck.

Joanne

Now That I'm The Breadwinner...

Dear Elders,

I'm a 40-year-old woman married to a recently unemployed disabled military veteran. When I was in my 20s and 30s, I had a professional career as a publications manager in state government. I gave that up, gladly, when I found I had melanoma. (Luckily, it was caught in time.) I just felt that I was not doing much to help anyone, and I wasn't enjoying my life or my work.

I moved in with an elderly couple who are dear friends; their lives were in transition and they needed someone in the house to help with chores and writing. Six months later, my husband found me.

For the first two years of our marriage, he was my rock. He had a good job that paid well, and although we had moved 4,000 miles away from friends and family, we were making a life here together. All of that gradually fell apart: first we had a devastating house fire, then his health began to deteriorate, and finally he lost his job about six months ago.

When we got together, I made it clear that I'd had my career and didn't want that kind of life again. Instead, I wanted to do work that I enjoyed and that was meaningful, no matter how little it paid. Because he was well-paid and had great benefits, it didn't matter.

All that is a long-winded intro to my question:

How can I get back into a well-paying job after spending nearly a decade doing work that others consider "menial"? I have been a silversmith, I've clerked in a country store, and for the past 2 1/2 years I've been a respite worker for elders. Unfortunately, that position pays little and is considered on-call, so it has no benefits and no set hours.

I must find some way to support us, because my husband's disability check covers our mortgage and that's all. He also has a sizeable child support payment, plus considerable credit card debt.

I've applied for many positions, but I've had not one interview yet. I know that my age and the gap between now and my "career" days are working against me, but I don't know how to overcome them. I'm also very unsure where I fit into the job market anymore, and since I live in Alaska, opportunities are very limited.

Any advice will be a great help…I'd welcome everything from specific job-seeking advice to advice on how to maintain my relationship with my husband in these trying times. Stress is a big problem for both of us.

Thanks so much.

Elder Response

thank you for this oppurtunity to advise. my advise would be:take a darn good look at government again. it is a pretty fertile field right now. especially in the security field. with experience in that area you might find some thing that fits into your life pretty well.websites are pretty fruitful.i am retired but am taking a real look at many of the good ones i am finding.

Best regards,

Frank

Law School vs. Teaching

Dear Elders,

I am currently a college student. I would like to be a lawyer because I know that lawyers get paid a lot and that they are always looked upon prestigiously. However, deep down in my heart, I would like to be an elementary school teacher. I love working with kids and I feel fulfilled when I do. The thing that is holding me back from pursuing teaching is the low salary. Especially with the high prices in the Bay Area I wouldn't know how to survive and live the life I want. What should I do? I would be really grateful for your help.

Elder Response

Hi,

It would appear that the ONLY reason you are considering a career in Law is the potentiality of substantial financial reward and prestige.

On the other hand, you appear to have passion for teaching.

Since money and prestige alone rarely bring happiness I would say that teaching is an odds-on favorite to bring you job satisfaction and fulfillment. Moreover, teachers' salaries are [now] quite respectable, and more so for those who hold a masters, and [at least in this area] 30 credits toward a PhD. Furthermore, since teaching is but a 10 month job, there is opportunity to supplement income in the summer.

I suggest that you look to your local bar association for direction to a public-spirited attorney willing to give you fifteen minutes of his time in order to point out the trials and tribulations not uncommon to a career in law—especially in the early stages.

Best of luck,

Peter

Feel Like Time Is Running Out

Dear Elders,

Well at age 37 I am once again hunting for employment. I was the victim of a company lay off after 12 years about two years ago, and we(my daughter and I)lived off of my 401k for that first year.Now that is gone.I also had some savings but that is gone too.This past year I held several part-time jobs, and just finished a contract that was from September to end of December.They say they want to hire me but all new hires are being frozen right now. I can't wait forever, but I really want to work for this company they are one of a kind.I know I have to look elsewhere at the same time but the bills are coming in,and the stress is hitting me hard. My biggest fear is my home (condo) going into forclosure. I can't borrow money from anyone as times are tough all around. Any suggestions and inspirational words would be appreciated.

Thank you for your help.

Elder Response

You have to put your daughter and yourself first. If this company, for whatever reason, cannot hire you now—move on. Particularly in this economy, there is no guarantee that they will ever hire you. It may look like a great job and a great company, but if they don't hire you now, they are not doing you any good. In addition, I know from personal experience and experiences of my friends that if they wanted you that badly, they would find a way to hire you as an exception to the job freeze. My advise is to put this company on the back burner and put your job search back into high gear. If this company should contact you later, you can always consider them. I hope this helps.

Best regards,

Linda

Parachute

Dear Elders,

Hmm. Not sure where to start. I've spent the past 6 months trying a variety of ways to get a tech/web marketing job such as my previous one. I spent several years prior to this getting an MBA with marketing in mind. I still have a lot of debt to pay off from this course of study and have been going on the assumption that a marketing job would be the best way to pay it off.

On the other hand, its not my dream job. Cubicle-land is a bit dull and never really got me 'pumped' for the daily grind. I ready to take a step back and find out what I really want to do—a path that would simultaneously help me fulfill my financial _and_ social obligations while making me happy and allowing me to grow. I guess I'm wondering how to start finding this out. Creative writing or thought mapping? Talk to someone? Hmmm. Any thoughts?

Elder Response

It is hard to advise you in this matter because there is some information that I don't have. If you're in your mid to late 20s then situation is not all that uncommon and advise is relatively simple, not easy, but clearly definable. If you're in your 30s, 40's or 50's then it is a more serious situation and the advice quite different.

Since your situation is more common to someone in his 20s, I'll answer it that way; if you're not, then you need to write again and let us know that so that we can give you more accurate advice.

The point to your issue is really that you have invested a lot of time, effort and resources (money especially) in a career field that you're still not sure is for you. AND, the field you're talking about doesn't have the future potential as it seemed to have not too long ago. Add to that financial responsibilities and it makes you feel trapped. You've got financial obligations, the seemingly best way to deal with those is to stick with what you're educated in since it would seem that the potential income level there would be higher than in a field you're not well trained in.

OK, so here's the advice. First get on board with one of those Temp Agencies. This will help to address the immediate financial needs. I am very sure, with your education, you'd be very much in demand. This will give you a chance to look at other businesses and perhaps other career paths.

Additionally, while "stepping back," try some volunteer work. Most places have a central volunteer coordinator office. The Red Cross, the United Way, and others maintain databases on organizations looking for volunteers. This is another way to explore different careers. I've often volunteered and been offered jobs with the organizations I volunteered with, so it can also lead to other employment.

You need to determine what you enjoy doing, try to relate that to a career field. If you're not sure what that could be, then it is because you have not experienced very much, so get out there, through the temp service and volunteering, and experience. If you do, you're bound to find a path that is fulfilling and rewarding.

Hope this helps,

Gene

Didn't Make It....

Dear Elders,

I've been dancing (ballet) since i was 6. Well now, i didn't make Officer over the drill team i'm on at school. It wasn't judged fairly at all. Well i quit the team. Yes i love it and i know i have alot to offer, but i can't deal with it. It will be my senior year and i can't handle all of the drama, i need to concentrate on school work. i think i would cause more problems if i stayed because i would be so jealous. i need to know if i made the right decision and how to deal. my best friend made it and i didn't. i didnt make it because im a strong person and i stand up for what i believe in. all the girls who made it are in the directors palm. im proud of myself for being me but upset for not making it. help!

Elder Response

My dear girl, you have a problem you must acknowledge and work out so that you have a happy and satisfying life. Each time you fail (as we all do) and quit, you have acknowledged failure by removing yourself from the field. Do not go this way anymore....

You couldn't handle all the drama, but you were creating it! You didn't make the right choice; you should have hung in and found a way to accept not being chosen. Now you have no way back and no way to participate because of your envy. You should not be proud of yourself for how you acted in this situation, because you hurt yourself. Why? Because you wanted to be special and number one, and you weren't chosen to be.

Had you been reasonable about this, you could have stayed on the team and enjoyed the activity, friendship and sharing. Baloney on all the girls who made it being in the director's palm. You know better, and must stop excusing yourself.

You must not react this way again to not getting what you want, because it will have a very negative effect on your life. Learn to deal with reality and then learn to do better, no matter what.

I wish you the best, good luck, and hope that you will mature to where you can accept yourself as you are, others as they are without excuses, and enjoy your life.

Best regards,

Bonnie

Hands-On Work vs. Management

Dear Elders,

I have been working for the past 4 years as a manager within Information Technology. Prior to that, for 12 years I was a computer programmer. I enjoyed being a programmer, but because of my ability to mentor others I was offered a position in management. My instinct told me that was not what I wanted to do, so I declined. However, due to the encouragement of co-workers and my husband, and a promise by upper management I could remain "hands-on", I finally accepted.

The problem is I really hate it. I don't enjoy having to convince people they need to do their job, or having to do the tons of paperwork and human resource issues involved. I've been told I'm good at it, however, I disagree.

Now the real problem. I rarely get any "hands-on" time. I've had technical training to keep up with the times, but in the Information Technology field if you don't work with it every day because of changing times you become a obsolete. I have lost all confidence in myself and my abilities. I want to go back to the development of software and have asked my current employer to do so. I stepped down from the management position last April, 2001, but still find that because the team was used to taking my direction and my replacement found that convenient, I'm still doing the project management. I may not have to sign the paper, but I'm still approving or disapproving.

I have asked to look at other opportunities within the company, but there really isn't anything available. Plus, my gut tells me because I'm overseeing a "highly visible project" I will not be allowed to be moved to another position for awhile. (I now know how these things work from being in management).

Sorry so long winded. It's hard to get out. Anyway, my dilemma is I'm afraid to look for another job in a different company because I feel I have lost any skill set or I'm too rusty for consideration within a computer programming position. I have been unhappy for the entire 4 years, but the last 2 have taken it's toll. I'm really depressed and having difficulty with my attitude. I feel trapped.

How do I get my self-confidence back? I'd quit and go back to school, but the situation doesn't afford it.

Any suggestions would be greatly appreciated.

P.S. Forgive any typos, after years of being on the computer, my eyes are kinda shot.

Elder Response

Have you kept your resume up to date? If not, that is the first thing you need to do. As an information technologist, I am sure that you are aware of the vast resources open to you on the internet. Some great job sites for information technology professionals are dice.com, techies.com, monster.com, headhunter.com, computerjobs.com, computerwork.com, hotjobs.com and net-temps.com. On all of these sites, you can post your resume for prospective employers and headhunters to see and/or you can apply for specific jobs that are listed. I have found my last 4 jobs this way. It really works and when your telephone starts ringing with headhunters and employers eager to talk about your skills, your self-confidence will return. Don't be stuck in a job you hate!!! It will end up affecting the other parts of your life and life is too short for that. I hope these ideas are of some help.

Best regards,

Jim

Public or Private

Dear Elders,

I graduated from college in December and accepted a position teaching in a public school...the same school that I student taught in...well i am also very interested in religious education and have ambitions to return to college to work towards my masters in theology...well lately i have been feeling that yes i am called to be a teacher...i feel like i am in the right field but im not so sure that I am teaching where i am called to teach...you see i do teach presently 2 classes in my parish faith formation class...i also am the coordinator of our singles ministry and i receive more strength and wisdom from those volunteer positions then i do in my day teaching job...so i am just wondering if perhaps i need to be working in my parish...full time and only teaching in the public schools part time like as a sub...or perhaps i should be teaching in a private school where i can teach about my faith as well as all the other topics etc.... as well...i just get so confused as to what i am being called to do...Teach yes but what and where...

Elder Response

Hi!

I am convinced that "teaching" is almost something in your blood, so to speak and the rewards are great. However, teaching something that is very important to you makes the rewards even greater. Most all students can decipher if the teacher really and truly believes in what is being taught and it's important. Would I rather have a mechanic work on my car who is good, or a mechanic who is good and LOVES his work?

Three of my children are teachers, both my wife and I had taught, my mother-in-law was a teacher. Each of us, thank goodness taught or are teaching in areas and grade levels that are unique and best express not only the love of the classroom but the love of the subject being taught.

My friend, don't be so confused. You are being called not only to teach, but to teach of things that you consider important and are close to your heart.

Good Luck!

Paul

What's Important In Life?

Dear Elders,

At this stage in your life, what is most important to you? Right now I am concerned about my career and trying to find out what is my purpose in life. Trying to discover something that I can excel at or something special that I can offer. Should I be worried about this?

Elder Response

Hi!

Well, at this stage of my life the things that are most important to me are most likely not so important to you. Although I wish I could convince you otherwise, LOL! Being concerned about your career should involve being concerned about what makes you happy and feel fulfilled. So what's the purpose of life? I guess it's to live it in a way that gives you some measure of self satisfaction. We all, each and everyone of us has value, to recognize this value and find a way to live it is the real challenge. What are you good at? What do you enjoy doing? What gives you a feeling of self worth?

Being worried accomplishes nothing. It is a state of mind that interrupts and destroys our ability to do just the opposite, be challenged and happy in the challenge, it's common to us all. Take heart in that my friend. We all face excelling at something "special". Often we do it but don't recognize it.

Best regards,

Treefrog

School Career

Dear Elders,

Actually my school career. Hello. My name is Leslie. I'm a freshmen in college and I'm a little worried that I won't make it as a Dermatologist. I'm not an "A" student but I'm determined, positive, and confident (sometimes). The benefits I have on my side I suppose is that I'm 29, a single mother and don't have to work full-time. That will help. Any advise from you?

Thanks for your time.

Elder Response

Hi there :-)

Well you seem to be on the right track except for maybe a couple of things. You have a goal, you have a positive frame of mind (but maybe not positive enough?), and you are confident (sometimes?). You have much in your favor. You have the goal in mind, get excited about it, and take one step at a time toward it. Stay focused on that goal and don't worry about not being an "A" student. The "A" is most often a subjective assessment by other people. If you must be an "A" student then identify how you might achieve that. I suppose there are many, many "B" and "C" dermatologists. In the final analysis what dermatolist hangs their GPA in the office? Remain positive, optimistic and excited. Share as much of your goal with close family or a close friend and tell them that if or when the "down" times, or doubts you will seek their support.

Good Luck!

Treefrog

What is "Work Ethic"?

Dear Elders,

I am a sophomore in high school, and am burdened by my honors classes, Advanced Placement courses, and extracurricular activities I have decided to pursue. I've found lately that its been harder for me to focus on my academics, mainly because I've found interests that I would like to pursue professionally some day. However, I've heard of the concept of a 'Work Ethic' and am wondering if it is something that will help me focus and organize my life, or at least my work; I was wondering if the Elder Wisdom Circle can provide me with a clear definition of a work ethic and propose a virtuous one that will help me achieve my goals.

Thank You

Elder Response

Hello,

It sounds like you have lots on your plate and that your new-found professionally related interests seem more exciting than your school work. That often happens to lots of students and it's nothing to worry about as long as you see the link between schooling and career. When that link weakens it can undermine your work ethic.

Speaking of that, my understanding of a work ethic is a sense of responsibility to one's duties that encourages thoroughness, creativity, enthusiasm, insight and competence. It means working hard but joyfully and fully doing the best you can do. It means being willing to learn, to extend oneself, to accept criticism, etc. You seem to have it, but it's being threatened at school. Keep up your school work by seeing that it, in the long run, will link you up with the skills and qualities you want to have later on as an adult.

Best regards,

Cindy

Is The Ministry For Me?

Dear Elders,

hi. i'm 22 years old, and i feel very very new at life. i think the ministry is something that i'd really like to do, maybe not in the very near future, but at some point in my life. how can i be sure that i'm on the correct path? i mean, i guess you can never be sure of anything, but how can i be sure-ish?

Elder Response

Far too many people are asking "How can I be sure?" You can't—life has no certainty. "How do I know I'm on the right path?" You can't—there is no right PATH…there are many right PATHS for each of us.

You will know if your desire to become a minister continues, or continues to grow in strength. You will also know if your interest lessens or fades away.

I admire you for thinking serious at this point, and know that whatever you eventually decide to do (perhaps many things), you will do well and be happy.

Best wishes,

Donna

What Makes Me Happy Is What Makes Me Sad

Dear Elders,

Today I am seeking advice in regards to my college experiences and career choice. I am currently a 3rd year University student, majoring in 'Society, Ethics & Human Behavior'. I had originally enrolled at the University as a Business student, however through the past 3 years have determined that I find sociology and psychology much more intriguing. Needless to say, I changed my focus of study, and am now taking numerous classes which focus on the development of identity, sexuality and society.

Upon speaking with a number of my professors and scouting Graduate schools, I have found quite a few professions which relate to my area of study. Perhaps most important, I have been looking into Social Work and Child/Teen/Family counseling.

My question is this: Careers such as those in the field of Social Work have a particularly high burn-out rate, meaning that a large number of people become overwhelmed and change careers, therefore how can I be sure that this field is for me and that I won't burn out in 10 or 20 years?

Social Work and counseling can be extremely demanding and emotionally draining, especially when dealing with domestic abuse or drug addiction, and I am not so sure that I am cut out for that kind of work. I love helping people, and know that I would find no greater joy in life than to help others improve their lives and relationships, but how can I be sure that I will succeed?

Please respond if you have been faced with similar decisions, and let me know what your experience has been. I am indeed interested in hearing from anybody you has work experience in these fields. Thank you so much for your time!

Elder Response

Hello. Good that you are giving much thought to such an important decision. The helping professions are quite challenging and rewarding, although they are also demanding. If you find great joy in helping others, you will definitely succeed in this field.

From my own observations, I believe there are 2 main reasons for burnout:

1) Unrealistic goals. There are bound to be many "failures" in this profession because not everyone can be helped to the degree we strive for, and they are not necessarily ready to accept help at the time we are working with them. Not acknowledging these limitations causes many professionals to become frustrated and cynical. People who are victims of crime, illness, domestic violence and other unfortunate twists of fate always benefit greatly from a relationship with a caring, dedicated professional. That is the hallmark of success, no matter the outcome of the counseling itself.

2) Lack of Balance in one's personal life. It is crucial to have a solid network of support and love to replenish your own energy and vitality. Pursuing other interests that are nurturing to you will certainly keep you from burning out.

All the best to you in your career.

Frangi

Stay In The Military Or Not?

Dear Elders,

I have come to a crossroads in my life. I have been in the Navy for three years now, and have one year left. Soon, I have to make the decision to get out or stay in. I do have a successful career thusfar and love the Navy. But the frequent deployments and the fact that I am stationed in Virginia while my husband is stationed in Florida is very hard on our marriage. I feel like that if I get out, I might regret it for the rest of my life. Could you give me your point of view? Thank you so much, and God bless you.

Elder Response

Hello…

What a difficult decision this must be, but how wonderful to have both a person and a career that you love! If you're absolutely sure that you can't get a more stable positoin in the Navy where you husband is located and vice versa, then one of you will have to make a change in career.

Have you thought about asking your husband to consider changing his work? Lots of women have moved to follow their husband's work; some men have done the same for their wives. You sound like you really love the Navy and maybe your husband could make the change. Also, have you thought of marriage counseling to help you both find a better way to make this long-distance marriage easier on you both? Again, many couples do this well.

I'd consider many options before quitting the Navy. At least give yourself this chance to think of other options so bitterness and resentment and regret don't haunt you later in life.

Best regards,

Cindy

I Don't Know What I Want To Be When I Grow Up

Dear Elders,

Hi. I am a 20-year-old college student, majoring in psychology, but recently discovered that I am not as interested in pursuing a career in psychology as I am taking psychology courses. I would consider myself a creative person. I love to write and do creative things, such as little art projects with my room. For the past few months I decided that I would graduate with a bachelor's degree in psychology, but then pursue a writing career. Of course, I know that I will not be published right away, if at all, and what will I do for income? I'm feeling a little trapped, because there are things I am interested in getting involved in and I only wish I could have realized these things before I collected 86 credits towards a psychology degree. I would love to be an author, a photographer, anything creative that will allow me to travel and be a 'free spirit', because I cannot stand '9-5 jobs'. I plan on graduating form college in Spring of 2004 and hoping to join the Americorps program, to give back to the community and earn some money to pay off student loans. What I am going to do after that is beyond me. I know I am not the first person to have these thoughts, but I really don't want to settle for a job or career I am not happy with just to earn money. Any advice or suggestions?

Elder Response

Hello there and thanks for writing:

Just because you majored in psych, it doesn't mean you have to pursue that as a career! As a college professor for 35 years I've tried to explain to students that liberal arts degrees are to "liberate" the spirit and love of learning that you seem to have accomplished quite well. You are widely versed, have a good sense of the larger world around you, want to get involved in your life in a meaningful way, want to "give back" by joining americorp (many students I know just loved that project)so…you've already gained what a college degree as a liberal arts major can provide. Hooray!!!

Now, you can finish up your degree in psych without worrying, ok? Most folks, especially parents, believe that college, especially liberal arts, is job training. It's not and it's so much MORE than that…it's LIFE TRAINING! It prepares you with skills, knowledge, values and insights to lead a successful life, which includes a career, but also so much more than that.

So…do enjoy the whole range of career options that will open up to you. Most employers want folks who can THINK, can write and speak well, are eager and curious, bright and hard working. They'll train you for a specific JOB, but you bring to them YOUSELF, competent, eager, creative, thoughtful, skilled, etc.

What to do next? How about pursuing some of your interests right now by writing for the school paper, e.g., or gaining some experience through an intership/club with the things that matter to you. Take any elective courses you might have in subjects that broaden your interests or expose you to new things. Do some research on how to get started in publishing. Take a "study abroad" course/semester if you can fit it in with your program, etc.

Relax, enjoy the rest of college and keep being you…

Cindy

How To Start A Woodworking Business

Dear Elders,

I am a 20 year old college student and i really am intrested in starting a woodworking business. I have been woodworking off and on for about 8 years and it has become a bit of an obession lately. I need some information on how to sell my work, pay taxes on the business, and advertise my products. Please send any information that you can obtain. Thanks,

Elder Response

Hi,

I don't want to rain on your parade, but: 95% of new businesses fail within the first 5 years for lack of capital and/or experience and know-how. You obviously lack the requisite administrative skills.

My best suggestion to you is to seek employment in a wood working shop for a year or two before venturing in business. Additionally, I urge you not to jeopardize your college education. That should be JOB #1.

Best regards,

WO Owl

Mid-Life Career Change

Dear Elders,

Hi wise elder. First of all, I want to commend all of you for participating in this site. I just discovered it and think the idea is a great one. My dilemma has to do with deciding what path to choose. First I must give you a little background on myself. I am a woman in mid 50s still trying to figure out what 'I want to do when I grow up.' When most people my age are looking towards retirement, I feel that I want to 'work' forever. However, the problem is in which direction should I go. I have been working in law firms for the past 25 or so years as a legal assistant and/or supervisor. I finally completed my degree in Business Management last year hoping to finally get out of law and use my skills in another area. However, the market where I live (Las Vegas) is entirely different than where I moved from (San Francisco)and there does not seem to be much opportunity here. The thing is that I am much more service oriented than product oriented and of course most of those organizations do not pay very well. The things I am most interested in are human rights, i.e., eliminating racism, child and domestic abuse, illiteracy, poverty, etc. and business in developing countries. I really think that I would like to form some type of foundation, or be a speaker or write articles or something like that. As I cannot actually quit my job in order to spend the time to investigate this more, I feel frustrated as I do not feel that I am really contributing to society in a positive way, yet I feel that I have definite gifts to offer which are not being utilized to the fullest extent. I meditate and have always read extensively on many different subjects and have done much personal development work. One of my issues is finding one thing to do or one path, as I am interested in doing everything. I just cannot seem to pinpoint one area where I would most like to be working. I do not have a wide network of influential or successful people in my life either. I certainly do not and cannot expect a pat answer to all of this but would be most grateful if 'you' could perhaps offer me a place to at least start. I hope that these ramblings do not sound like a 'pity party' because I feel extremely blessed and grateful for everything in my life. I just want to make a more meaningful contribution than I feel I am at the present. Thank you in advance for taking the time to read this.

Elder Response

Hi and thanks for writing:

Congratulations on finishing up your degree! With your business management and legal skills you could definitely make major contributions to human rights by, as you say, writing articles, giving workshops, lecturing, etc.

How to best do this in your situation is another issue, eh? I, too, wouldn't quit my day job yet. You're right in noting that many human rights organizations don't pay well. Have you considered volunteering some of your time and talents to help out such groups? Most of them are DESPERATE for someone with you talents and experience—-I wish I knew some of the things that you do to help with animal rights work, which is my interest of late!

By volunteering, you not only give something back, but you also gain additional skills, make future job contacts, and meet wonderful people who share your interests and values. There's a great Website that links you with your local agencies/groups that need volunteers:

www.volunteermatch.org

Just type in your zip code, select the areas you're interested in, and viola, a list appears that near you.

Also, you could list yourself with local "speakers bureaus" who need people to talk to groups about specific issues. Try contacting the local colleges/universities near you too. They might be interested in you talking to a school club on campus, many of which are humanitarian in theme.

Getting a job in a non-profit agency/organization is another option. Here's a Web site that has job opportunities, links and other resources:

http://www.idealist.org/

Even the title of the web site, The Idealist, should interest you!

Hope this helps.

Cindy

Job for 12 Year Old

Dear Elders,

I am a 12 year old boy, i need money, is there any job I can get that is easy and offer a lot of money.

Elder Response

Dear Boy,

You have come face to face with one of the facts of life; namely, there are no easy jobs that "offer" a lot of money. For that matter, the easier the job, the less the money. Conversely, the more difficult the job, the more the money.

However, if you can devise a means of making a lot of money easily, let me know. I'll patent, bottle, sell it, and split the profits with you.

As concerns a means for a 12 year old boy to earn "some" money: shoveling snow, cutting grass, caddying, baby sitting, car washing come to mind.

Best regards,

Harry

Take More Time Off?

Dear Elders,

I'm a little embarrassed to be asking for advice on what is basically a no lose situation. I think the fact that I'm not up against a wall is what is making this a tough choice.

I work for a good company and have a good job. However when the economy started to dip, my company offered a "leave program". Basically you get 20% pay for 0% work for a year. I jumped at the opportunity. I was a bit of a workaholic and needed to develop more of a life outside work. Well, 10 months have gone by and I was getting ready to go back to work. Looking forward to seeing old friends, making money, etc…Now they have offered another 3 months to the deal. My dilemma is that I don't know if I should take the extra time. On one hand this is still a once in a lifetime opportunity, I don't really like my job all that much, and I could use the time to find something new. On the other hand, I said all those things 10 months ago, and don't really expect the next two or five months to be any different. I may be the kind of person who needs to be doing five things to get even one done.

Any thoughts on to work or not to work?

Elder Response

You suffer from procrastination. Weigh things out and make a decision. Time does not stand still. You have to take a job and get used to the discipline of holding a job. You don't want to drift through life doing nothing. Take charge and do something.

Best regards,

Scott

End Of My Rope...

Dear Elders,

I am currently enrolled at school. I am a single mother and I live in a homeless shelter. I really need to get some money but I have 3 mths left of school. I don't really have the time to work a job during the week-days or on Sunday because of my responsibilities at the shelter and to my baby. I don't know what to do.

Elder Response

Hello,

You are already carrying many big burdens and I'm sorry to hear that you can't make the money that you need. I'm not sure about where you live but I wonder if you've considered applying for welfare or pub-lic assistance? In most places I know of, and I was once a social case worker, single mothers who are going to school are eligible for housing benefits, food, clothing and money for the child. Have you applied for these benefits? If you've been denied you can appeal the decision; there are many free legal aid socieites that can help you out. Check with the Dept. of Children Services in your local community.

Hopefully you'll be able to see your way through the next 3 months until school is done. Bless you and let us know anything more specific so we can help you out.

Best regards,

Cindy

Money Or Meaning

Dear Elders,

I have a very meaningful job. However, I barely make enough money to get by. I have a family and I am concerned. Should I find a job that pays more and give up a true passion? In other words, should I choose money over meaning? Thanks

Elder Response

You need to find balance & set your priorities, is more money a priority over doing something meaningful? Try to explore ways of making more in your current position.

What kind of support do you have from your family? are they pushing you to make more money? that could be an issue. You state that you barely get by, I hate to tell you this but that's most of the country. I would rather do what I enjoy & be poor than hate what I do & be rich.

Best regards,

David

Friendships At Work

Dear Elders,

Do you think it is possible, or advisable, to make close friends out of acquaintances you meet at work? I work in an office, and I try to keep business and private matters separate; but sometimes I think I am missing out on the chance to make good friendships. Do you have any advice on how to do this, or should I keep my work and personal life separate?

Elder Response

First of all, if you met these people outside of work would you want them as friends? if the answer is yes then you want them as friends period.

Before you begin any close office friendship make sure that it will not interfere with work, this may be difficult if someone ends up reporting to the other. If you feel keeping your friendship out of business matters would be too difficult with someone then I would avoid developing a close friendship with that person.

I have had some wonderful friendships develop from working friendships. Just make sure you know someone well before jumping head on with all the details of your life.

Best regards,

Sam

Fighting Ageism in Business

Dear Elders,

I'm a 'semi retired' music composer / arranger with over 40 years of experience in the tv, film , and adevertising industries . As others in the creative trades can tell you, (such as actors,screen writers, etc) there is a strong unspoked 'agism ' practiced in these businesses.due to the fact that creative decisions are basically made by people close to 30 in many…make that most ,situations…and'old' is like leprosy!

Being 64, and recently widowed, I'd like to still do some work now and then just to keep my hand in (fortunately, I don't meed the money,(thanks to a union pension, SSA, and some ASCAP royalties and other investments…) I just would like to keep busy doing what I have had years of experience doing…and….if I must say somyself, am pretty good at. :)

I've tried to get some part time college teaching jobs doing seminars on film scoring and commercial music, but since I'm in WA state, there aren't many schools that need what I have to offer. (Plus, I was always so busy working, I don't have a complete advanced degree…so I possess no academic prestige…just experience in the real world.)

I'd love to hear what other creative types in my age group (actors, writers, dancers, musicians , etc) have foud to do…or any successful methods they've found to combat the 'over 30' problem…which really is strong in TV and Advertising.

THanks for whatever you all come up with…

Gray haired, but still quite capable :)

Elder Response

Well, first, stay active. Keep learning. Reading, studying, assessing your views. Document them, perhaps here at the Elders Circle. We get technical questions all the time. Having seen any specifically on your field, but I've seen questions about writing, archeology, veterinarian, horticulture, etc...Only a matter of time before someone comes in with your field in mind. Also, you may well see questions on advice on some of life's issues that you have experience with too. It helps to keep your mind active and you'll be surprised what you think now about things you lived through years ago.

Volunteering too, a lot of organizations I'm sure could use your expertise and would love to have it.

Hope this helps. Best regards,

John

Asking For A Raise

Dear Elders,

What is an appropriate way to ask for a raise at work? I have been with my company for 3 years, and have completed many projects. I have received recognition for these projects, and feel that I deserve a raise. I am sure that my employer will agree. However, any advice you can give me as to appropriate behavior would be helpful. Thank you for your time and advice.

Elder Response

Hello,

A good time to ask for a raise is during your annual performance evaluation. If you don't have one at your job, set up a time when things are fairly quiet at work and prepare for it by:

1. make a list of the things you've done for the company that have improved it

2. indicate the ways in which your skills and knowledge have improved since your last raise

3. tell your supervisor/boss about the things you're planning to do in the next year to enchance the company and to grow your skills

Hope this helps.

Cindy

Work Too Much

Dear Elders,

I have a full time career job at the United Way and I also work about 30 hours a week at a bar in Minneapolis, because I make really good money. i feel like my life is consumed with work, although I am not unhappy. I was wondering if you had any advise on 'working too much'. I feel that I am very successful for my age and I am trying to develop a good life. What do you think.

Elder Response

Hello and thanks for writing…

As someone who loves to work I was intrigued by your letter. It makes me think about the issue of what it means to be "working too much." I re-read your email several times and I noted that you say "I am not unhappy" but you don't say, "I'm happy" and I wonder if that's telling at all. You seem to like your day job and enjoy the money of your "part time" job and there are many people who work 60 hours/week and like it too! Much depends, I guess, on whether or not you're happy with the rest of your life. Assuming you want some things like friendship, companionship, intimacy, time to yourself, time to read a good book or be in nature or whatever then if you also have time for these things in your life then I guess you're not working too much. Maybe you're very good at managing the time you spend when you're not working and maybe you don't want many of the other things you can't fit into a 60 hour week. Only you know the answer for sure, but a good life is a balanced life. One that, should we die next week, we can say that we lived as fully as we wanted to, doing the things we wanted to do.

I try to keep my life in this balance and don't always succeed in doing so, of course, but it's a wonderful question and reminds me to check in with my life too.

Best regards,

Cindy

A Mean Boss

Dear Elders,

I am wondering if you have any advice on how to put up with a mean, cranky boss. I have worked for my boss for a year and a half, and I have seen her smile once, maybe twice. Usually she is frowning and scowling and yelling at people and slamming things around on her desk. I have tried the 'overly nice' approach and nothing changes. I'm just looking for ideas to maybe make her smile a little—or anything—to make the work place a little easier to work in. Any ideas??? :-) Thanks!

Elder Response

People are going to be who and what they are because that's the way they want to be. You can't change them, all you can do is enjoy your own life. Don't try to change other people, you can help them in some ways, but you can't change them, and if they perceive that your trying to, whether you are or not, it is likely only to make it worse.

I have learned, over the years, as much from people who acted in ways that I didn't think were right, as I have learned from people who did things well. From those I didn't think did things very well I learned how not to do them when I got into their position. From people who did well I learned how to do it well when I got to be in their position.

Watch what this boss does and notice the effects it has. Then, resolve not to be that way when you are a supervisor of others.

Hope this helps,

Gene

Laid Off

Dear Elders,

I was laid off from my job two months ago. I'm having a hard time staying positive. My career has been very important to me and I haven't been without a job since I was 15 years old. I am very proud of this accomplishment. I made very good money prior to being laid off. In two months I have had only one interview and nothing has come of it. I'm really good at what I do and I am a dedicated, hard worker. All of my previous supervisors, peers and subordinates and ready and waiting to offer references. I am okay financially, so at least this is not an immediate concern. I know I won't be unemployed forever, but being out of work is becoming very difficult. My self esteem is suffering and I'm having a very hard time staying positive. How can I have a better outlook in this temporary but difficult situation?

Elder Response

Hi

Believe me, I can relate to that, especially the deterioration of self esteem. Your concept of value to others seems to disappear. That's how we grade ourselves, isn't it? How others value us. We seem to lose sight of our own self worth. It is curious how we measure our self worth, Is it solely measured by a job? By receiving a paycheck? By getting up in the morning and going to a place to work? Our value is NOT diminished by a lay-off. Only our pride is. And that damn pride affects our self esteem. You gotta work at and maintain an optimism that says "I am good at what I do....I enjoy what I do and there is a place for me". Look for and expect good things to happen. We live in a country that makes that trek possible. Set up a plan to job hunt. Don't be shy about tapping all those friends, peers, etc. to help your. Pester them even! And while you do this, volunteer for something, anything. It makes you feel "needed" and of value, and gives you a better outlook "in this temporary but difficult situation".

The Best to You,

Treefrog

Teaching

Dear Elders,

I am a teenager and interested in teaching as a job when I graduate from college. I need to know, what type of classes should I take, or is there any specific college I will want to look at? How do you start teaching? Also, if you are an experienced teacher, what do you find to be the perks of teaching?

Elder Response

Hi there…in many States you have to major in both education and the subject/area you're going to teach in, e.g. math, history, sociology, etc.

You should go to the best college you can find, one with a strong school of education and liberal arts. In your 2nd, 3rd or 4th year you'll do "student teaching" and apply for a job in your senior year. Your advisors will help you out with this part. As a college professor myself, and with many friends in the teaching field, the "perks" of teaching are: freedom and creativity at work, the joy of sharing and helping others to learn to love learning, having an intellectually stimulating career and, although the salary is low, having pretty good benefits. Teaching is also HARD work, not very respected in the U.S. so…be sure you really want to teach! Good luck…

Best regards,

Claudia

Need A Mentor

Dear Elders,

I am very glad I found Elder Wisdom Circle. I want to first thank you for volunteering to offer invaluable advice and helping the later generations overcome those curve balls that life throws at us.

I have been laid off for 14 months now. In the past few months, I became very very tired of sending out resumes, cover letters and asking people to help me look. And I'm tired of rejections. So my brilliant solution to my problem is to give myself a job. So I started my own little business at home. I currently help people (notably those uninsured or underinsured) find affordable heathcare so that they don't have to worry about the high cost of going to the doctors or hospitals. However, this business has just started and I have not yet established a steady income.

I'm sorry if I seem like I'm rambling. I just wanted to give you a little bit of my background. What I'm leading to is that I want to learn real estate investing, as it will become my career and will supplement my income. I am reading books to learn the jargons and how the business works, but what I desperately need is a mentor who is skilled and has expertise in the real estate investment arena. Like all things, I need a teacher who's willing to teach me and guide me. Now, I don't know what you do for a living, but would you know how and where I can go find someone in this profession who would be willing to pass on his knowledge as a mentor and as a friend? Unfortunately most of my friends are in technology of some sort, so they can't offer me any help.

Again, I want to thank you for volunteering your advice and wisdom. I really appreciate your time and efforts whether or not you can help me find a mentor.

Elder Response

Hi,

I realy don't want to rain on your parade, but would be remiss were I not to hoist the "danger" flags.

Although the rules and regulations governing insurance agents vary from state to state, I urge you to assure that a license is not required for the concept at hand.

AS for real estate investment: not knowing anything about the business, and having to buck up against highly knowledgeable and sophisticated players, your chances of success—not to speak of losing your shirt—are slim.

Moreover, in the world of commerce [business] it is axiomatic that any venture relying on expertese via reading books and mentors is DOA. [Dead on arrival.]

Since you have an interest in real estate, have you considered getting a license to sell real estate?

Best wishes and good luck,

Frank

What Makes A Good Teacher?

Dear Elders,

I graduated from college in 1998 and have been in the workforce since. Lately I've felt like something's missing nd have decided to become a teacher. I'm presently researching the lateral-entry program of my state and wanted to know from you, since you're a former teacher, what are the number-one qualities to be a teacher?

Elder Response

Hmmmmm....How did you know I was a teacher? And so was my wife, and two of my three children and my mother-in-law. It seems to be genetic in my family, a curse, so to speak, the curse of wanting to build the future not of bricks, morter, steel, wires, computers....but of intelligent, caring minds. Without these minds, and some values to go with them, all the silicon chips in the world are but dust.

What are the #1 qualities to be a teacher? Not a hard question at all. You gotta want to face each day with a new challenge. You gotta yearn to get others excited about what you are excited about. You gotta sometimes rely on just one student smiling at what you've just said and see a "light bulb" glow over their head for a day's satisfaction. You gotta accept the challenge of digging deep into a bag of tricks to bring a young, recalitrant mind into the passion of life and discovery. You gotta accept long hours and, unfortunately, unacceptable remuneration. To tell you the truth, it's most exciting.

#1 requirement....you gotta be patient and love kids and the chance to "make a difference".

Good Luck

Jack

Interviewing for Jobs

Dear Elders,

Recently I changed careers and am in the process of interviewing for a new job. Getting through the door is the easy part, however, the interview is the part that always gets me. When the interviewer asks me a question about my work experience at a previous job that I did not like. I have a hard time saying anything positive. I know the cardinal rule of interviewing is, "never say anythign negative about your previous employer." However, its difficult to say anything positive about one's work experience, when one did not really do anything of significance in that particular position. I would like advice on how to impress my interviewer with out being negative and without having to lie about what I really did in my old job.

Elder Response

I interview people on a regular basis as part of my job, and you are correct in assuming that you should not speak negatively about your former employer. It is definitely not what the interviewer wants to hear. When they ask you about your past job I sure you can tell them something positive. Each and every experience we have working is a lesson for us, even if the job taught us that this is not where we want to be. I always look at it as a stepping stone to better things. Most people want to better themselves and that requires experience, experience is what you are getting in some form no matter what job you have held in the past. Maybe you did not find he past job challenging enough and are ready to move on to new things to reach the potential you know you can reach. Maybe you have updated your skills and are looking to put them to work and were unable to do this in the past jobs. Or you are looking for a position that has potential for promotion. I don't know what line of work you are in, but any of these reasons is a good answer for an interviewer, I'm sure you can find an answer that applies to your situation.

Hope this is helpful and good luck in your job search.

Best regards,

Paul

Searching For A Job In Uneasy Times

Dear Elders,

Along with a majority of the population right now, I'm currently looking for a new job. The search is limited with our economic situation being unstable and my motivation is slimming down. I recently graduated (okay not too recently, 2000 to be exact, but I'm still a new inductee into the "real world" syndrome) and am actively pursuing a writing career. Unfortunately, the market in San Diego (my residence) is not conducive to a steady and profitable journalism career. I work for a business newspaper now, but the pay is horrendous. While I understand that I am just a babe, and must start at the bottom of the totem pole like everyone else, it's put a strain on how to go about achieving some sort of financial and professional success. Also, I'm not exactly doing what it is I've dreamed of doing and that is becoming a journalist.

I've looked into it all, I do freelance and am seeking a part-time job on top of my full-time one if my job search has no leads by March. In my search, I have gotten several offers from companies, where the pay is right, but the position isn't. I'm willing to sacrafice the writing full-time (My freelancing will help keep my writing portfolio up to date) and work for the sole purpose of saving money and moving to the East by the end of the year (where the writing markets are more plentiful). My question is though, how do I go about deciding which job is right for my temporary situation? I don't want to be too quick to accept a job that may last for only 3 months, but at the same time, how do I go about making the right decision? Also, if you have any other routes for me to take (I may be going about it the wrong way) that would be most helpful too!

Thanks!

Elder Response

Thanks for writing.

Journalism, like most professions, requires that people begin at the bottom and prove their abilities before they gain significant recognition. This takes time, and hard work. The Boulder Daily Camera told Stephen King that he had no ability; look where he is now. There are two different avenues to the same goal in journalism. First, you can take a job at a less prestigious newspaper, prove yourself more quickly against less-skilled writers, and move from paper to paper as you become a "name" in writing.

Or, you can join an upper-tier newspaper, and slowly move up, because you are already competing with the better writers. However, thinking that you can enter the market and immediately command a large salary or prestigious position, is irrational.

Good luck.

Sam

No Purpose

Dear Elders,

I worked full-time as an Administrative Assistant to pay for college. I decided to return to school because I wanted more opportunity. I was consistently told that I have wonderful skills, but am "underqualified."

I am currently studying for my MBA in Human Resources, but have a passion for Not-for-profit work and am considering changing my major to Business & E-Commerce and Public Administration. Nonetheless, I still have the same barriers because I cannot even get an entry-level position outside administrative assistance.

The problem is that I have been rejected by EVERY single company I have applied to as being "overqualified" for Executive Assistant or "not experienced" enough to branch in new areas. It is a gross understatement to say I am frustrated and feel that the more I try to better myself, the more I am harming my chances. I even removed my higher education and some experience to get back in administrative work and an interviewer commented that I "sound like I have more experience than reflected on my resume." Geez!

I understand that we are in a tough economy and the market is in the employers' favor. Nonetheless, I am at a loss and am curious if there was ever a point in your transition period that you regretted pursuing more education? Do you have any words of wisdom that can help me figure out if I should just give up this pursuit for the right opportunity and take the next "stapler" job I can find?

Right now, I feel like my life has no purpose and I don't fit in anywhere. How did you learn to overcome this and find your passion?

Thank you in advance.

Elder Response

:-) Hi!

Back in 1964 I graduated a college seminary with a major in philosophy. Discovered there wasn't much of a market for "philosophers". So I drifted back into post grad work, psych., then business, finally ended up in education since I did land a job at a private school teaching. Figured a "master's" would be my ticket. Did get my M.Ed, but the economy in 1970 went into recession. I applied for many teaching positions and none could afford a "master". I ended up eliminating my hard work from my resume.

My Dad was in construction so I gave up my desired future and worked for him. Managed to raise a family and do ok. BUT, to this day, I wish I would have hung out the recession, took any job close to what I wanted to do and "paid my dues". You know you always have to "pay the dues".

I never understood why HR people fail to consider an application due to "over-qualified". I'd love to have a carpenter working for me who has a B.A.,LOL! Maybe they figure you will not be happy?

NEVER, EVER will you regret getting a post grad degree. You, initially, may or may not wish to include it in your resume. There IS a position out there for you. It may be slightly off "target" but you gotta get something to prove to the human resources gods that you can perform and accomplish. If you get rejected for being "over-qualified" don't be shy in calling and asking them what you can do to be "qualified".And for those positions that say "not enough experience", tell them you will work on 30, 60 day probation, no strings.

Don't dispair. The whole business of "lacking experience" or being "over-qualified" are sometimes excuses given to dismiss your application. Think over your resume, maybe have a "pro" look it over? Search out suggestions from the Net. There are several very good resources there. Just search "careers" or some such thing. Just don't give up! Things will change and turn around, trust me, they do. Just keep that final goal of doing something you enjoy in mind. And while you pursue that opportunity you might just have to keep that "stapler" at hand.

Good Luck!

Treefrog

Distracted

Dear Elders,

I work as a paralegal and work in a cubby. It would be nice to have an office, but the company I work for doesn't have the room to give paralegals their own offices. My work sometimes requires me draft legal documents, read lengthy documents, reports, etc. I have been findng lately that I am not able to concentrate on my work due to the commotion around me. In particular, one girl who is constantly talking—to herself, to anyone that walks by, or anyone else. I have gone to my manager about the problem, but I fear that he will not do anything about it. He's the type that likes to make everyone happy. Other people int he office also have the same problem as me. We have tried to make light jokes about her never shutting up, but she doesn't think we're serious. What can I do to keep her quiet? Please help before I lose my mind!!!!

Thanks.

Elder Response

Hi….have you tried going to lunch with her, building up some good rapport and then talking this out with her? Often we don't realize the problem or don't/can't find a way to change the way we are, but if we like people we generally try to do so. Good luck,

Frank

Finding My Calling

Dear Elders,

Thanks for taking the time to read my email…It's going to be a long one so get comfortable! I am 34 years old and have had a very full life already. I have been through serious depressions, suicide attempts (mostly due to the feeling that life had no meaning and that it was more pain than pleasure), YEARS of therapy and soul searching, many boyfriends, college (degree in psychology), and lots and lots of travel. I am happier now than I ever have been but feel sort of at a loss on what I should (or even want) to be doing for a career. I have tried many different occupations from working with emotionally disturbed kids, to Mortgage banking, to advertising sales exec, to tv newscasting, to my current position as a bartender (which I have been doing for 9 years). I enjoy the freedom that this job gives me (I only work nights and get 3 days off in a row every week). It allows me to travel and enjoy lots of leisure time. I am an excellent bartender but feel that I am sort of wasting my life and that someday I will look up and I will realize that my life has passed me by and I haven't done anything meaningful or fulfilled my life purpose (whatever the heck that is!). I am writing a couple novels, but procrastinate a great deal and don't seem to be getting anywhere very quickly on them (I'm talking 10 chapters at most in 3 years…not exactly speed writing). I keep vowing that I will write for at least 30 minutes every day but quickly fall out of the habit.

My grandfather told me at one point when I was embarrassed that all I was doing with my college degree was bartending that: 'if you are happy, then it doesn't matter what you are doing.' Well, I am much happier than I ever was before at any of the other jobs I've had (in fact learned that a 9 to 5 office job would drive me completely crazy with boredom and misery). This can't be all there is to life though, can it? I keep thinking maybe I should go back to school to get my Master's Degree but I have no idea what subject to take.

I feel stagnant and that I am no longer growing and becoming a 'better' person. I'm tired of feeling lost and searching for 'the meaning of life' and 'Mr. Right' and 'the perfect career.' I'm starting to realize that there usually are no absolutes in life and that nothing is flawless. At the same time I believe that everyone is put here to fulfill some purpose (whether or not we ever figure what that purpose is). I'm sort of at a loss on what to do now. I feel like I've tried so many different things and am still floundering. I'm also reluctant to leave my current job because the money is so wonderful and the freedom it gives me is amazing. So what I am wondering is where to go from here? If you can offer me any advice on how to find my true calling or 'passion' I would really appreciate it. Thanks.

Elder Response

Hello,

What a wonderful life you seem to be having...full of rich and varied experiences! I'm not sure that there's any "meaning in life" or "deep purpose" that you're missing up on. We all try, in our jobs and lives, to infuse them with meaning and purpose. This can be done by doing brain surgery, selling cars, writing poetry or collecting garbage, in my view. How one does one's work matters much more than what one does. You enjoy tending bar, are good at it, and provide service and sociability to others. Your work has meaning and you seem to give it your best. You say, however, that you're getting stagnant. Maybe it's nothing to do with your job?

Maybe you need to set yourself other goals to reach? I don't know you at all, but some people want to learn a foreign language, others want to give something back by volunteering, etc. Maybe you can spend some quiet time with yourself and really ask yourself what is missing in your life that you'd like to pursue. It might not be a change in work but a change in your life...you friends, your relationship to your body, to nature, to spirituality, to your community.

I wouldn't quit the job either but do listen to that inner voice and see if it's telling you something.

Best regards,

Cindy

Trusting Myself

Dear Elders,

I promise to give your advice serious consideration. I also wish to thank you in advance.

I too am getting on in years. I'm fifty one. I've never had to push myself very hard. I've been blessed with a mind that is just enough faster than most of those around me to enable me to arrange my life to suit me. Lately I've been haunted by the idea that I have wasted 90% of what came to me naturally, and haven't live up to my potential. Now I seem to be driven to achieve something larger than myself, so that I can be remembered. I have lived an ordinary life because it was easy not to excel.

Here's the question my wise friend. Should I put out the effort to write, and see produced, a series of motion pictures for posterity? Or should I succumb to a lifetime of relatively negative inertia, and comfort myself with the old fable of Sour Grapes?

If you can avoid telling me to go screw myself...I'd really appreciate any words of guidance, inspiration, direction, and or encouragment.

Thanks.

Elder Response

Hello, it's nice to hear from you. I'm not sure exactly what you perceive your problem to be...is it whether you should exert more energy than is normal for you in hopes of giving something of value to the world? Or achieving fame?

Regardless, the important issue is that you do not feel you are continuing in your 'habitual lifetime of relatively negative inertia.'

I emphathize with your feeling the waste of not having lived up to your potential, but in fact, you did—you did exactly what your individual potential directed you to do—as little as you needed to achieve what you wanted.

Nothing wrong with that, many of us do it.

The danger now is that you feel you've wasted a greater potential, and wonder if you can somehow make up for it. Surely you can, in doing what will make you feel useful, not in doing something to make others see how great was your potential.

If you now feel you want to make that effort, do it because you want to, not to "make up" for not having knocked yourself out in living your life.

You're a lucky man, and I hope you appreciate that fact. I am also a lucky woman, but I feel my life has been full and fulfilling, even though I didn't achieve world-renowned fame for my accomplishments. I simply thank fate every day that I was endowed with the ability to succeed (in my opinion), and be happy with it.

I would like to hear again from you after you've decided what your path will be from here. I hope you will be happy and fulfilled, and I wish you good luck and send my best wishes.

Arianne

What Really Matters?

Dear Elders,

I'm not sure what direction to take with my future…

I have been working as a graphic designer for 4 1/2 years with an associates degree. Lately I have become very unsettled when I think about my future. My job is just that…a job. I find myself volunteering on the outside of work to fill the void and sometimes that doesn't seem to be enough. I want to do more.

I have been thinking about going back to school to change professions. I was always interested in costume designing, even from a young age (drawing outfits of every range). I also love volunteering and giving something back to the community. I catch myself checking the Defenders of Wildlife web site for job openings sometimes.

I don't have a strong sense of which path to go down. If I go back to school for costume design, hopefully I would be making good money and in my spare time I could continue to volunteer. Then again, I could go back to school (or not) and work for a non-profit organization. The only fear I have is that with working full time for a non-profit I wouldn't be able to live a comfortable life style (I'm trying to save for the future).

So, the question is—what really matters?

Elder Response

Hi! Thanks for writing.

"What really matters?"

What really matters is identifying what you are good at and what gives you a sense of accomplishment. It could be a simple matter of digging a perfect ditch, or it could be a matter of designing a great costume.

Each requires some discipline, sacrifice, and training. I've always preached that if you love something and pursue it with confidence to be excellent and it brings peace to you, the world will have a place for your dream and enthusiasm. It may sound idealistic, but the alternative is to live a life not of your own choosing and not necesarily a happy one. As an old, long gone friend of my once said...."sometimes you gotta pull down your pants and slide on the ice...." It can be an exhilerating ride if you so dare.

Keep Well!

Paul

Conflict At The New Job

Dear Elders,

Hi there. I'm trying to decide how to handle an irritating situation. I start a new job in two weeks in another state. During my job interview, my boss mentioned off-handedly that the company would pay for my moving expenses. He repeated the offer again when I called to accept the job, and told me to contact the head of human resources for the details. Given the many expenses associated with a new apartment, a new car, etc., this offer was really helpful.

I finally did talk with the woman from HR (I'll call her 'Beth') when I stopped by the office a couple of weeks ago. She seemed to bristle when I asked her how to go about arranging for the moving company, and told me that any offer to pay for my expenses should have been written into my contract, and that the company doesn't usually pay these expenses.

I went back to my boss who told me that the offer still stood—that I should just find the least expensive mover, and he'd work it out. He simply assumed the company would pay for my move, because they had paid for his. He said he'd talk to Beth. So everything seemed to be fine again.

However, I felt uncomfortable that Beth had treated me as if I had done something wrong. She had been so friendly when I first interviewed with her that the change in her attitude was obvious. This is a small company, and I didn't want the head of HR angry with me. So I emailed her a couple of weeks ago just saying that I was sorry if my question came as a surprise, and I updated her on the situation. I still haven't heard back from her.

Now I'm angry that she seems to be blaming me for all of this. I don't think I should confront her about it, but I'm upset that I already have this conflict to deal with—and I haven't even started the job!!! After all, it's nerve-wracking enough to start a new job without someone being angry with you for another person's mistake.

What do you think I should do now?

Elder Response

Hi,

I assume that you have made the move. In the event you have not, I suggest that you look for a job near your home. If you have, and already are in the employ of the company in question, I'd roll with the punches for a while in order to ascertain whether the evident personality clash with the HR person will transcend to your standing in the company. If it will, I'd seek other employment.

At any rate, you don't have much choice but to pay for the move; chalk it up to experience, and in the future "get it in writing."

Best wishes and good luck.

Frank

Work Guilt

Dear Elders,

I am feeling terrible about something I had to do at work. I got a promotion and had to fire a friend. I feel like an outsider at work, like everyone looks at me like a trader for getting rid of one of our own. I had to do it, or the whole ship would have gone down. What can I do to smooth things over with my co-workers?

Elder Response

Hello,

This is a difficult situation I can imagine. Apparently you are in a supervisory position of recent vintage and still feel a natural bond to your "co-workers". There are no easy answers and much depends on your own style, but I've been in situations where a brief, gentle but firm explanation of the situation is helpful. Remember that you are not asking for their approval but, out of respect for them and a hope for the future of the company, you'd like to explain the reasoning behind this difficult decision. Workers need to know that good, trusting people are generally not fired but sometimes, "the whole ship would have gone down."

Best of luck…

Sam

Help Me Find The Way

Dear Elders,

My fiance and I have been together for five years. He is in the military and is currently overseas. When he is not he flies for a living. I am a bit younger and I am just beginning to find a career. I recently finished a degree in biology and my goal is to be a wildlife biologist. Most entry-level positions require traveling to wherever the field work needs to be done and in many cases living in remote areas. It has become increasingly difficult to plan a life together where we can actually live together. I feel that until now, I have set my goals aside so that we can be together since I don't have an established career but, I do want to pursue my dream, too. I am fustrated and may not be looking at all the options. I was wondering if any of you have experienced situations similiar to this and would be willing to share how they dealt with it or if anyone had any advice. Thanks!

Elder Response

Hi!

Well, you say it yourself, "I just haven't figured it out yet". Your comment shows a positive attitude. You have every right to pursue a career and to work at achieving your dreams. Both of your careers "may", (it hasn't happened yet), interfere with being together as much as you would like. This can put a great strain on a relationship if there isn't good communication and giving on the part of both of you.

Have you exhausted all the possibilities regarding your entrance into the field of wildlife biology? In our area we have many parks, hiking trails and nature preserves. They are all staffed by "naturalists". They also teach at local community colleges, conduct field trips for schools, give presentations and conduct nature hikes, field trips, write articles for local papers, etc. Perhaps you are more interested in field research?

In any case, look at all the possible options, do a bit of networking, discuss possibilities with your teachers and peers. Leave no stone unturned!

Best regards,

Julia

Differences In Opinion

Dear Elders,

I am an Accounting Manager at a Law Firm, and I have recently laid off two employees who did not do much and were far from motivated. I plan on hiring one quality person to replace the two which will make the team a great one! My issue is that my boss, the CFO, the Executive Director and I all have different ideas of who this person should be (qualifications as well as responsibilities). In the end, this person reports to me, so I need to get what I need and want taking their needs and opinions into consideration. Any tips on how to handle the situation best? I don't want any of these people (all higher level than me) to hold this against me. Thanks!

Elder Response

Hi. Thanks for writing.

Well, let's see. You had the job of dispensing with two employees and you had no problem with that because you saw lack of performance. Was your CFO involved in this decision? Should it not be a "quid pro quo". If you have the authority to "dispense" should you not have the authority to be involved in the replacement? Not all CFOs understand exactly what is involved in "account managing". It takes a bit of delicate maneuvering to suggest that trust in you will not be misplaced. A face to face meeting with your CFO convincing him/her that you understand what the firm "needs" is in order. Make them understand that you are working to make things "happen" with your properly motivated people and that you can do the job if you are involved in the "process".

Good Luck,

Sherry

Unemployed & Unhappy

Dear Elders,

I really like the idea of going to elders for their wisdom and life long experience. I've been feeling overwhelmed the last few months. I'm a 25 year old woman that was laid off in January from my software developer job. I have been job hunting the last few months and the job opportunities I have been presented are nothing I want to do. The company either turns out to be shady or it's a long commute. I've also been unhappy in my stage of life. I pictured myself at this age to be settled in my career, on the steps of marriage, and moved out. Now, I don't know what I am going to do with my career. Do I want to do web development or go to public relations? I really like writing. Do I continue sticking in my 6 year relationship? I'm just so confused. I try to remain optimistic and happy, but deep down inside I'm overwhelmed and unhappy about my life situation. I know I'm young and things should turn up soon, but I'm tired of waiting. Any advice?

Elder Response

Hello and thanks for writing…

Sometimes we reach a stage in our lives where we realize that things aren't working out as we planned and dreamed and yes, it can be scary and frustrating! When I was in my late twenties I had similar experiences and looking back on it now, I see that it was time for me to make some changes, which I did, to improve my life.

You seem at such a stage right now and while it's difficult and unpleasant to be out of work, for example, this can also be seen as a chance to try out something new. The public relations field is very broad and you might want to do homework, researching the field: try this web site…

www.wetfeet.com for good tips on career changes in general and PR in particular. Something to keep in mind is that most young people will have several careers in their lifetime unlike older times where we stayed in just one. Don't panic; see this as a step in self-discovery, realizing that only by trying something out will we know if we like it and are good at it.

Also, you seem to be questioning a 6-year relationship. That, too, is not uncommon…the "7 year itch" gets it name from that time in a relationship when we DO face some issues and events that require re-evaluation. Again, this is both scary and exciting a time. It would help to check in with a counselor for a short time, say a few months, and see what you can learn about this relationship. Some need some fine-tuning, while others need a major re-haul. Again,use this as a time for reflection and change to make you live richer and fuller.

Most people, at some times in their lives, face these overwhelming situations and the ones who do well move THROUGH them, not around them! Yes, it's tough at times, but believe me, it's much worse to live blindly and just go through the motions.

On a more practical level, how about trying to get more exercise/active fun in your life. How about a change in your eating habits that will give you more energy? Take a different route to a store, visit a local neighborhood or park for some variety. These small things can help ease your stress (as will quiet meditation)and help you in making decisions. Also, be KIND to yourself, patient and gentle…these changes ARE hard, will challenge you and you'll need lots of self-love to forge ahead.

Best of luck…

Cindy

Burned Out Doctor Seeks New Career

Dear Elders,

I am 45 years old, and i have had my fill of the practice of medicine (anesthesiology) in this day and age. I have the personal freedom to choose to leave a high paying career and start anew (no wife or children, no huge financial obligations).

I enjoy learning, and my ideal is to have a new career in which i am paid to learn new things. I have a strong interest in the process of financing for new and early stage companies. I think my experience and skills would be useful to venture capitalists and other investment professionals in helping them to understand the science and technology behind the companies they are evaluating for investment.

I do not know how to best pursue such a career shift.

I have broad experience in medicine, touching on many specialties, including a year of experience in a molecular biology laboratory. My communication skills are excellent. In particular I am skilled at explaining complex scientific concepts and issues in simple language that laymen can easily grasp.

Over the past five years I have worked part-time as a consultant for lawyers, evaluating their malpractice cases for merit, analyzing other kinds of cases that have medical issues, performing library research and teaching attorneys the medicine they require to intelligently prosecute or defend a particular case. I have also had a couple of investment clients for whom i have analyzed and explained technology behind a company's products and assisted in their investment decisions.

If you are a venture capital or other investment professional, or a physician who has made a similar career change in mid-life, I welcome your wisdom and insight. Thank you very much.

Elder Response

Dear Doctor,

I am not a venture capitalist, other investment professional or physician, but I have been around the block a couple of times.

Were I in your shoes, I'd stay clear of venture capitalists. On the other hand, I believe that the consultant to attorneys concept holds promise. 1) Your knowledge and experience as such is an essential element in successful defense or prosecution of malpractice suits.

2) you have a client base on which to build. [Reads: Networking and word-of-mouth.] Insurance companies should also be fertile "hunting grounds." You may also want to consider advertising in a local Law Journal. [Suggest that you have an advertising agency frame the ad.]

I wish you the best of luck.

WO Owl

Should I Hang My Shingle?

Dear Elders,

Hello. Next month I will graduate from law school and face the daunting task of finding a job. However, I have always wanted to run my own business and I have a friend who is graduating 6 months after me who asked if I would like to start a law practice with her. I would love to do this, but am afraid. I like the security of getting a paycheck every week, but in the long term I would value building something for myself more. Originally, I thought that I would work for a law firm for a few years to get experience, but that may be a mistake because I may get too comfortable to leave. Also, I worked for several years as a paralegal, so do have some legal background. The areas my friend and I would focus on would be environmental law (I worked for Dept. of Env. Protection for 5 years), real estate and business. I know there are organizations to help small business owners, such as SCORE, SBA and my state (Mass.) has an office for minority and women business assistance to help business owners bid on state contracts. I would appreciate any advice you could offer on whether or not I should 'go for it' and hang my shingle. Thank you very much.

Elder Response

Hello:

In response to your inquiry, I would offer this:

Henry Ford once said, "Yes, if you start on your own, you assume the risks. However, you are in control and are eligible for your share of the pie." I would go further to say. You get to cut it. Go for it. The cost of security is that the organization makes the calls. You are the puppet of their wishes. Who says you are not every bit as qualified to make even better decisions.

i have found that in life their are many dictators very willing to get between your talents and the payoff. They give you a pittance and continually tell you how unworthy you are. Their jealousy causes them to undermine you.

G O F O R I T.

Thank you for the opportunity to share.

Frank

Unemployed In Changing World

Dear Elders,

I was recently (last week!) laid off from a high-tech company. I have about 3 1/2 years' experience in computer programming. However, the market is really tough right now. It seems like there is a glut of programmers out there. Honestly, I never thought I would be in this situation: I always assumed that since programming requires 'hard' skills (math, programming languages, computer skills), I would always be in demand. However, that does not seem to be the case right now. I really love programming, frankly I can't imagine doing anything else, but after my severance package runs out I need to get a job doing *something*. Have any of you 'elders' been in this situation, where you feel like you have a skill that is useful, and within a couple of years it will probably be in demand again, but you can't afford to wait that long? If so, what did you do about it? Because the high-tech field changes so quickly, I don't think it's an option for me to wait it out and hope to find a job in a year or two. I think by that time my skills would be out of date.

Thanks so much!

Elder Response

Thanks for writing.

Welcome to the real world of high-tech. This has been the story of the industry for several decades. Technology changes faster than any other industry; always has, always will. It's also a volatile industry, because to the average consumer, technology (at least latest technology) is a luxury that is first to be abandoned during tumultuous times.

The first time I was laid off from a high-tech job, I drove taxi-cab for three years. Many fellow drivers also had higher educations or training in esoteric fields. But soon, the demand returned, and because I'd continued studying and reading papers on my field, it wasn't difficult to step up to the new level.

I wish you the best of luck, and know that if you keep the faith, and keep up on your reading, technology won't leave you in the dust. (My father continued with his technological training well into his 70s, and when he passed on he was learning COBOL)

Best regards,

John

Balance In Career & Life

Dear Elders,

I have a great job working at a Bank. I have a lot of responsibility (sometimes too much!) and enjoy working through the projects and the problems that I'm given. I'm in my mid-30s right now—no husband and no kids. I'm wondering how to find a life outside of work. It seems that more and more, I want to find fulfillment and direction outside of my job. Is it too late? And how do I go about finding a 'life direction' that doesn't involve me staying late at my desk working on the computer? Thanks for your advice!

Elder Response

Hello and thanks for writing…

How great it is that love your work…maybe even too much, eh? Balancing work with other parts of life was a major challenge for me too. And, no it's NEVER too late to change our lives. Here's some tips that worked for me:

Nothing works better for leaving work at the end of the day than having another appointment! Join a health club/gym, book club, church club, etc., make an appointment to be there/somewhere at 6pm or so and, then….GO! If you do this only once a week for starters, that'll help.

Call a family member/friend and make an appointment for dinner/drinks/shopping/coffee one night a week and……GO. That's 2 nights.

Pick a night to stay at time with your favorite TV program, home movie, good book,plants, new hobbie,etc. and then schedule it in your appointment book and then……DO IT!

Pick a night to volunteer 2 hours after dinner at your a community group (visit: **www.volunteermatch.org** for a place near you) and then….DO IT.

That's 4 nights where you can't stay late because someone or something needs you! On night 5 stay late at work….:)

In order not to overwhelm yourself, I'd suggest doing this slowly….at first, you'll find this a bit harder, but as you get used to having a life beyond work it'll be easier, you'll enjoy work more and expand your life too. If we believe that we only have a month to live, it helps to put lots of things in perspective too. Meditating on the meaning of a full life, knowing how precious life is, can help us keep in balance.

Hope this helps…

Cindy

Maintaining Objectivity

Dear Elders,

I jave recently been promoted to a job where I am in charge of 5 people. Things go well most of the time but eventually in any atmosphere there is conflict. Here's my trouble: I seem to take everything personally. I know that I should but it's tough to stay objective. How can I stay objective and calm?

Elder Response

Hi, thanks for writing. I've made it a mantra in my life that I may not be able to control how I feel, but I certainly can control what I do.

For this to be successful, you have to learn to create a calm in the center of yourself when stress gets too high. You have to acknowledge that you are in a superior position (in charge of 5 people), and that you have that position because you are capable of being what you must be.

If this doesn't work for you, than pretend that you are calm and in control. Do not lose control of the situation, other people or yourself where anyone else can witness it.

By training yourself to follow these rules, the time will surely come when you are in control, and will no longer have this habit of taking everything personally. You are not operating on a personal level here, it is all business and being professional. Now stick to it!

Best regards,

Lydia

It's The Staff, Again

Dear Elders,

When I was hired by this company as project manager, I was assigned two subordinates to help with my project. At the time, I was told that I would only have to supervise personnel for the project duration. Heard that story before? As the company has exponentially grown over the last year, more and more administrative and office management tasks needed to be taken care of and no one was in place to do so. Guess who gradually took on those duties—in addition to my original responsibilities? My project is now completed and I am currently Office Manager and Assistant to the President. I still have two direct subordinates and serve in loco parentis for the remaining staff when the 'big guys' aren't here. I like using my skills and contributing to company operations. However, I still LOATHE personnel supervision!

As it comes with the territory, and the company needs someone with my skills to run the place, I can't very well get out of having subordinates. Can you give me some advice on how I can maintain my enthusiasm for the overall job and minimize the reluctance and dislike for this particular part of my task list? Part of the problem stems from the fact that my staff is inexperienced and needs lots of guidance. Unfortunately, they have a habit of not remembering the guidance and training that they have been given and I can't depend on them to get their jobs done. Those lapses, in turn, trigger my impatience and I have to remember to be fair and not squash the efforts that they ARE making. I plan to change the methods that I use to direct them, like using more written communication instead of just verbal requests and I have asked them to research additional, outside training that they might be interested in attending. But, I REALLY REALLY want to tell them to JUST DO YOUR JOB!!!! Bad, bad manager…

Last week's issue was in regard to a disorganized employee and one of the suggestions was to go to the HR department for assistance. Since I

AM the HR department (and accounting and administration and...), that option is somewhere down the road and can't be utilized in this case either. Any other suggestions that you can give would be greatly appreciated. Thanks in advance for your response.

Elder Response

Thanks for writing.

It sounds as if you have a handful. It also appears as if you may already have found a partial solution to the problem. Put everything in writing.

Doing so will allow you to document that you've given these people the direction that comes with your job. There is nothing wrong with telling them to do their jobs, as long as they know exactly what they're supposed to do. (Make sure you keep copies of this documentation!)

If these employees continue in their failures to comply with directives, their behaviour could be considered insubordinate. The documentation you have amassed should, at that time, be taken to your boss. At that point, if he doesn't support your efforts to solve this problem, you might consider a new boss.

Good Luck!

Paul

Beginning A Career

Dear Elders,

I am 21 years old and have just graduated from the University of California Santa Barbara. I did extremely well in school, including my graphic design classes. I want to start my career as a graphic designer, but my creative talents are rather weak. I know all the tools of the trade and even have a modest portfolio. How do I build the self-confidence to keep looking for an entry-level job when the competition is fierce and the economy is slow?

Elder Response

Congratulations on your graduation, you must be very proud.

It is wonderful that you can take a look at your skills and see where you are weak. Ask yourself this very important question, are you weak in the creative talent area due to a lack of ability or is it lack of experience?

Creativity & passion are linked, if you are passionate about design but lack experience promote your passion & desire to make your mark, an employer will see that. If you feel you lack creative talent but enjoy the business try to find a fit within your chosen industry that won't rely so much on your creative skills.

Starting out is always tough in any market, don't use that as an excuse. If you have a passion please follow it, the world needs more people who love what they do! Make it a goal to not stop til you get the foot in the door.

Best regards,

Jonathan

I Hate My Job

Dear Elders,

I have been unhappy at my present job for a couple of months. It is at the point that I do not want to go to work. I have told my present supervisors of my unhappiness and they assure me that they would support me in what I am wanting. I have gone on a couple of interviews within the same company and feel like they have ruined one of my chances at a position I wanted because another girl from the same department is going to that job as well. I was told this would cause a strain on the department if both of us left, but I don't feel like this is a reason to hold someone back, do you?

Elder Response

Your first mistake was in telling you managers that you were unhappy in your job and wanted to look for something else. My experience has taught me over the years that managers see this as betrayal, not honesty. Managers will look after their own self-interest first; not yours. While their holding you back is definitely not fair, their own self-interest dictates that they try to avoid the loss of two employees at the same time. Heaven forbid…they might have to do some work themselves!! If you are not able to find something more to your liking with this company, I would look outside. The internet is an excellent source of jobs. I have found my last 4 jobs through the internet. In the future, I would suggest keeping your feelings to yourself and telling your manager you are not happy when you tell him you have another job.

Best regards,

Sam

Staying Competitive In This Job Market

Dear Elders,

Two years ago I accepted a job in New York City as a writer and editor for a new media startup company. It was an amazing, chaotic experience—I picked up my life in Texas and moved 2000 miles away to the most expensive city in the world. Unfortunately my company suffered the same fate as so many others in the tech sector, and eventually all staff was laid off and the company closed its doors in March 2001. Since then, I have had a great deal of trouble finding a permanent position, even though I know I have the skills, qualifications, and can-do attitude employers want…there just aren't enough jobs, and the job market has become highly competitive (I usually battle with 60 others just for an interview).

Since it has now been 11 months since my dot-com dreams hit the skids, I am starting to lose hope and question my abilities. I am not a salesperson at heart, and I hate puffing out my chest, but I can't help thinking that employers hire someone else simply because they can sell themselves better at the interview. Last winter I started to run into financial trouble with the high New York rent and cost of living, so I moved back in with my parents for 3 months. I plan to get back on my feet as soon as possible, but I continue to have trouble in my job search. When I find a job I am qualified for, there are too many candidates. When I find a job I would accept because I just need to make the bills and get back on my feet, employers are skeptical because they think I am 'over qualified' for an entry-level position.

Can you offer me some advice on how to proceed in my job search? Rejection at interview after interview wears on my self-esteem.

Elder Response

Thanks for writing. You're correct when you say that employers hire someone else because they sell themselves better at the interview. Instead of this being a barrier for you, it should tell you one strong thing you can do to be a better interview—SELL YOURSELF! That's the way of the world, and to succeed we do the necessary (within our good ethics, of course).

Secondly, you need to present yourself in such a way that the interviewer sees you as someone to hire, even if the job isn't quite a good fit. You should display perhaps a desire to learn some facet of your profession that you can learn better by taking a lower level job, that would negate his feeling that you are overqualified. You have to convince the interviewer that your desire to work for the company will offset their fear that you will shortly leave because you won't be challenged by this job you've accepted below your qualifications.

Remember, the most critical impact we make on other people is the first impression. Work on that—smile, be confident (very important), be open to change, truly believe you are the best person that can be hired for that position. Believe the company would be grateful to have you work for them. Psych yourself up.

Never go in with a poor me or a I'm not going to get this job attitude. Walk proud, talk proud, and you will succeed, perhaps sooner than later.

Prepare yourself well. Know the company. Dress impeccably. Watch your grammar and speech patterns, which by the way are very good. Sit and stand tall. Remind yourself that failing to obtain a particular job is not a personal rejection, but purely business and economically based. No need to lose any self-esteem.

I send you all my wishes for good luck in your search, and my hopes that your life be long and fulfilling.

Best regards,

Julia

Frustrated Nanny

Dear Elders,

This could fall under children as well, but beings as how it's mainly a problem with my boss...

Anyhoo....I'm a part-time nanny. I work about 6 hours a day taking care of 3 kids, ages 3, 5, and 7. Here's my problem: When it comes to discipline the parents tell me that I'm more than free to spank them. The parents do all the time, and when they're not spanking, they're screaming their heads off at them. No matter what they tell me, I refuse to hit the kids. I just don't feel right about it. If they were my kids, I may feel different, but they're not. So I've tried to come up with creative forms of discipline. Writing sentences, restricting television and video game access, things along those lines. Unfortunately, every-thing I do is somehow wrong to the parents and they wind up nixing it all. Basically, I'm down to the point that I can't think of anything else to do but forget about discipline altogether, or start whacking them on a daily basis (which of course, I can't bring my self to do).

So, any advice?

Elder Response

Hi,

I am certain that this dysfunctional family does not pay you enough to put up with all the gaff. I am equally certain that you can find another nanny position at the snap of your fingers. If I were you, I'd check out. Whatever you do, irrespective of the parents' permission to whack the kids, DON'T DO IT!!!! You could end up in a heap of trouble.

Best wishes,

David

Instant Gratification

Dear Elders,

I don't when I developed it but I am a person who needs instant gratification. If I ask someone to do something, I like it done right then. My thought is, if I wanted it done later I would ask later or do it myself. I am this way at home too. If I want to further my career, I do it right when I have the feeling to do it…I am determined. But yesterday I had someone tell me 'NO' that I couldn't do it now, I had to wait. I need advise as to what to do. Do I just except the 'NO'? How do I tell them to let me do it now!?

Elder Response

Hi. Why should everyone in the world do what YOU want them to do? Why do you expect to be able to do everything you want to do WHEN you want to do it? Only a baby is entitled to instant gratification, and you certainly don't NEED it—you WANT it!

You NEED to do a lot of thinking about being a mature person, contemplate the fact that other people have a right to their wishes as much as you do, and stop being so childish. Yes, sometimes we do have to "accept" the NO from others. It's called Life.

Best wishes and good luck.

Claudia

Transfer??

Dear Elders,

I'm faced with a difficult decision that I would love some help with.

I've been working for a company for 7 weeks now in a position that I'm not terribly happy with (turnover is very high for the position, so I know it's not just me). That being said, I intend to leave the company in about 5 months regardless to pursue a Masters. I have not said anything about this yet.

There is an opportunity to move over to a short-term, project based research position that sounds much more appealing than my current position and one that I know would give me considerable, applicable professional experience for future jobs and advancement should I return to the company after my masters(whereas my current position gives me almost none). I am thinking about applying for the research position but still fully intend to leave in early-mid September. I believe I could make the transition fairly easily (no one in my current department would suffer because of the move) but seeing as how it would only be for a very short time, I feel a little uncomfortable about making the move, especially since I have only been here a short time.

I have never felt good about not revealing my plans to leave but I was admitted after I accepted the job and believe that it would have jeopardized my employment if I had revealed it. Likewise, revealing it in applying for the research position would almost certainly keep me from getting the job and very likely, damage my standing in my current position. Since I am not under contract and I or my employer may terminate employment without any notice, I know I don't have any contractual obligations here—but it does make me feel uncomfortable.

What do you think? Thanks for your advice.

Elder Response

Thanks for writing.

You can't in good faith take the research position without informing them of your intentions of resigning in five months. Not only would it be dishonest, it could do irreparable harm to the firm if a major contributor to said research project were to abandon it without seeing it to its conclusion. This could, in turn, drastically tarnish your reputation, and prevent good job offerings in the future.

As I see it, you have three choices.... stay in your current position; it's only five months and almost anything can be endured for that long.... ask for the new position, honestly informing them of your future intentions...or...changing your post-grad plans, doing the research project, which may put another feather in your cap, and continue with school upon completion of said project.

I know which I would do, given the opportunity; but it's not my decision.

Good luck!

Jim

Need Inspiration

Dear Elders,

Hi again! I've sent a couple of e-mails in the past regarding career questions. But right now I could really use some inspirational or encouraging advice. I'm in a job I've grown to really dislike. I have a 3 hour commute every day too, due to a recent transfer to another branch, and I hate to drive. Basically I'm stuck in the corporate cogs, and am being sensible by keeping the job while I look for something else, and doing my best at it (because after all they are paying me). But I'm becoming really discouraged. I'm starting to feel like this situation will never end, and if I do something radical and risky I could be alot happier a lot faster. I don't have any dependents, and life is short, right? But I guess it would be like running away from a problem…I just need to be patient. Any words of wisdom to encourage some patient feelings to grow? What have you held onto when you were trying to tough out a situation? Or am I being too cautious?

Thanks in advance for your advice.

Elder Response

Hi! Thanks for writing.

Well, it is indeed the hope of many to end up in a career that they enjoy. You know, you wake up in the morning and actually WANT to go to work? Experience indicates that there are different degrees of this "ideal", the lowest degree being "I don't want to get up in the morning".

You have the advantage of having no dependents and that's pretty important. Many find themselves in situations that they dislike but the responsibilities of a spouse and children have them somewhat "tied up".

In your situation you have to determine for yourself if there is any future in where you are working, is there a chance to advance? a chance to prove your worth and grow, and feel a sense of self-worth? If, after careful thought, the chance for you to gain some satisfaction in your situation does not seem possible then there doesn't seem to be much sense in going on (in my opinion). Read something in the paper today…"I do not intend to tiptoe through life only to arrive safely at death". Not a bad thought, huh?

Good Luck!

Peter

Dealing With Incompetence

Dear Elders,

Where do I start? I have had the same supervisor for 2 years. The first year she was an intern/teacher. This year she is director/teacher. The situation basically is that I have been at the same job for 5 years. In that time I have had 3 different supervisors. The workplace is an alternative high school. She is the administrator and I am a teacher. There have been many instances where the supervisor has been incompetent in her job. I have spoken to her as well as her immediate supervisor

(superintendent of the school) of my concerns. Am I asking too much for a supervisor to do their job or do I just shrug my shoulders and let it go? My big concern is the students and their education. I am also concerned for my sanity.

Elder Response

Hello,

In response to your inquiry:

First you may want to examine your values and expectations. If they are impossible to achieve then you may want to change. I applaud you for your desire to want the students educated. You cannot change anyone but your self and your own values. If these will not fix within the structure of where you teach, you may want to either change jobs or become a supervisor yourself and make the changes you feel are necessary.

Good luck.

Frank

Inappropriate Touching

Dear Elders,

I have a girlfriend who has been married for 18 years.

She is quite histronic and extremely affectionate and touchy feely with many people, and has actually had a male co-worker complain to management about how uncomfortable he feels with all of her touching. She is also in a management position with her employer.

She has struck up a friendship with a woman, and while recently on vacation was witness to how much kissing on the cheek, hugging, grabbing of hands she was doing with this woman. My friend has a very strict 7th Day Adventist background and might be horrified to find out what others are thinking of her at her employement regarding my next question.

My sister is friends with another of this woman's co-workers who asked my sister whether my friend was lesbian as she has indeed exhibited VERY friendly behavior towards the aforementioned female co-worker.

My sister's friend has suggested that some people believe my friend is lesbian based on the level of touching going on at work. My question is…do I tell my friend that there seems to be some confusion about her sexual status by her co-workers.

Elder Response

Hi,

Whatever, if any your friend's problem may be; it's not yours. I suggest that YOU NOT MAKE SUCH by getting involved.

Best wishes,

Margaret

Job Boredom

Dear Elders,

I have a really great boss. We usually get along. But lately, we haven't really spoken. More than that, I have been left with little or nothing to do throughout the day. I hate feeling useless, and that's exactly how I feel.

My question is how do you go about telling your boss that you would like more to do and that you are feeling like you are getting paid to watch the clock go by?

Elder Response

"Boss, I have been left with little or nothing to do throughout the day. I hate feeling useless, and that's exactly how I feel. I would like more to do. I feel as if I am being paid to watch the clock go by, and I don't like that. Please give me more work to do so I can contribute to the company."

Why haven't you and your boss spoken lately?

Best regards,

Pat

Dog Training

Dear Elders,

Hi, I'm not sure whether this should fall under career or other. I was wondering if any of you have ever trained dogs and might have some insight for me. I have long had the dream of becoming a dog trainer and obedience training dogs in shelters to make them more adoptable. My husband and I recently acquired 2 English Pointers and have had the oldest one (she's just over a yr now) started as a bird dog by a professional trainer. I find training fascinating and my husband and I talked about the possibility that perhaps training bird dogs might be an option on the financial side to help me realize my dream of being able to afford to volunteer my time to train shelter dogs. I tried speaking to our trainer about it and she said that to really be good at training, you had to grow up and be around dogs your whole life so that you could read them and understand their personalities and what is going on inside their heads. I had gotten pretty excited about our idea up to that point and she kind of burst my bubble. I do love dogs, but I have no practical training experience. I am willing to work hard and learn all that I can, but she made me feel that it wouldn't be enough. I am fairly intelligent and there are many other things that I could find success in, but I really like pursuits that are more hands-on (literally). I have 3 young children, so this is not something that I will be jumping into anytime soon. I was just wondering if any of you have had any experience in this area and might have some insight for me. Do you believe that desire and hard work will not be enough for me to be successful in this particular field; that I have just missed out because I wasn't raised into a dog training family? Or should I plow on ahead, taking my lumps, learning all that I can and hope for the best?

Thanks for your time and thoughtfulness.

Elder Response

Hello,

What a great idea you have and it's too bad you got such wrong advice! Several people I know in the past 5 years have started successful dog training businesses. None of them had any extensive experiences with dogs, except for 3 who had a dog as a pet when they were younger. There are many schools that will help train you and I see absolutely no reason for you not to pursue this wonderful idea. I volunteer at a shelter and they sure do need people at all shelters to help with obedience and other training. There are many books/videos/conferences/workshops on starting this training. Clearly knowing about the different breeds of dogs/temperaments, etc. will help and you can start to get this knowledge now. Absolutely do NOT give up this dream. Your own dogs will be great teachers :)......

woof, woof...

Jeremy

Just Getting By In Life

Dear Elders,

For the last 19 years I have been an electronics tech. This last August, I was laid off after seven years. I have been on unemployment for the last nine months. I was fortunate enough to qualify for retraining in a newer field (Information Technologies—Networking) I am now being told I either have too much experience from being in electronics or not enough experience for network work. It's hard just trying to stay positive and try and meet the weekly requirements of my unemployment. On top of that, I am dealing with diabetes and other health issues on my own (I have no family)

Just need some advice to make it through the day and find some hope which there doesn't seem to be much of.

Elder Response

Hello and thanks for writing.

Sorry to hear about your job loss. This is a very devastating situation for most people and can really erode one's self-esteem! It's great that you took the opportunity to enhance your skills, but now you find yourself between a "rock and a hard place" in seeking employment, eh?

Clearly, the first thing I'd do is be sure to keep yourself in good health. Diabetes is made worse by stress and depression, so do make every effort to watch what you eat, monitor your sugar levels, etc.

Regarding the job situation, you might not want to reveal right now your training in networks and just try to find a job where your experience will impress employers. You can keep searching for a network job, but if they feel your experience is lacking, they won't be likely to offer a position in these difficult times for IT. Here's a good Web site for getting another view of employment options:

http://www.wetfeet.com/asp/home.asp

It has LOTS of good links, tips, resources, etc. For many people in computer technology, the market is grim right now. It's important to not let this erode your confidence! Find something else in life to comfort you right now...family, religion, sports, music...and know that this too, will pass.

Stay positive and best wishes...

Carol

Should I Quit My Job

Dear Elders,

I quit my job because I was unhappy with my boss and position. I am 50 years old and trying to decide how I can be sure that my next job won't lead to the same problems. That is if I can find another job.

I am independent and like working by myself. I worked for many years at one company and lost my previous job due to a merger.

Please tell me any wisdom you have on this topic. Thank you.

Elder Response

Hi! Thanks for writing.

Sometimes I wish they would change the title of this website to "Elder Experience Circle", the idea that age necessarily brings wisdom is argumentable, LOL!

In any case I've got a few years on you, decided to retire early, then 9/11 and the stock market, etc. now forces me to consider re-entering the job market. And I was an independent contractor. You don't say what it is that you do. But I presume it not a matter of disliking your work but more of disliking the "management"?

Perhaps increasing, broadening your idea of what you can do with what talents you have can open up more options? Maybe there are areas where the pay may not be up to snuff but the working conditions are enjoyably rewarding. I know many construction contractors who traded the hassle of working in the field with irate people and deadlines for a job sharing their experience at Home Depot.

Check out "**www.daretochange.com**"

Good Luck!

Michael

Team Transition

Dear Elders,

I am presently in a very comfortable position with my job. I have the opportunity in the next couple of weeks or so to move into a position that would be quite different and involve an entire new team to manage. Any suggestions on how to ease the transition for both the rest of the team and myself. Thank you.

Elder Response

Hi! Thanks for writing.

Well, moving from "comfort" to "challenge" always presents some perplexing thought processes.

We find peace and security in reaching that stage of going to work and knowing how the day will go and how it will end. That's fine for many, the comfort and stability are important. But then there are always the few who have an "itch". They feel there are more and better things to accomplish. They feel they have the talent to do more, they just need a bit of "chutzpah", a smile on their face as they decide to "pull down their pants and slide on the ice". The talent to ease the "transition" is already in you....you just have to recognize it. You already know what I'm talking about, don't you? Ease the transition in friendship and understanding.

Be Well,

Treefrog

2

Home

Apartment-Friendly Plants

Dear Elders,

Hello,

Thank you in advance for any ideas you have to share. I live in an apartment with an abundance of natural light provided by several large windows and a sky light. Except for a Lavender Heather plant (which prefers almost no attention) and an African Violet (which hasn't produced a flower in months), I have not been able to keep any plants alive. Can you suggest some potted plants that will thrive in the conditions I described? I'd like to have a green, vine-like plant and a flowering plant. These guys really have to love light because they really won't find any shadows in which to hide. I appreciate any light you can shed on this topic. :)

Thank you,

Sherry

Elder Response

Hi Sherry!

You don't say where you live but it sounds like you have enough light. Other important things are humidity, temperature, watering habits, fertilizing. I have a feeling that your apartment might be very dry? You might need some dishes of water around or a portable humidifier. When the sun shines the plants work hard at making food for themselves and in the process they lose water in what's called "transpiration"....kinda like sweating.

First, African Violets love "filtered sun". They don't like to have their leaves wet but they need humidity. Placing them over dishes filled with gravel and water does the trick. If the soil feels at all dry then use water with one of those special A. Violet gentle fertilizers.

As far as vining plants I highly recommend one that is called "Golden Pothos" (Epipremnum aureum). They are most hearty, pest resistant, grow fast. They can climb and they can hang. I've got a couple in hanging baskets that trail for 15—20 feet! You can train them to go anywhere.

Other plants I have that pretty much take care of themselves are succulents such as, "Burro's Tail" and "Buttons-on-a-String".

Good Luck,

Bill

Home Improvement: Tuckpointing

Dear Elders,

I'm wondering if I can learn how to tuckpoint the exterior mortar in my 95-year old house or if I should hire an expert. The mortar on my house is beginning to disinegrate in certain places and I want to address the problem before it becomes a huge issue to deal with. Thank you!

Elder Response

Hi!

Well it doesn't take a rocket scientist to tuckpoint. If the house is 95 years old chances are your biggest challenge will be to mix a blend of store bought "redi-mix" masonry mortar and then find some powdered dyes to try to blend in and match the color of the aged mortar in your house. Different dyes can be found at places that sell masonry materials (brick, block, etc). Of course your experimental mixing has to dry before comparing colors.

If matching color is no problem then you have the following options:

Clean, wirebrush out ALL loose mortar. You might want to invest in a "tuckpointing" tool. It's basically a trowel but only about 1/4" in width. With the mortar placed on a flat board or something you use the tuckpointer to push and smooth the void joint. Before tuckpointing the joint moist up (damp) the void with a brush and a bit of water.

Another alternative is to simply purchase a tube of "mortar caulk" (Home Depot, Lowe's) and use the ol' caulking gun.

Happy Tuckpointing! Best regards,

John

I Hate To Cook!!

Dear Elders,

HI!!

Thank You for helping out!

I got married two years ago, when I was 16yrs, I'm really happy with my marriage, but i think their is a big problem, I don't like to cook. I've never, ever cooked before, nor I cook now. But i have a feeling that i should learn. my 30yr old husband cooks, but i feel bad.

Do you think this might end my marriage?, or is their a cure for my hateness? How do i get over this?

Thank You

Elder Response

I suspect the main reason you don't like to cook is because you never learned….now is the time. If you can't get to a cooking class (community colleges usually have some kind of cooking classes), then get yourself some books and get started! Don't try complicated meals with lots of ingredients—"The Joy of Cooking" is not the book you should start with……just a simple old Betty Crocker cookbook might be just the thing.

It won't end your marriage unless it has lots of other problems too—but learning to cook—or at least trying to learn and trying to like it, may go a long way towards cementing the good parts of your marriage.

Give it a try—you might find out it's a lot of fun once you know what you're doing.

Take care...

Julia

Deer Me

Dear Elders,

Okay, what is it about my garden that screams 'Deer Fest'—they wait until night to sneak into my garden and eat the tops off of my pansies. They only eat the yellow ones, mind you, but something else is digging up the ones the deer don't eat. Is there a flower variety that is distasteful to deer? Or is there a remedy other than poison to deter deer from entering my garden?

Elder Response

Hello and welcome to the world of deer-dominance!

Seriously, I have been down this road for many years and the only advice I have is: plant christmas trees…deer don't like them….or fence off your plants with wire high enough to keep them out. There are many remedies out there and I think I've tried almost all of them. Why not live in peace with the deer…DON'T feed them…and buy some good fencing…

Best regards,

Julia

Pie Crust Help

Dear Elders,

I have tried several different recipes for pie crust, but mine always turn out heavy and tough. My grandmother used to make piecrust that was so light and fluffy! I wish I knew her secret. Can anyone tell me what I might be doing wrong? Thanks for your advice!

Elder Response

Hi, how are you? I've answered this question many times, but I'll answer it again, since it's a popular one.

Pie crust should not be worked very much; you should combine the ingredients, barely get it mixed together, and then roll it out, put it in the pie pan and—finished! I don't approve of kneading pie crust, I think it toughens the dough.

My other suggestion (and I admit to using this myself most of the time) is that you use a packaged pie crust mix. I totally recommend the Jiffy brand. One box makes a double or single crust, they are very well priced, all you add is water, and the crusts are uniformly good and tender.

It's so good to know people are still baking out there! Pass it on.

Best regards,

Carol

Facial Mask

Dear Elders,

I am looking for a recipe to make my own facial mask. I am interested in either the traditional clay mask or any other variation. Thanks for your advice!

Erica

Elder Response

Hello,

Here are some that I've used with much success. They are healthy, easy to make and feel wonderful:

Make a paste from a little oatmeal and water. Apply to face and allow to dry. Gently wipe off with a damp wash cloth.

Mash 1/2 banana and add 1 tablespoon honey and 2 tablespoons sour cream. Apply to face and let set for about 10 minutes. Gently wipe off with a damp wash cloth.

Two tablespoons of cornmeal mixed with enough water to make a thick paste makes a great inexpensive facial mask. Gently apply to face and wash off.

To loosen blackheads, combine equal parts baking soda and water in your hand and rub gently on your skin for 2 to 3 minutes. Rinse with warm water.

Mash half of an avocado and apply to entire face. Let set for about 20 minutes and then gently wipe off with a damp wash cloth.

Puree 1/2 peeled, sliced cucumber in a blender or food processor and add 1 tablespoon yogurt. Apply to face and let set about 20 minutes. Gently wipe off with a damp wash cloth.

These are just options...try one each week and have fun!

Cindy

Running Out of Dinner Ideas....

Dear Elders,

Hello. I am boring my family to death with what I serve for dinner.

I'm not much of a cook to begin with. Having a restricted budget makes it even worse. The natives are getting restless and I'm afraid they're going to revolt if I don't start serving something different. Does anyone know any tasty, yet very inexpensive recipes for me to try out?

Elder Response

Hi...I know what you mean! Italian food can be very quick and inexpensive. Try: pasta and beans...

...sautee 2-3 garlic cloves in 2-3 TBS of olive oil

....take 2 cans of cannolini beans/Navy beans and drain them well; add them to the olive oil and add a half can of water or veggie stock and let simmer for 20 minutes; add salt/pepper to taste

...cook a box of your favorite small pasta/macaroni (I like "elbows") until almost done; drain the water and pour the pasta into the beans and then let them cook on low for another 5 minutes to mix their tastes.

Serve with garlic bread and a nice salad!

Also, I like this web site:

http://www.mommysavers.com/cooking_on_a_shoestring.htm

It has lots of recipes that are inexpensive and fast to make.

Best regards,

Cindy

Looking Back on Your House Choice

Dear Elders,

I twice bought houses that I thought I would live in for the rest of my life, putting money and labor into making them home. Both were sold. Now I am in the market for another house. I know that I probably won't live in this next house forever, so I might choose a smaller, less expensive house.

It's not the same for everyone, but from your experience, over the years do you become more satisfied with the house you bought or do you regret that you didn't stretch a bit further financially to get something better or bigger?

Elder Response

Hi, it's nice to hear from you. We have always bought houses we could afford, and then spent a lot of time and money in making them into the house we wanted it to be. We did the same when we bought the house we now live in and expect to live in when we retire.

However, we moved into the house which needed nothing, and haven't yet stopped improving it. The fact is, you either are or are not that type of person—we are definitely both that type of person. We want to make the house ours, not someone else's, so we immediately begin to transform it. This is our life's pleasure; it takes the place of many vacations and other activities, because it is what we want to do.

Here, we immediately took out and had replaced the master bathroom cabinets. They were so ugly I couldn't live with them! Then we had built into the living room on both sides of the fireplace, cabinets and bookshelves I had designed. Then we had a skylight put into my office, which is small and was very dark. We also had a very large window installed in the family room (which we completely re-did, my husband designing, making and installing a wall of bookshelves and fireplace) that looks onto the most beautiful part of the "backyard".

We just finished redecorating the foyer, and will soon start on the back hall and laundry room.

We completely changed the landscaping, adding many flowers and starting vines over the tennis court fence to mask it. We installed a great lily pond right beside the patio (dug by my husband and sons with a small landmover) and I partially cleared the bank behind the house so I could make a wildflower garden on the path that we made to go along the bank.

Most of the work and all the planning were done by us, although we had professionals build the bookshelves in the living room, install the large family room window, the bathroom cabinets, and the skylight in my office. Everything else we do ourselves. We are experts in painting, planning, wallpapering and other decorative arts. I recently painted a faux stained glass window in the laundry room and have one planned for the powder room.

It is the great joy of our life, and we do it only to please ourselves. We sold our former house in one day at the price we listed it, and it was a bargain at that! Actually, we had a second bid for higher than we asked!

I guess some of us are just nuts. Pleasure is where you get it, though.

To answer your question (sorry, I got carried away), we have never regretted a house we've bought (3 in all), we've never regretted selling them, and we are very happy with our present home, and plan to stay here until we can no longer.

I hope you've enjoyed hearing about my home, and perhaps have a clearer idea of what you will do in the future. Never regret doing something, just make sure it's good for you.

Best wishes, good luck, and enjoy your life.

Arianne

Strawberries

Dear Elders,

Three years ago I planted a patch of strawberries next to my house. Last year my plants had next to no fruit on them, yet, the actual plants were very large and lush. I was wondering what I might have done wrong, and what I might try this Spring to improve their fruit output. Any information would be greatly appreciated!

~Spring

Elder Response

Hi!

Well, if the plants are large and lush then you must be in full sun (required). Lots of leaves but no fruit? And no pests are observed? If you use a fertilizer that is balanced or higher in nitrogen it makes that plant want to produce more leaves and few flowers. Suggest you use a fertilizer high on "Phosphate" (the middle number). Use a tomato fertilizer. Strawberries have very shallow roots and need lots of water, but keep the water off the leaves and flowers. The individual plants don't like to be too close together, check that out.

Good Luck!

Ellen

Orchids

Dear Elders,

Hello. How are you?

I just received an orchid from a friend of mine. I have never cared for an orchid. Any advice? Do they like water? Sun? I look forward to hearing from you. Thank you.

Elder Response

Hi! Just fine at this end of the line :-)

I guess you have an orchid growing in some sort of container? To tell you the truth orchids are a different sort of plant. I've tried growing, "nurturing" them and had only minimal success. They are much different from the everyday plants we are used to growing. There are thousands of varieties. They grow in tropical type forests and root in "debris" that often collects in the crotches of trees. They like filtered light, and high humidity. It's kinda hard to create an atmosphere in the normal home that these plants thrive in. Did you get a little note with the plant telling you how to care for it? IMHO they are indeed a "specialty" plant and are pretty fussy about proper conditions for continued blooming. Maybe there are some out there who would take exception to my observations but all I can do is speak from "trial & error" experience.

You might try going to a website "plantfacts.osu.edu", type in "orchid" and get a lot of advice.

Good Luck! And best regards,

Julia

Shoofly Pie

Dear Elders,

Thanks so much for the previous recipes, I cant wait to try them. So I was wondering if you also had the recipe to Shoofly pie.

Elder Response

Of course. This recipe was given to me by my husband's grandmother who got it from a friend who was Pennsylvania Dutch.

In case you don't know who they are, they're descendants of 17th and 18th century settlers from southwest Germany and Switzerland, who do not use many modern things. They use horses and buggies for transportation, do not use electricity or many more things we are accustomed to using. They are a deeply religious and close sect, and wonderful farmers. They live in one of the most beautiful areas of Pennsylvania and many are great artists.

I have numerous recipes for this pie, but this is my favorite, and my family LOVES it. It is best served the day after it is made, if you can keep it that long. I prefer to use dark molasses, but you can choose lighter, if you wish.

Shoofly Pie, Pennsylvania Dutch—Best and Original

Make large piecrust, set aside. Mix together:

—3/4 cup molasses
—3/4 cup hot water
—1 teaspoon baking soda dissolved in small amount of vinegar
—Flavor with cinnamon.

Now mix together, cutting in butter (or margarine):

1/2 cup sugar
1/4 cup margarine
1-1/2 cups flour
Pinch of salt

Add all except a small handful to first mix. Pour into pie crust and sprinkle remaining crumbs on top. Bake at 350º for 20-25 minutes. It is best when it still has a wet bottom.

Enjoy!

Anna

Cats and Houseplants

Dear Elders,

I have two indoor cats that keep eating my plants and killing them. Any suggestions on indoor plants that aren't too difficult to take care of that cats will leave alone? Or some treatment for plants to repel cats? Thank you.

Elder Response

Hi!

There are a number of products at nurseries that are touted as "cat repellents" (maybe they are dog scents). Three things that might work if scattered around the base of the plants; 1) human hair, 2)cayenne pepper, 3)tobacco. Give it a try and,

Good Luck!

Treefrog

Moles

Dear Elders,

I have moles in my back yard and I have tried everything to get rid of them. However nothing has helped. I've tried moth balls, amonium, chewing gun and all the usual things in the store that they sell. The one thing I haven't tried is a sound thing that sets off some kind of noice that the moles don't like.

Any ideas are gladly accepted.

Thanks!

Elder Response

Hi! Talk about moles! I've been battling them for years with everything you've talked about, including the electronic thingie (don't waste your money). You gotta get rid of the grubs that the moles are feeding on. There are a couple of products out there that do the job. One is called "Grubex". But it's got to be put on at the proper time. Here in the midwest it's July.

Actually I've developed my own game plan. I go out and stomp down the tunnels. Go away for 20 mins. or so. Then I come back with a lawn chair and a cold beer and watch the tunnels I've stomped. At my side is a nicely sharpened hatchet. The mole starts "re-constructing" it's tunnel and you can see the sod "humping". I take great pleasure in the "execution". You'd be surprised at how much ground one mole can disrupt! The neighbors, however, do wonder what I am doing sitting in a lawn chair, staring at the lawn, drinking a beer and periodically "hatcheting" the lawn. LOL!

Good Luck!

Peter

Beautiful Back Yard

Dear Elders,

Hello, Now that it is Spring I am ready to do some work in my yard. My family and I have a pretty big backyard near Chicago. We have a pond and some flower beds that are ready to be used for planting. I am wondering what would be the best flowers to plant that will also come back next year? I am looking for anything that will brighten up our garden. Thank you and have a wonderful day!

Elder Response

Hi! Thanks for writing :-)

To tell you the truth you've presented a question that's almost impossible to answer! Your choices of what perennials (plants that return year after year) are in the thousands. Your choices are narrowed by the the amount of sunlight the various beds receive since plants differ in how much sun they need to grow well. I presume you have nice, loose organic type soil?

I guess you would like to have a yard with various plants blooming all spring, summer and fall? That takes a bit of planning, research, and maybe talking with the local nursery people. A lot of major nurseries publish catalogs that show pictures of the perennials and what they like and when they bloom. They often show which plants attract butterflys and hummingbirds.

Since perennials are expensive to purchase (but worth it in the long run) you might want to do a bit of research and purchase one of several good books on them. Ortho has a good one called "Successful Perennial Gardening". You might also visit "**www.nationalgardening.com**" or "**www.ohioline.ag.ohio-state.edu**." Once they are in the ground you gotta know how to make them happy!

Good Luck!

Julia

Buying and Selling a House

Dear Elders,

My family & I are putting our house on the market in a couple of days. We have found a larger house that we would like to buy. Do you have any advice on selling & buying a house because this is our first time selling!

Thank You!

Elder Response

Congratulations! You are either facing a most exciting adventure or something most traumatic. You don't say whether you are using a real estate agent or going it on your own. Big difference. A good agent will handle just about everything, including telling you what you might do to make your house more saleable. Always keep in mind when dealing with agents "who" they are representing, the buyer or the seller. Home inspections are pretty much standard and good, especially if the home is 15 years old or more. Many "systems" start needing attention from there on. In my humble opinion, a good agent does earn his/her commission, it leaves you free to consider the other stuff, like packing and moving.

If you are selling your home on your own then it's vital to have a good real estate attorney, unless you are one. It takes about 1/2 or more to sign the dozen or so documents that are required by enough laws to choke a horse. There are a number of packages out there that deal with selling your own home. A little research on the net or in the library will lead you to these. They will also tell you what to do to your home to make it a "good sell". Good Luck!

Best regards,

Tony

How to Make Soup

Dear Elders,

Does anyone know why when I make milk base soup, sometimes it curdles?

I love homemade Tomato soup, but hate it when it curdles.

Elder Response

Hi. The milk curdles because you're boiling it. You must make the soup, cooking everything before you put in the milk, and after adding the milk, heat the soup gently but do not allow it to come to a boil. Then the milk will not curdle and the soup will be delicious.

Best wishes,

Skye

Quilting/Sewing

Dear Elders,

I recently took up quilting as a hobby and I have a very old machine (about 20 years old) that is very basic. I can adjust to about 12 different stitches and how many stitches to the inch. For a beginning quilter is this machine good enough or do I need to invest in a newer more complex machine. I am not sure how involved I am going to get in this as I am just starting out. I am also planning on learning how to sew garments too.

Thank you.

Elder Response

Hi. I've had my sewing machine since 1971, one of the first things I bought when my husband graduated from college. It's doing fine and has done everything I ever wanted it to do. I have sewed draperies, done upholstery, made all my clothes, and some of my husband's (tailoring)and children's clothes in the early days.

I still use it about every day. I'm currently making pillows and cushions and curtains. It is still great. I have also done quilting on it. I imagine it is similar to your machine, and I have found nothing that it can't do. If you have the basic operations, the rest of the talent is up to you. I would recommend you treat it well and use it forever.

Best wishes, good luck and enjoy life.

Arianne

Ink Stain

Dear Elders,

I need a miracle recipe for getting out ink stains!!

Thanks!

Elder Response

Well, the only process I've found that works at least some of the time is to:

Sponge the stain with alcohol,

Rub detergent into the stain,

Rinse and launder.

If this doesn't work (and I hope you haven't tried other ways to get it out, which might set the stain), I have nothing else to suggest.

Good luck and best wishes,

Paul

Caring For Old Oak Floors

Dear Elders,

We recently bought an old 1915 colonial with beautiful old luminous oak hardwoods. I am not sure how to care for them…I use pledge and a swiffer broom, and that gets them 'surface' clean, but should I wet mop them? Also, what about wax? I think one should wax hardwood floors, but I have looked at every hardware, etc, store around and I see only cleansing soaps like Murphy's oil, but no wax. Is there a once or twice yearly routine I should perform to keep them in top shape? Should I buff them sometimes?

Thanks for any advice!

Elder Response

Thanks for writing.

When we had hardwood floors, we used a dust mop to clean them weekly. Then, once every couple of months, we used Murphy Oil Soap to clean them completely, let it dry, applied Simonize paste wax (in the pale yellow can) and then buff with a machine and lambswool pads.

It is a lot of work, but the rewards are well worth the effort.

Happy cleaning!

Arthur

Furniture Re-finishing Help

Dear Elders,

Recently, my spouse and I purchased a lovely armoire at a church garage sale. The armoire is awfully heavy, of a decent quality and made of sturdy wooden fronts and bottoms. It also is ornately detailed on the two cabinet doors and has similarly detailed medallions on each drawer front.

We wanted to uncover the original finish, as the armoire was painted at least twice before, so we purchased the standard stripping materials and went to work on one of the drawers. While the wood we found beneath was quite lovely, there were two problems: the armoire was initially finished in a 'Celadon Green' stain, and perhaps more importantly, the medallions (and therefore, most likely the detail work on the cabinet doors) are of a material other than wood. That material is firm and grainy like wood, but seems to deteriorate beneath the stripping chemical.

I would hate to lose these decorative touches, and am wondering if there's a better way to uncover the wood's beauty, without ruining the artificial scrolling.

If not, what is the best way to sand the scrolling, so that another layer of paint (dread the thought) can be applied?

I appreciate your help.

Most sincerely,

Susan

Elder Response

Hi Susan! Thanks for writing. I'm into woodworking and do a lot of refinishing. Your problem is a bit curious. Especially the thing about "material other than wood? i.e. before plastic? Can the scrolling be removed and treated seperately?

When I work on scrolling stuff I depend much on a tool called "Dremmel". It's a small tool that rotates with several small accessories for different jobs. I don't care for chemicals because they seem to somewhat inhibit application of new stains.

Am wondering what type of wood the basic armoire is? Is it a softwood(like pine) or a hardwood(like oak)? If you can press you finger nail into it and leave an impression it's a softwood. It's easy to remove stuff from softwoods.

In any case, if it's a beautiful piece, you might consider checking out a pro to strip it well.

Best regards,

Laura

Sun-bleaching Stains?

Dear Elders,

I heard recently that if you put stained articles out in the sun, the sun bleaches out the stains. So I've tried it on my white table cloth and napkins and it seems to be working well! However, I think I may *also* have heard that lemon juice and/or baking soda can help accelerate or deepen the process. I'm curious to try either of these, if they work, but I'm reluctant to do anything that either sets the stains more or creates new ones. If anybody there has experience with any of these approaches I'd love to know! Thanks in advance.

Elder Response

Hi. Yes, the sun bleaching does work; it used to be the only bleaching available. I still recall that my grandmother and the women who came to help her with the laundry always draped white clothes and linens over bushes to dry while the sun bleached them—about 50 years ago.

I agree that lemon juice will help the process, and is particularly effective in removing rust when bleach will just set the stain. I haven't heard anything about using baking soda for bleaching.

Other additives that might help (but should be tested on unimportant pieces first) are alcohol, vinegar and ammonia.

Best wishes, and enjoy life.

Arianne

Germinating Herbs

Dear Elders,

Thank you in advance for your advice!

I am attempting container gardening for the first time, and I've had success with germinating all my seeds except the mint and oregano seeds I planted. I planted the seeds in potting soil, and I've been watering regularly. The seeds are getting direct sun for most of the day, and the temperatures have been mild (probably lows of 50s and highs of 70s). What could I be doing wrong?

Elder Response

Hi! Thanks for writing.

Most seeds, bulbs of any type, like consistently warm soil and slightly moist but not "wet" soil. If you hit the low 50s and the soil is wet the seeds might be rotting before germinating. A good bet is to start the container indoors with a constant warm temp until you see the first shoots come up.

Good Luck!

David

Cleaning Kitchen Pans

Dear Elders,

I forgot to clean the pan after broiling something and boy is it tough! I've tried scrubbing and soaking but nothing seems to work. Is there a cleaning product (or a secret solution) that might help?

Thank you so much!

Elder Response

Hi...wonder what you cooked that wouldn't come out? Hmmm...life is short, so I'd buy a new pan and keep a watchful eye.

Best regards,

Brian

Painting a Room with Crown Molding

Dear Elders,

I am preparing to paint a bathroom in my house. The room has crown molding and I am wondering whether it is easier to paint the walls first or the molding first. I am concerned about taping anything off, as I am afraid that the tape might pull off the freshly dried paint. Any suggestions?

Elder Response

I have handled both ways. My preference: paint the walls first and give them a week or so to "cure". Then use a paper paint tape to edge off for the molding. If you are using good paint and have allowed it to cure, there should be no paint pull-off. If there is any, it should be minimal and can be touched up easily with an artist's brush.

Good luck!

Pat

Spider City

Dear Elders,

Hi! I live in a very humid area next to a pond. Consequently, my lawn is absolutely filled with little black spiders (some not so little, but big and furry). They sometimes get in the house. I hate to spray toxic chemicals because I have a dog and because there is a great deal of wild-life in the immediate area. Do you know of any natural predators I might introduce into the yard to help control this problem? Perhaps there is an all-natural spider repellant I could try? Thanks.

Elder Response

You don't say what part of the country you live in so I have no idea what kind of spiders these might be. In any event, if you live close to a pond, those spiders are keeping down the mosquito population which is, as you know, potentially very dangerous and at the least, very irritating!

Thank you for not spraying toxic chemicals!! You are right to be concerned about the environment and obviously understand how the balance of nature works.

Spiders have many natural enemies, some of which are other spiders, birds, frogs, snakes, certain kinds of bees. Also, considering the time of year, I suspect there is a lot of spider hatching going on and in time, if you can wait, the situation should even out.

I guess I haven't really helped a lot. In my family killing spiders is almost a sin! The insects they consume are so much worse than whatever kind of fears the spiders arouse in us.

Well, maybe I have helped you look at them in a different light. I hope so. Take care and good luck!!

Cheryl

Fishy Smell!!!!!

Dear Elders,

Hello!

I love to cook fish in the house but I always have a problem with the SMELL!!! Do you have any advice for how to either prevent it or get rid of it once it has permeated the house!!

Thank you,

Alyssa

Elder Response

Hi…

I, too, love fish but not the odor! Here's what works for me…choose fish that don't have a strong odor—e.g. fillet of sole, monkfish (avoid strong ones like salmon, bluefish). Odor usually is as strong as the taste. Keep your house/apt. windows open a bit, letting air circulate; instead of frying try grilling or baking; don't use lots of oil; after eating, burn some incense or spray with an orange-scented odor masker and leave the windows open overnight.

Not sure if you like shellfish, but if you boil shrimp, lobster, clams, muscles they don't have a strong odor and are fun to eat!

enjoy….

Cindy

3

Family

Sons

Dear Elders,

Hi,

I need help with my son. He is 8 yo. He is always in a terrible mood at home. He fights with his sisters all of the time and is extremely jealous of the sister that is younger than him. He resents his older sister b/c she is sometimes bossy, though she is getting better. He has a terrible temper and yells all of the time. Please help. I know many of you have raised boys.

Thanks so much!

Elder Response

You have a potentially serious problem here. Why is he being allowed to be moody, jealous, have a terrible temper and yell all the time??? I wouldn't allow it in a son—or daughter—of mine. He would soon find out that his behavior is not only unacceptable, but not allowed. He would suffer from attempting to act without regard for others. Frankly, I'm shocked by the number of children today who seem to rule the household. Don't you know that you're the adult and you're the one who is older and wiser and bigger and stronger and you're supposed to be training and encouraging your children to be good people and not horrors?

I raised two sons and a daughter, and not a single one of them would ever have tried that kind of behavior in our home at any time. I don't know why you have it, except I never for a minute considered allowing it and you do allow it, all the time. It never occurred to me that my home was going to be run by anyone except me. I never considered that any of my children were smarter than me, or stronger than me, or more competent than me to set the rules of our home and family.

What is happening today that so many parents are letting their not-knowledgeable young children run their lives and homes????

Come on people, start thinking. YOU are there to protect, train, encourage, love, respect, and teach your children the wisdom you have accumulated throughout the days of your life. If you can't do this, then for heaven's sake, don't have children. If you want children, then accept the FULL responsibility of being a parent. Parent your children!! Stop being irresponsible yourself. And know, beyond any doubt, that your children WANT your guidance, they WANT you to control them, they WANT to be liked and taught how to act, they WANT to be part of a good and loving family, and you're failing them if you allow them to act as bullies in your home. Best wishes, good luck, and get control of your life so you can enjoy it.

Arianne

Balancing Career and New Baby

Dear Elders,

Hi there,

I am a new mother. I am 30 years old and have a 5 month old son. He is the sunshine of my life, that is for sure. I have a wonderful husband that is totally supportive. The situation we face is that about 9 months ago, my husband lost his job. This happened while I was pregnant, and right after we bought a home. We thought he would get a job fairly soon, but as the ecomomy got worse and worse, the job market followed.

Our son was born in November and after 3 months of maternity leave, I headed back to work. I make a very good living in sales. Obviously, working right now is not a choice, but a neccesity. Our mortgage is quite high, and someone has to pay the bills.

I am struggling with the guilt I feel leaving my son (even though he is taken care of by my husband and my parents help out) to go to work and the guilt I feel in not being able to work as many as hours as some others do. Also, when my husband does find a job, we will have to put my son in childcare. I like my work (most days anyway) and bring in very significant income. However, I do not want to feel as if I have missed out on the precious years of my baby.

Any advice?

Elder Response

Hello,

Congratulations on your baby! I wonder why you feel guilty leaving your son with his father? What a wonderful gift for him and his son to have a bond that so few fathers and sons ever have! Pat yourself on the back for that one! Have you considered continuing to work at your good-paying job, which you really like, and asking if your husband would like to stay and home? Some men really enjoy this much more than their work…why not think about it, at least for a few months or a year? If that's not possible for either of you, then I'd vote for staying at home with your son until he's ready for school. You can continue working part-time/volunteer,etc. to keep your toes in the water, career-wise, and resume work later on.

Best of luck…

Linda

Being a Mommy

Dear Elders,

Aloha! Being a Mother is new to me…I've been doing it for about 5 months now and I love it. My husband and I just moved to a new location and there is soo much to do! Our little one needs attention and love like everybody does…but how can I find time to put things away and clean up without neglecting my little one? If I put him in the swing (he sits next to me while I do dishes) or sit him on the floor next to me while I fold laundry I end up feeling guilty for not paying more attention to him. He also objects to spending anymore than 15 min. without interaction. I talk to him while I do things but its very hard to get much accomplished. I would much rather spend my time discovering new things with him than clean out cupboards and put away dishes. Do you have any suggestions that could help??? Thx.

Elder Response

Hello. You absolutely do NOT want to be entertaining the little one every minute he is awake. It is important that he learn to find entertainment, too. Your company is sometimes all he wants, and sometimes he'll want you to play with him.

It is unreasonable to think that your entire attention must be directed at him at all time. If he is already objecting to your not having interaction with him after 15 minutes, I think you might already have overdone it.

Give him a chance to learn about his environment without your always being in front of him; give him time to contemplate and study and recognize objects, people and just plain space, sometime.

Remember that it is not good for you to be engrossed only in him, because children are on loan to us, and the time will come when they will fly the nest. So keep your individuality, too.

I'm sure you're doing a great job.

Best regards,

Bonnie

Breaking Away From the Nest...

Dear Elders,

I think I'm going to become a frequent user to this service since it is as theraputic as it is enlightening. Thank you so much for all the time you put in for those of us in need.

The purpose for today's gripe is quite a common problem, actually. Basically, it comes down to me having parents that seem to over worry themselves and can't seem to let go. Being the younger of two children, I guess I have always been overnurtured as a child and young adult. That is why after college, I decided to move out on my own. I realize that parents will always be parents no matter what age you get to be, but I'm looking for a way not to get angry when I talk to my parents anymore. It seems that whenever we have a conversation, I always seem to feel that they're not letting me make my own decisions in life and are trying hard to control me. I have tried explaining to them that I need a little room to breath once in a while, but that doesn't seem to help. I love my parents very much and can totally understand where they are coming from because if I had children, I would be worried for them as well. I have read advice other wise elders have given to this problem by acknowledging their comments and moving away from the discussion, but when I do that, I still get a very angry feeling inside me. What makes me even angrier (and quite embarassed) is that the independence that I currently have trouble obtaining are some of the same ones granted to most young adults living throughout the country, such as saving money on rent by finding roomates. They seem to have a strict set of thoughts in their minds for how I should live my life without any regard for my own feelings. I thought that I had demonstrated my independence by moving out and living by myself for the past two years, but I'm afraid that it has really done nothing. To them, I am still as naive as a two year old child. Sadly, I had to end my last two phone calls by saying that they are stressing me out and that I can no longer talk. At the end of each call, all I feel is anger and guilt. Anger for their lack of consideration and understanding of my needs and guilt for ending the call on an unhappy note because they will probably have trouble sleeping knowing that they've upset me.

I work a full time job and have enough problems/stress in my life. The last thing I need is to have stress from my family, which I consider to be my most precious possession. Having been sons/daughters as well as parents yourselves, I hope you can give me some advice on how to not to be angry and break away from the nest (so to speak). Thank you for giving me the chance to unload. :)

Yours humbly.

Elder Response

Thanks for writing.

Parents can be like that, unfortunately. When mine started with their constant criticism of every decision I made, I asked them to refrain. I told them to only make comments that would be construed as supportive and positive; I appreciated them caring for me, but that I HAD to make my own mistakes at my own time to learn from them.

After that, every time they attempted to criticize something I'd done or was contemplating, I would thank them for caring, but when I wanted their advice I would ask for it, and terminate the conversation.

It took a few tries, but finally they realized that I was going to keep my word, and not communicate with them if all they had were negative comments.

Good luck!

George

Teaching a Child Responsibility

Dear Elders,

I have a 5 year old, almost 6 years old, who is taking on a lot of 'older' things without permission. She thinks that almost being a first grader warrants much bigger responsibilities…without understanding that it also means being responsible for her actions. How can I leverage this time in her life? What kind of responsibilities can I give her that will help her understand what responsibility is?

Elder Response

Thanks for writing.

If the first responsibility you gave her was a chore, or something else she didn't find pleasurable, and stipulated that she had to earn her next responsibility by first fulfilling that one, you might slow down her demands.

Things that come to mind are making her own bed, and if she has a younger sibling, the bed of that sibling as well; or maybe a light weekly or daily cleaning project that is within her physical ability.

Once she has successfully met this responsibility for a month or two, add another one to her list. Continue, one responsibility at a time, and if she fails to complete them all in the time stipulated, a loss of a reward would teach her the importance of being responsible.

Hope that helps. Best regards,

Helen

Missing Dad

Dear Elders,

My dad passed away very suddenly almost 1 year ago. Do you think that he knows what is happening in my life now, or has anything to do with the things that happen to me?

Elder Response

my dad passed away many years ago but i know that he is always with me and the good things that have happened to me are the result of his teachings.

Best regards,

Jim

Help—My Daughter Misbehaves

Dear Elders,

My daughter is 7 years old and over the last couple of years she has really developed an attitude, more like a teenager. She talks back to me, yells at me and will not do as she is told. I want to stop this before it gets worse, and definately before she gets any older, but not sure what to do. Time out never worked and grounding her doesn't work either. Any advice would be helpful.

Elder Response

What do you mean grounding doesn't work? If you've told her she can't go somewhere because she's grounded, then why hasn't it worked? Do you give in, or change your mind, or let her have her way?

You have a serious problem in the making here. If you think she's difficult now, how do you intend to control her when she is a teenager?

You are the parent, the adult, and you must be the one to set the rules and see that they are followed. If she doesn't adhere to this, then it is your responsibility to see that somewhere she realizes she loses by not following rules. I assume you have not made this clear to her.

This is your problem, not hers. YOU have to take the position as the power person, because if you don't, she is in for a very bad and difficult life, not having learned rules must be followed. Do your really want her to grow into an adult with that attitude? If not, you'd better find something what works to control her power with you and your household.

I suggest you talk with a therapist about her attitude; she, or you, or all of you, may need professional help.

Best regards,

Margaret

Annoying Little Sister

Dear Elders,

My little sister is 15 months younger than me and very annoying. People mistake us for twins and that bothers both of us. She and I fight a lot and sometimes hurt each other. One time she sent me to the emergency room. My parents just ignor us when we fight and that makes things worse. I think we would fight less if we didn't have to share a room, except my parents always say, 'Learn to get along and then will think about it'. I need to be alone but our house is so small that I cant go anywhere without being bothered. My sister and I try to get along but she always gets mad a the silliest thing. How can I get my sister and I to stop fighting even though my parents have been trying for 12 years?

Elder Response

Hi! Thanks for writing :-)

Well, I'm not sure how old you are? Maybe 12 or so? In any case both you and your sister have to decide that hurting each other and fighting is not a good thing at all. Sometimes sharing things, like a room, is a good opportunity to practice patience, understanding, and love. But this can only happen if you talk to each other, and talk without being mean. Really listen to each other….REALLY listen. You say "she always gets mad at the silliest thing"….do you do so too? Think about it. Don't talk about each other, talk about your dreams and hopes. Talk about teachers and friends. Talk about how you want to be friends for life….sisters forever. And always be prepared to forgive each other's stupid comments. When the years pass "15 months" will just be a tiny click of the clock.

"Learn to get along" simply means we are looking for opportunities to do those random acts of kindness and speaking gentle words to each other at every chance we get. And we ignore all that would be otherwise.

You Can Do It!

Best regards,

Angela

How do I Ask My Dad?

Dear Elders,

Hi! Recently, two of my uncles have needed angioplasty. As they are my father's brothers, he has been having tests run to check the condition of his health. This is a good thing. However, he refuses to inform us (being my brother and I as our parents are divorced) until after the fact. I would like to help him, or at least go with him, but this is impossible. How can I approach him to let him know that I would like to know before he goes and not after. He is a very quiet person and difficult to talk to about certain issues. Thank you for your time and knowledge.

Elder Response

Hello,

Maybe your dad has his own, good private reasons for wanting to tell you after the tests. Why not just respect his wishes and wait until the tests are done? He's doing the right thing by getting a check-up and may not want the added stress of you going with him. We all handle things in a different way and since he's clear about how he feels, let the issue drop. Trust him and respect his wishes.

best of luck,

Michael

Grandma Wants To Move

Dear Elders,

We moved here from AZ about 7 years ago to bring our children closer to their grandparents. We live 5 minutes away and the children are as close to them as can be. Recently my brother who has no children, announced he is buying a lot of property in PA. My Mom was invited to sell her house and move there since it is much cheaper than here. My sister and her husband are also picking up and moving too. Now we are going to be the only ones on Long Island. I don't wnat to move to the sticks where we not ahve any hopes of getting teh professional jobs we have here. We are all in an uproar about it. I think my parents are being selfish but I think I am too. I have 5 children that will be heartbroken. My parents seem to think we will go there every weekend. My kids play soccer on teams on the weekends so this would not be possible. They also think I would sned them for months in the summer. I don't wnat to be away from my children for months (even weeks would be too long). HELP!!

Elder Response

Hi,

Everything else aside—if your family were to decide to go swimming at Jones Beach on January 1st, would you join them?

Of overriding importance: How does your husband feel about joining the exodus?

As for the children: The sooner they learn that the road of life is not a paved super highway, the better off they'll be.

In my opinion, the idea of joining them is preposterous.

Best wishes,

Jack

Kids & Medicine

Dear Elders,

My 3 1/2 year old yesterday started with a new way of 'manipulating' me. That is, holding his side, crying at the top if his lungs (in front of my friends) and claiming he needed medicine immediately to feel better....the good tasting stuff.

How do I instill the in him the proper respect (time, place, use) for medicine?

Thanks.

Elder Response

Hi,

The next time your son demands medicine, I'd feign a phone call to the doctor and tell the boy that the doctor said that he cannot take the medicine any longer and that when he is in pain, he will need a shot.

Thereupon I'd pack him into the car and drive in the direction of the doctor's office. Betcha a dollar that when he realizes that the jig is up, the pain will go away. [Repeat as necessary.]

Best wishes,

Pat

Death of Father

Dear Elders,

Hi, My dad passed away a month ago. Although he was sick, it came as a shock to the family. He and my mom had been married 57 years. I know its only been a month, but does it get easier for both the children and my mom? She's having such a hard time adjusting to the loss. They did EVERYTHING together. She does not drive, so she relies on family to take her places. Is there anything we can do to make it a little easier for her?

Thank you.

Elder Response

Hi! and thanks for writing.

We have experienced much the same in the last couple of years. Wow! 57 years! They sure must have been in love and it's not hard to understand the loss felt when someone you've seen every morning and gone to bed with every night for 57 years is now gone. Everything seems suddenly so empty and meaningless. There's a gigantic mental and emotional "void". Time for the family to understand that she has to learn to accept and find reasons to go on. It's a "touchy" process because at first it's "you don't understand". Then it's "no reason for me to go on". But I know you do understand and there are many reasons for her to go on with the rest of her life. Dad has to remain a "presence".

My dad passed away 9 years ago. Today my mom is 85 years old and we constantly celebrate dad's life. We joke, and smile and have rememberances, and include him in all our thoughts. But this didn't happen overnight. It took the children to help mom understand and celebrate dad's life, what he accomplished, what drove him. It takes time. Be patient with your mom and be there to fill the void and get her slowly back to a new life, one that can include your dad in a very real way. I'm sure you can do it.

Be Well and then share it! Best regards,

Claudia

Mother's Day

Dear Elders,

Mother's day, though fairly far from now, is an important day for me. I have given my mom something every year and am running out of ideas. I've already given flowers and other traditional items. Would you have any other interesting ideas??

Elder Response

The best gift you can give your mom is yourself, a whole day with just you and her, no need to spend a lot of money or even any—go someplace and have your picture taken together—give it to her in a nice frame. Do what she likes to do—in my own case, I would love it if my kids would take me to one of the big nurseries around here and just spend a few hours looking at the plants and seeds and even the dirt! Then come home with me and dig in the garden for a while, maybe take my car for a wash (it's hard for me to do now) or ask me if I could have anything in the world, what would it be—and then talk about it. Get the drift?

You're very considerate to ask; take care and have fun!

Best regards,

Karen

Caring for Ailing Mother

Dear Elders,

My mom is 82 years old and suffers from Myasthenia Gravis. She has always been fiercely independent. My sister and I are dealing with the multiple issues of how to best take care of her without making her feel like a child (of which we are often accused). She still lives by herself. My sis and I and our children take turns going each day to help her (when we get off work) and we make all her meals. She is beginning to admit that she needs help a couple of days a week with housekeeping but we feel she needs live-in help. This is so difficult for everyone involved and is draining emotionally for all of us.

My mother is an extremely private person and doesn't like even us touching her things or going into her rooms and is obsessive-compulsive about her 'stuff'.

I know there are many people who must deal with these issues. I would like some information and support on these matters.

My mother has expressed feeling like a burden to us and many times she says she doesn't understand why God just doesn't let her die. She jokes and states that my dad and my other sister, are in Heaven and they have their feet on the 'pearly gates' because they don't want her to go up and interrupt their peace and quiet!

If there is anything we can do to make this easier on her we would like to know.

Elder Response

Hello,

I had similar problems with my aging mother and here's what I'd suggest. Talk with your mother about getting her some help for a few hours/day at first. It may be harder to have her accept full-time "live in", which you may have to do later on. When you search for a home health aide be sure to check references and tell them about your mom's privacy needs. Sometimes you have to try out several aides before you find the right one. My mother had a hard time for 3-5 months accepting a "stranger" living in her home. She resented the loss of her "control" over her home, but had to accept some of the needed help. Eventually, with my sister and me, we made it work, but you need to make frequent visits to establish a friendly relationship with the aide. You also may need to "mediate" her relationship with your mother and learn that there are always "2 sides to every story". Our aide was wonderful, mom eventually accepted her and she lived with my mother for the last 3 years of her life. It became a very close, nurturing relationship, after such a rocky start, but it can be done. Don't get discouraged and don't try to take any of your mom's independence away…let her do anything she can for as long as she can. Give her a chance to rant/vent about losing her freedoms, options, etc. This is a very stressful change for many people, who if they can admit it, will have an easier time adjusting.

best of luck…

Linda

My Children's Friends

Dear Elders,

I have a five year old son. Since I am a single mother, I work very hard teaching my son good morals and manners. He is a very polite and intelligent child who gets compliments constantly. I am proud of him. I also keep a good eye on him. Never does he play outside without my supervision and we do everything together. I am not the kind to have others watch my son while I live my life. He is my life and I value his well being more than anything or anyone else.

However, the little friends that he has in the neighborhood and from school aren't as well behaved as my son. They are really bad! I told myself that he could no longer play with them, but that didn't work because there are no other children in our area. Then, he is lonely. I tried not letting them inside and just play time outside, but that is dull at times and my son likes to play inside.

One family allows their son to speak to them with NO respect. He knows not to try that over here, but we do have some trying times. Another family has allowed their daughter (4yr.s) to roam the neighborhood since she was three. At times she leaves the house and they don't even know where she has gone. Yes, our neighbors in the area are wonderful, but you NEVER know when an evil person is out looking for little kids. HORRIBLE!

Parents that we know leave their children with me. Some parents from school who have NEVER been to my home or met my family, have allowed their young sons to stay over night. It doesn't bother me because I know that I will take care of them and my son is safe. But, it bothers me that parents are so trusting when we don't know each other as well as we should.

Ok, so my main problem is this: should I slowly end these relation-ships? I kind of feel that God sends these children to me and my family because we do love children (no matter how tired we are of having them around), and we WILL keep them safe from harm. Some parents these days act like they don't have to take any precautions in this DANGEROUS world.

On the other hand, I am constantly trying provide some "home train-ing" for these handful of children who are not mine, but who are friends that my son LOVES!!

How do I handle these situations? My son is only 5, but it makes me wonder will I always be the one to provide the safe environment for kids as he gets older. And do I have to try so hard to "raise" them when they go home and get nothing?

Take as long as you want to answer because I value your advice. I know that many of you have probably gone through things with your kids! But I feel I have a conflict because in my heart I feel responsible but my head says that their parents need to be responsible. OH! I am also an elementary teacher, so you probably can see why I am concerned for these children.

Elder Response

Hi!

Yes, I sure can understand your concern. We have three wonderful children, all grown and two grandchildren. Believe it or not I both my wife and were teachers, my mother-in-law was a teacher and two of our children currently teach. Teaching and being a parent is a bit like a two edged sword. You have a pretty good idea about values and a pretty good idea on how to teach them. But other parents aren't so blessed and that frustrates the heck out of you.

As you know there's a lot of good and bad out there. And on certain days it's hard to tell which is more prevalent. As hard as a parent might try, it's impossible to protect their child from either. The best that can be done is to communicate constantly those values that will enable them to eventually sort out the good and avoid the bad. If done at the earlier ages the job is much easier and eventually proves rewarding.

We used to have our children's friends over all the time. Our home was always warm and friendly. Their friends seemed to prefer coming to our home. And you know from experience in the classroom & neighborhood that there are parents out there that could sure do a better job! We didn't try to raise other's children. If we were approached to provide a bit of "daycare" and the child was familiar with our children's values then no problem. Otherwise we graciously declined. If one of the children's friends proved difficult we explained that it was not acceptable. Eventually both the neighbor parents and our children got the picture.

In anycase, you seem to definitely be on the right track. The older they get the less they seem to listen and what you instill in them now will be tested in the years to come (just wait til he/she gets a driver's license! LOL!)

Good Luck!

Treefrog

They're Spoiling My Child!

Dear Elders,

My three-year-old son is the first (and only) grandchild for both sides of the family. Despite promises from my mother and my wife's parents not to spoil him too much, I still see a pattern of extravagant gifts and lack of discipline that is beginning to affect his personality. Now he's trying to extort gifts from me just for brushing his teeth or getting into bed! I can understand and welcome a small gift for him every so often, but the grandparents all live very close and see him regularly. Their little gifts upon every visit are literally overflowing our house.

How can I put my foot down without stomping on their feelings?

Elder Response

A Grandparents joy is to spoil a Grandchild, but you are going to need to be the kill-joy. You must sit down with both sets of Grandparents seperately and have an open discussion, the fact is you are the parent and will determine the standards & rules for conduct.

Your son is like most children wise to the game and probably can play Grandma & Grandpa pretty well and gets frustrated when it doesn't work on you. Be kind but lay down the law, I'm sure your parents have good intentions and will cooperate.

Best regards,

Peter

Christmas After Losing A Loved One

Dear Elders,

Our family has suffered a deep loss recently and as we head into Christmas we are unsure of how to handle gifts during this difficult time.

John, my husband's brother, was 30 years old and a firefighter who died tragically in the trade center.

The children are not sure how to handle Christmas and what sort of gift might be appropriate and meaningful. We are putting together a "remembrances book" which will be filled with stories. This will be one gift.

Do you have any thoughts on an additional gift that might be appropriate and bring them hope or solace this Christmas season?

Thanks for your help.

Lisa

Elder Response

I am so very sorry for your loss—the advice I offer will be from my own experience as I lost my first-born son when he was 31. Let me tell you this, first of all, your book of remembrance is the greatest tangible thing you can give right now. Never be afraid to mention his name—this will be balm on all the hearts that are broken. There is no such thing as "reminding" someone of their loss—believe this, it is always there. Talk about him as if he were just in the other room, when you feel it is appropriate, laugh about funny things he may have said or done, cry often and never hold tears back. You do not say if his parents are still alive—be aware that their pain will never end, nor will his siblings, but it will be a different kind of pain. Those things that meant the most to me, and still do, are any words written down of experiences shared, even simple things. I know you may be feeling immensely inadequate to this pain—you are not—You may have had grief counseling—what to say—what to do. The truth is, there is nothing anyone can do to take away this kind of pain—people half a world away are crying with you, I'm crying right now....just be there, it is the greatest gift you have. Peace,

Sam

Who's Talking

Dear Elders,

At what age should a child start talking? Is there anything a parent can do to help a child start talking?

Elder Response

The best thing you can do is read to your child. Every day. Children who are read to begin talking and understanding conversation at a much younger age.

You also need to realize that talking is a motor skill NOT a sign of intelligence.

The average age for beginning words and short sentences is two. That means some start earlier and some later. I had four children, the youngest began using sentences at 10 months, the two in the middle (twins) didn't say anything until they were past two, the oldest started with a few words and simple sentences right around two.

It is important that you do not ridicule or shame your child in an effort to make him or her talk—that will usually result in putting off talking even longer.

Relax and enjoy your child at whatever age they are right now—

You do not state the age of your child—everything I have said is valid, but if your child has not started talking by the time s/he enters kindergarten, you might want to discuss it with a pediatrician.

Good luck—take care.

Cheryl

Pressure on Teens

Dear Elders,

Hi. I am fourteen years old, and a freshman in high school. I have always been pushed by my parents to be the perfect child. To please them, I do everything. I am a straight A student, I run three seasons of varsity track at a national level, I write for the newspaper, am in various clubs, and try my hardest a everything I do. But it's never enough. If I get a 98 on a test, the first thing they think of is where the other two points went. I have never heard "as long as you try your best". This was alays imply ow things were, but now that i am in high school, I find my interests changing. There are more important things to be right now than a perfect math exam. I love the outdoors, and go hikin and back-packing whenever I can. I am involved in activist organizations, adam thininhg that i might want to pursue work in that sector. To me, the things that they hae always emphasized are just not as important. But, everytime I try to bring the subject up, they go crazy. One day i suggested i might want to go to the University of Colorade in Denver got college, and they told me that ws ridiculos, that I was going to Princeton. I am wondering if you have any advice for me to help me make them realize what a burden it is to carry their expectations, ecasue they don't seem to listen to a thing I say. Thanks.

Elder Response

Hi! I can relate to your predicament very well. My oldest son graduated as valedictorian. But when he was a junior in H.S. he holed up in his room a lot. I got worried and asked him what was the problem. He broke down and admitted that our expectations were too great and it was too hard to meet them and he was not happy. He talked much, even cried (and that's not easy for a varsity baseball and football player. He kinda forced us to listen to him. We finally understood that we were indeed putting too much pressure on him, but here's the key…we didn't realize it!

Your parents love you much otherwise they would not care and put on the pressure. But you must approach them and tell them that you love them but, in all honesty, the pressure hurts. By the way our son ended up in Boulder, Colorado even though we wanted him to go to Cornell. You can do it!

Best regards,

James

First-Time Father

Dear Elders,

We are expecting our first child in three weeks and are excited to welcome this gift into our lives. Still, I am anxious about how dramatically our lives will change. I perceive that we will have little time alone to enjoy one another, just reading a book, watching television. I am concerned that my wife will be stressed out a lot of the time. How did you respond with your first?

Elder Response

Hi...and congratulations! Gotta tell you a story. Back in 1966 my wife, ok "we" were "expecting". Those days no way to tell what the sex was and birthing programs were none existant. But the bonding between us was great. Your excitement tells me the same.

Yes, your lives will change but, happily, for the better. At the early stages, the husband has to understand that the wife has carried a child for nine months and now it's come to a completion. As far as I can figure that can be depressing. Haven't figured out why after three children....but it is so. You gotta just understand, and back rubs are most therapeutic and necessary (not for you....her).

For awhile everything is centered around the newborn....but that doesn't mean that you can't at least show all the love and appreciation you can. Some flowers, some special hugs....nothing really "overt". Make some soup . We martians feel particularly inept at this time. But it does change and "paternal" instincts do surface.

You will adapt, and if you have had good parents then you will remember, and if you forget, and they are still around, give them a call.

Your lives will change, but if love is there, it will change for things far beyond your expectations.

Best regards,

Chuck

My Son Is Trying To Move Back Into The House

Dear Elders,

I am the mother of a 27 year old that has moved back home on several occasions. I would like my husband and I to finally be 'free' after so many years raising kids. How can I tell him WITHOUT hurting his feelings that I do not want him living us?

Elder Response

Hi,

I am afraid that there is no easy way of telling a 27 year old child that you don't want him to live with you any longer.

If I were you, I'd tell him outright that it's time for him to become independent.

If you can afford to do so, throwing some $$$$ at him [with the strict understanding that it's a one time shot] might ease his "pain."

Best of luck,

WO Owl

Facing Fear

Dear Elders,

I know that I am truly blessed with a loving husband and delightful young son. We have tried for four years to have a second child experiencing 4 inexplicable miscarriages in the process. This experience has been quite difficult on me. We picked ourselves up, dusted ourselves off and tried again, this time through adoption. We have a beautiful baby girl waiting to come home to us. The closer it gets to her arrival the more anxious I become. We love parenting and believe we are doing a very good job, I just can't help but be afraid that something traumatic may happen again and I will have to go through some other kind of horrible emotional pain. I realize this is irrational, but it feels real. That in conjunction with Sept. 11th is tough. I love my children so much and want to give them a safe world without fear. Feeling like I can't do that allows the fear to get to me sometimes. Any suggestions for developing a bright, optimistic outlook once again? Thank you very much.

Elder Response

Hi!

Congratulations on your growing family. Yes, 9/11 took a lot away from all of us and added an insecurity that is not really definable. But we have to go on, not with the past, it's done and over, but with the present and those we love here and now, and what you call a "bright" outlook and future. Methinks that's what makes us as a human species "unique". We can recognize loss, disappointment and suffer it all but at the same time maintain hope as we recognize what blessings we have and presume more to come. Be positive and presume the best. To do otherwise puts you in a "limbo" of doubt and frustration.

We all want to "give" our children a safe world. I'm not so sure that's entirely possible. But what is possible is to give them love and life and the desire to make it a better world. Congratulations on taking on the responsibility of giving hope for the future.

Keep Well,

Bonnie

Preschoolers

Dear Elders,

Need advice—have 4 yo twin boys very inquisitive about their bodies—particularly private parts. Have talked to them about "playing with their pee pee" but they continue to do it—what should I do.

Elder Response

The title of your letter gives me a few clues! You are concerned that your little boys are playing with themselves, and I hate to tell you but they are. Even at the young age of 4 a little boy can figure out that touching down there may feel pleasant, that coupled with your constant "Don't do that" will make it all the more appealing.

Here is what I would do, first see your family doctor to make sure there is not any type of medical condition (rash etc)I doubt it but just to be safe. Next I would talk to your boys about being private with their bodies, maybe "We don't touch ourselves in front of other people" or something of that nature, tailor it to your family values.

In closing this is very common and if you make a big deal about it they will do it all the more. Your doctor may also have some good tips and after talking to you can tailor something more comfortable for you to follow. Good Luck!

Best regards,

Lydia

Sleeping Patterns

Dear Elders,

I have a 3 yr. old a 5 yr. old and a 6 yr. old. All three do not want to go to bed at night, but my 3 yr. old is the worse. She will sometimes go to sleep at bedtime, but she wakes up before midnight. I am writing this at 2am. She is wide awake. How can I help her establish a healthy sleep pattern?

Elder Response

Hello. The basic rule of having bedtime not become a difficult time is to gradually slow down the pace of the children. Often this means no television an hour before bedtime (playing quietly replaces it), next giving relaxed baths and ending with reading a bedtime story in a quiet time. Then, you turn out the lights and leave the room. The test is yours. Children are very skilled at keeping their parents' attention. Most will make several attempts to bring the parents back into their room with various tricks, questions and complaints. I suspect this is what you are experiencing.

Secondly, you have to train yorself not to respond to each attept to get you back. You have to give them time to wind down into sleep, and dithering back and forth doesn't do it. You need to instiute a rule that this will not be acceptable behavior on their part (or on yours. You do deserve some time alone, you know.)

The problem with your daughter is the same, except with another time frame. She goes to sleep, then wakes up in the middle of the night and expects you to come entertain her. On this I had to have advice from my pediatrician, and I pass it on to you.

This is if you have no reason to believe she is in trouble or has had a terrible nightmare, in wich case you respond quickly. She will let you know if either of these conditions exist. When she cries for you, ignore her. Keep ignoring her. When she continues to cry, keep ignoring her. Ignore her up to a half-hour. She probably will have dropped off to sleep by then. The success of this is to outlast her crying. The good news is that after the first time she has gone back to sleep without your going in to her, the next night will be better, add the night after that, and the night after…

It is an extremely hard task to ignore your crying child, but very effective. And how old do you want your child to be to continue to disturb you at night without good reason?

The other suggestion is that no child is allowed out of the bedroom after having been put to bed. If an emergency occurs, you will know. You have to stop this behavior before it convinces the children they rule the roost, and before you begin to resent their attitude toward your getting rest necessary to take care of them the next day. Good luck, and best wishes.

Julia

Teenage Driver

Dear Elders,

I could like to know what rules we should have for our 17 year-old who will be driving in about 2 months. (She will graduate from high school in '03.) Our family has one car to share. She will not need to drive unless I send her on an errand.

Our daughter has earned the privilege of taking driving lessons because she earned a very high A in all her classes this semester; and has shown a remarkable improvement in her overall responsibility and attitude. She has earned our trust.

What do you think?

Thanks very much.

Elder Response

Thanks for writing.

Many of us learned to drive while we were teen-agers, and survived to tell about it. Obviously, because of the significantly greater number of cars on the road, risks have increased somewhat. These are the rules I would expect my grandchildren to obey:

1) You are taking the car to travel to a specific destination. Do not make any detours.

2) You may only carry those passengers that were already agreed upon.

3) Under no circumstances are you to violate any traffic laws.

4) You must wear your seatbelt, as must all passengers.

5) Return the car with at least as much gas as it had when you left, also in at least as clean a condition. If you desire to return it cleaner or with more gas, we won't complain.

6) Your continued good grades and improved attitude must be retained to keep your driving privelages.

7) You must give us a time when you intend on returning. Unless there is an emergency, you are expected to keep that timetable. If you must be late, you are required to call before the time you are expected home.

Those are a start. Driving is a serious responsibility. Make sure your daughter remembers that. Best regards,

Tony

Balance

Dear Elders,

I am married and have a 2 month old son. I have opted to stay at home with him. He is so precious to me. He has a huge appetite and can spend the better part of the day nursing. Do you have any advice on how to balance a husband, a young child, and household duties without becoming half crazy…lol. I'd appreciate your thoughts…Thanks.

Elder Response

Hi, there. Boy, do I remember those days!

First off, I hope you're telling your pediatrician about the time you spend nursing, in case your baby may be overeating.

It's hard for a new mother, no matter how much help she has, and not many of us have help. I know my husband thought caring for children was entirely my job. Ha!

The best advice I can give you is to be very, very careful that you maintain relationships outside your home. It is well worth the extra effort and planning to keep yourself anchored to the world outside family, at any age or stage.

You need breaks from the demands of husband, child and household, and a reminder to yourself that you are an interesting person outside those familial relationships.

You and your husband must be careful to continue to set aside time for just the two of you, because otherwise you might fall into the bad habit of never having time alone together, except when you sleep.

I was a stay-at-home mother for some years, and my only regret is that I spent too much time cleaning. Although I was a good mother, with results proving that, I still regret that I didn't spend more time with my children. Perhaps all parents feel this way.

Best of luck and I wish you and your family much happiness.

Bonnie

Young Married Issues

Dear Elders,

A little background to start off…

I am 24-years old (American) and my husband is 27 (Turkish-German). We have been married since 02/16/01 (in NYC). We met at a party in Manhattan. Dated and got married (about 1 year).

Due to immigration issues, he is now in Germany and I in the US. It took us from April till early December for his visa to get approved but now it is APPROVED! We are just waiting for the final paperwork to come in from the consulate. As soon as everything is approved he will get the next plane back here!

Here is my problem…we have allot going on in our life right here or rather I do. I am trying to get a job. Have decided to go back to school and have allot of debt. Besides that I am very lonely without him. I have moved out of Manhattan and am now staying at my family's house (trying to get a job, want to wait till he returns to get a job). I feel like I should be able to call him anytime I want or email him whenever and I feel like I should be able to get a response ASAP. He seems to have his phone (I call him on his cell) turned off more then its turned on. Somedays I go for 3 or 4 days without being able to get in contact with him. It drives me completely crazy! Sometimes there are little things going on that I want to discuss with him or maybe I just feel off and want to reach out to him. When I get him on the phone he always seems calm…like nothing is going on. I get so upset because I have tried to call him for 4 days and by the time I get him on the phone I am sometimes close to tears (if it something important) and then the conversation doesn't go very well.

I have asked him multiple times to please keep his phone on. He doesn't seem to think that I should have to get in contact with him.

That everyone that I have to say can wait till he is in person (sometimes I want to bounce job leads, etc off of him).

Am I wrong to think that I should be able to contact him anytime I want? Am I just being selfish? Sometimes I think he doesn't care about me anymore. When he first was away we would talk everyday….

What do you suggest? I really miss him. I can't wait to see him again. It just drives me crazy that he is not an everyday part of my life. I just want to talk to him.

Sorry if this is so long! Thanks!

Elder Response

I think you will have more success at keeping in contact with your husband if you withhold initiating any attempts for at least one month.

Let HIM try to figure out where YOU are.

You're a grown up, you don't need to "bounce job leads, etc." off him. I suggest you get a copy of "A Woman of Independent Means" by Elizabeth Forsythe Hailey as quickly as you can and read it immediately. Be careful, there are two books with this title, only one by this author. The book is over 20 years old. You need to absorb it.

A little wisdom for your future, absolutely nothing thrives in a cage, not one made of steel nor one made of tears. To put that more graphically, if you squeeze a handful of sand, it all runs out your fingers….get the point?

Take care and have a great time with your life!!

Helen

My Son Died

Dear Elders,

My first child, my son died; he was 16 days old. Cause of death, unknown, he most likely aspirated but without warning (SIDS).

I am very sad. He still seems very close but it is hard to understand why I will spend the rest of my life without him with me physically. I am struggling to find meaning in such a senseless event.

Thank you for any advice you can give.

Elder Response

Hello and please accept my deepest sympathy for your loss. I don't think there is any meaning in these events—they are tragic and senseless. We mourn our losses as best we can until we can heal and recover. This takes much time. Searching for meaning is a natural part of grieving—it indicates that we are overwhelmed by the event and haven't accepted it yet—very natural for such a loss as yours. But try not to dwell on it too much as it can slow down the healing process.

One positive thing that can come from such traumatic events is that we emerge with a stronger sense of how precious our loved ones are and this helps us lead more meaningful lives. Your child will always be with you and how you live your life can honor his short one…

Be strong and patient and please let others comfort you.

Frangi

Understanding Dad

Dear Elders,

I'm from India. Here in the US for 6 years—Wife(28yrs) and one son (5yrs). Never been back home. My Mom and Dad live in Bombay(India) and have visited us twice.

My wife is from a conservative family. My wife does not like my Dad(66 yrs). She says he has kissed her on the lips twice. She does not like it. I have told her to turn her face and put her cheek forward next time we meet Dad and he tries to kiss her (this happens only when we meet or part). She says I should talk to him. I feel confronting Dad will only spoil my relationship with him, as we maybe misunderstanding him. My other option would be tell my Mom. I can be frank with her and she can somehow tell Dad without being specific that he should not be kissing (other women) on the lips.

Because of this sitation with my Dad, my wife does not want to visit them when We got to India this year. I haven't been back home in 6 years and my Mom and Dad expect us to visit them. My wife says she will stay with her parents and I can visit my parents with my son

Please advice.

Thanks.

Elder Response

Hi. It is your duty to support your wife in this problem and help solve it. I think you can find a way to tactfully and kindly explain to your father that your wife doesn't want to be kissed on her mouth. I wouldn't either, in this situation, and I question your father's motives in doing so. That's another reason you must stop it now, before it becomes a serious problem wherein your father may feel entitled to go farther in showing his affection for your wife.

I understand your wife's reluctance to stay in their home, as there are too many opportunities for your father to try to harrass your wife. I hope you take care of this before your visit. I think husband and wife should be together, especially on family visits. But you owe your greater allegience to your wife now.

Best wishes and good luck.

Jim

I Want To Know My Mother

Dear Elders,

Hello, I'm writing today because I wonder why people are scared of each other. My mother, 52, and I, 22, are really very close for the most part. Though when it comes to deeper issues we both become as non-confrontational as can be! There's so much I'd like to know about her and our family; I'm sure she'd also like to know me on a deeper level. I just don't understand what makes us shy away from the important topics. I wonder if it's fear of learning things we'd rather not, or just the discomfort of it all. What can I do to help both of us open up more to each other? Your advice is greatly appreciated!

Elder Response

Your letter caught my eye, and I began thinking about my own parents and similar issues.

I wonder if part of this "shyness" has to do with the fear of stepping out of the roles that we have played with each other all our lives. After all, Mom's role is to be a protector and provider and nurturer, often without a separate identity from children or spouse. Is this true in your case? On the other hand, a child may often always be perceived as the "child" by the parent and all that means…not as knowlegable, self-sufficient, wise, needing to be cared for.

I have several thoughts, in the way of games that might "break the ice". Although I do recognize people may not be comfortable with games.

Each of you write somthing down you would like to discuss about the other; take several days; schedule a time and "safe" place when you can discuss. Or audiotape in private your response.

Although I've found this to be difficult for people, you might try role reversal. When both of you can commit time and be in a safe and comfortable environment, pick a topic and talk about it in a switched role way. Don't spend too much time, conclude it if things get uncomfortable, and then talk about how you felt after it is over.

Use memorabilia, visit places significant to you and your mother, and use as stimulus to talk about past experience.

Use your own experiences as a 22 year old to ask your mother what she did, what she would have done as a 22 year old in similar circumstances.

And good luck!!! PS: lots of hugs and kisses also work!!

Pat

Unspoil a Child?

Dear Elders,

I understand that you dispense advice on any topic and I would like to ask if it would be possible to 'unspoil' a 9-year old only child, and how. My daughter and I are very close but I noticed recently that she has become quite tyrannical and expects me to be her slave. My husband worked abroad for a long time and that left me to deal with the child for most of her growing years. I would like my daughter to be more responsible and mature but I'm afraid that she has been babied by her grandparents and my husband (when he's around, probably to make up for his prolonged absences). Help!

Elder Response

Hi,

As a first step I'd tell the grandparents and husband that the spoiling must cease, NOW.

Next, I'd sit in a chair and have the child sit on the floor in front of me, looking up at me, and while glaring down at her, I'd explain to her that from now on "no" means NO, "maybe" means PERHAPS, at some future time. Repeat as often as needed, and each time you do, withhold a privilege.

Good luck,

WO Owl

No Time To Waste With Grandma

Dear Elders,

I am 27 and my wonderful grandmother is 93 years young. We are very close even though we might not always share the same opinion. I do have to be careful sometimes because she can wear her feelings on her shoulders at times either getting very defensive or getting sad (at certain descions I might have made). ie…living w/my boyfriend, which she does not know. Therefore, there are some things I choose not to tell her because I do not want to upset her.

She is an incredible lady, one who I greatly admire and I will miss tremindously when she is gone.

My question is…. she often tells me stories of when she grew up or what it was like when she met my grandfather (she was married for 49yrs and is widowed now). I have recently, the past 5 yrs or so, have found such an interest in finding out as much as possible.

When my grandfather died, I was devastated. I was just 12 and suddenly I felt as if my world had ended. We were also very close but things were different then. I was only 12 and did not care about history or other boring things!!

I have thought about asking her if I could film or tape her. This might sound silly but I would like these memories of her but more than that I would like info on when she was a child, the deppresion, being married ot info on her family. Of course I will not be able to have everything about her on tape but I think this would be a neat keepsake for me or if I ever have children.

I don't want her to take it wrong if I ask her to do this. Should I ask her and if so then how? And is this idea completely retarded?

She says she is ready to die and that she has been around for a long time and is ready to meet my grandfather. I just don't want her to think that I think she is going to die tomorrow. Bottom line I guess is I want to know if this is appropriate b/c I do not want to offend her.

Thank You for you advice!!

Elder Response

Thanks for writing.

I think you have a wonderful idea, that if presented properly to your grandmother, would make her feel wanted and possibly useful again.

I suggest that you tell her something along the lines of "you have so much life experience to offer, would you mind making a tape recording, so future generations can know first-hand what things were like when you were growing up?"

Good luck, and God bless.

Ward

Approval From Dad

Dear Elders,

Hi! i know im probably wrong, but i always feel like my dad doesnt appreciate me very much. he has never been affectionate with me, actually, he only calls me when he needs something, never to see how i'm doing. and i feel like i spend my life trying to get his approval, which i never get. its like i am never good enough. when i was younger he called me names like useless and stupid, so my self esteem has been always low. anyway, ive been married 5 years to a wonderful man (i married him because my dad told me to!!), but im very happy. he tells me not to let him get to me and not to live my life around him, but its hard not to, i just want his approval and his love. but i feel he will never love me.

i dont know what do do.

thanks for the help.

Elder Response

Hi,

It sounds like your father may not be very happy with himself and if so, is not able to be caring of others.

I think he has the problem, but you are making it your problem. Why not just be caring and kind to him and maybe he will change? If he doesn't there is nothing much else you can do except pray for him.

By trying to get his approval, you are turning your happiness over to your father. Don't let your father control your life anymore.

Your focus should be on your relationship with your husband.

I hope this is helpful.

God Bless you.

Bob

Focus on My Needs, or My Mothers?

Dear Elders,

I'm a college student in Boston. My mother immigrated from Guatemala when she was 16, but the cultural impressions are still very deep in her character. She lives in Florida, and has HIV. I love my mother very much, and want to know that should she become ill or die, I will not have any regrets and will have treated her right and loved her in the way that she deserves despite any sacrifices I may have to make. The problem is that in American culture, the family is not so nuclear. i am her only daughter and I cannot help but feel the responsibility of taking care for my mother on my shoulders. I love her so much and value everything she had sacrificed for my brother and I. She is always giving to the world, never taking. I want her to know that her spirit of giving and charity and kindness and selflessness lives on, by making her my priority. But this society makes it very difficult to do so; my bosses and friends don't understand why I send my mother money when i myself am struggling financially. They don't understand why I am willing to leave Boston for a semester to go spend time with her because she misses me. I start to wonder if perhaps I'm not making her TOO much of a priority?? Is it really 'her life' and should she really be vying for herself?? I realize that SHE is the adult, but so many times in her life, she has sacrificed everything she had—money, food, healthcare, time—for my brother and I even if it meant she had to go without. Her foremost goal has been to provide us with love and knowledge and morals, and she has succeeded incredibly. From this young naive low-income single parent sprung forth a lawyer(my brother) and myself (a student at one of the top colleges in teh country). Her hard work is the reason I am who I am. But I do find that giving her so much of myself is compromising my plans and goals for the time being. I don't mind this, but everyone around me insists that I'm not making the right decision. That I should help only as much as I can without hurting myself, and that it was her RESPONSIBILITY to care for us because she had us, whereas for me it should be something I do second to taking care of myself. My mother is HIV positive, so my actions now weigh heavily because time is something I cannot guess at…it could be thirty years, it could be one year. And I want my mother to realize that she will not die when her body dies, for her daughter will live with her mother's spirit and attitude in her honor. My mother took care of her father from the day she came to America at age 16…even if she could only send $15, every month, she sent him money that helped him to feel safe and loved. She would visit him when she could and help him with any needs he had. I know how much she loved him, and I want her to know I love her in the same way. Am I doing too much? Going too far? What should be my limitations? What if she holds it against me if I do more for myself? Where do I draw the lines between what I can do, what I should do and what I must do?

Elder Response

Hello. You're listening too much to other people, and here I am, another person, wanting to tell you how to live your life! That said, you are the only person who can decide who and what you are, and how you will live. I admire your obviously great love for your mother and your attempts to repay her for what she has given you, not the least your kind and loving character.

I urge you to do what your heart and mind tells you is the RIGHT thing for you to do. I think you should also suggest that your brother, the lawyer, join you in your support of your mother. She is ill and will die long before you; while you are fortunate enough to have her, you treat her and love her as you wish. Your time will come later to do everything for yourself.

I would like to tell you that many of us in this country enjoy and support close family relationships with great love and consideration. My husband and I would do anything for our children, and their feeling is reciprocal.

Someone with the capacity of loving that you have will never suffer for love in this life; you will nurture it and see it grow. I urge you to do for your mother all that you wish, without creating serious hardship for yourself. It is important to take care of yourself, also. Your mother is a very deserving woman to have a child such as you, and you are equally deserving.

I wish you only the best, and urge you to enjoy your life, even through the difficult times. You are an admirable young woman.

Best regards,

Carol

Getting Family Back Together

Dear Elders,

Hi! Thank you so much for taking time to answer all of our questions! Here is my question. We live 1200 miles from both mine and my husbands families. I speak to them daily and my mother visits every 2 months. My grandmother passed away 3 years ago and it was very unexpected. She was always the one to pull us all together for holidays...etc. This is now falling on my sholders. I honestly don't mind the new responsibilities until it comes to my brother and Grandfater. My grandmother was always giving us money and my brother asked her for help in getting him a truck 5 years ago. She did and nothing was ever really said about repayment until she passed and my grandfather has started to ask him about it. My brother made a few payments and then missed a few and my grandfather got mad at him (he said hurt)for no payments and not at least calling. My brother says he stopped calling because my grandfather just talked about the money. My grandfather says he doesn't even care about the money any more that he just wants to stay in touch with my brother but neither will make the first move and call. It has gone so far that we had seperate Christmas get togethers. My family is not confrontational so we just all pretend nothing is going on. I feel in the middle and don't know how to broach the subject to either without seeming to choose sides. Any advice would be greatly helpful! Thank you!

Elder Response

Hello. Get the entire family together, sit down and quietly discuss this situation with everyone, making sure that both your grandfather and your brother are paying attention and are not feeling defensive.

Emphasize how much the entire family is suffering because of the childish behavior of both of them. (I think your brother is greatly at fault here however, since he has a debt and refuses to pay it, and is punishing your grandfather for his insistence that it be paid. Very selfish behavior.) Do NOT go into the question of fault and guilt during the family meeting. Stress that everyone wants the family back to being close and sharing holidays and good times together. As evidenced by your grandmother's death, time is limited for all of us, so why waste it fighting about this?

I would make this a publicly-spoken issue to get it out in the open dealt with by all of you. Make both men aware that it is hurting all of the family and must stop.

Best wishes and good luck.

Ed

Help Me Respect Others

Dear Elders,

I tend to be alittle rude to my parents when it comes to not getting my way. Do you have any advice to help me treat them with the respect they deserve?

Thank you very much.

Elder Response

If you have no respect for your parents, you have even less for yourself, for you to treat them in a disrespectful way. I suggest you grow up and stop being such an ungrateful low-down fool.

Laura

Am I Spoiling My Kids?

Dear Elders,

I'm afraid I'm spoiling my children. I believe I'm firm when it comes to disipline and manners, but with material things, I'm afraid they have too much.

We did not have a lot as children. If my kids want something, I'll say; 'maybe for your birthday or Christmas'. But coming from a family of four kids, and my husband is one of five, they get a lot of presents on birthdays and holidays.

My concern is that they won't appreciate the value of their toys or clothes.

Elder Response

Hi there—it's wonderful that you can afford to give your children the things you didn't have when you were young. However, you are probably right when you sense that having too many things might spoil them. Most children today do have too much material things and research says that it's more important for them to have experiences than just things. Why not help them by getting them to donate their old toys/games to children who have less than they do. This way both poorer children and yours will benefit from the toys…Best of luck…

Frank

I Feel Lost, Alone & Like A Total Failure

Dear Elders,

After 3 miscarriages, I was blessed with a happy, healthy baby boy last year (the light of my life) and took off time from my career-oriented life to be a full-time Mom.

Now, my husbands' venture-funded start-up is closing (its was in the deregulated energy sector…need I say more?) and we are trying to make ends meet finacially while seriously evaluating our professional lives. I had recently decided to re-enter the job market to help out our family and was in the process of updating & mailing out resumes, contacting headhunters, etc.

Then, last week, I lost my dear father to a sudden heart attack and am working with my Mom to help close his practice, wind up his affairs, etc.…but I feel really lost, deeply saddened, yet unable to cry (I have been told by everyone I need to be string for my Mom, etc) and very, very lost……I seem to be only able to make it through the day keeping a positive, smiling attitude in front of my very active, constantly-moving 15 month old son…What is wrong with me?

I seem to have lost a sense of who I am, what I want and have any amazing loss of energy (though friends always have commented on my high-energy personality) and seem unable to focus on finding a job, making a smart professional/ move, etc. Any helpful thoughts, insight, etc. would be greatly appreciated!

THANKS for listening!

Elder Response

Hello and thanks for writing…

I'm so very sorry to hear about the death of your father. It must have been such a shock, too, which makes the death of a beloved parent so much harder to deal with. When my father died of a sudden heart attack I was devasted. It seemed to come out of nowhere and he was never sick a day in his life. I, too, had to struggle with mundane affairs and my mother's shock but I did make some private time for grieving and I'd suggest you do the same if possible. You need to cry, grieve, rage, etc. and trying to keep it all bottled up is not good for you or for your ability to help your mother.

Your symptoms of loss of energy, lack of concentration, etc. suggest that you might be having an acute episode of depression but of course you should check with your doctor. If it persists for a few more weeks, I'd suggest asking your doctor for a mild anti-depressant should that be the diagnosis.

Your feelings are not uncommon when other things, like your husband's career, are also unraveling and we feel somewhat overwhelmed/helpless/lost. Your baby is certainly the joy in your life but it also another demanding part of your life. Try to slow down, do only those things that are absolutely necessary, and give yourself some time to grieve, to rest, to enjoy your baby. This time of crisis will pass and you'll be able to do some of the re-evaluating that you mention. But, go EASY on yourself, be kind to yourself, take CARE of yourself and give yourself the space and time to deal with the loss of your beloved father.

This won't happen overnight, but don't rush into a career right away; your husband should be able to find some way to make the money you need to tied you over until things settle down at home.

Hang in there and my very best wishes for you...

Cindy

Don't Want My Kids To See Me Dieting

Dear Elders,

I've had a weight problem since college. I'm not obese, but I could always be 20 pounds lighter. Now I'm in my mid 30's with 2 kids. I have been exercising for a solid 3 years and have lost weight in between my kids. Now, after having my second child, I'm in the same boat. I'm still exercising, but with the kids snacking and the sleep deprevation. I can't loose these 20 pounds. I know Weight Watchers work, but I don't want to show my 4 year old daughter that I'm dieting. The snacks we have in the house are not 'junky' but I know I have to cut out so much. I just want to 'diet' without it effecting my children. I grew up with such self image problems, I don't want my kids to ever worry about it.

Elder Response

Hello. I can't imagine why you think it's bad for your children to know you're dieting. Actually, it's a sign that you're a healthy, well-motivated person who does what is necessary for your good health. And why would the opinion of your four-year old daughter cause you to not diet?????? Good grief!

The self-image your children will achieve will be partially based on a healthy image of their mother, too, who should be showing them that we need to have self-control and care for ourselves the best we can, not hide our problems from family.

Remember that as we all age we lose muscle tissue, and it is replaced, if we do nothing about it, by fat tissue. We have to do something to increase our energy expenditure or drop our caloric intake, or we will all (as many are doing now) end up overweight.

I applaud your consideration of controlling your weight, but simply don't understand your belief that healthy dieting is a bad thing that children shouldn't be aware of.

Best wishes, and good luck.

Lisa

Help Me With My Teen

Dear Elders,

Thank you in advance for your advice.

I am a single parent of a 17 year old son. I've raised him as a single parent since he was an infant. I come from a very strong european ethnic family. No one else in my family is divorced (no siblings, parents, aunts, uncles, cousins, etc.) I have 3 (2 brothers and a sister) siblings who basically cut us out of their lives about 14 years ago, and we haven't spoken in the past 10 years, basically because they organize their lives around mother/father, husband/wife activities, i.e. fathers take kids bowling or skiing, but no one invites my son. And, they all work for a family business which we are not a part of. All along, I have tried to be very pleasant whenever we run into each other, but I actually had a brother and sister-in-law turn and walk away from me last summer at a wedding when I went up to them to say hello. On top of all of this, I have just said nothing when I do happen to be out at funeral dinners or whatever sitting at a table with cousins, aunts and uncles when they discuss in depth in front of us how divorce and especially the children of divorce are the total ruination of our society (yes, i'm not kidding about this). It's like they just don't see my son and I, and don't acknowledge us.

On top of which my father (who died 10 years ago) had a very lucrative real estate developing business, which was left to my two brothers, who subsequently took in my brother-in-law many years ago, and I was told to get lost when I was first divorced and asked for help when I needed a job. Thereby, leaving me the only child of 4 who was cut completely out of the family business.

I've spent many years crying over the emotional pain of all of this. Just their turning their backs hurt so much. My mom just says nothing. She goes wherever she is invited and won't say anything about it. I spent years blaming my mother, who never overtly supported me and my son, but life is just too short and now, I have made my peace with this. I love her and try to spend as much time as possible with her, accepting the situation.

Now, my overall take on all this is that I actually have accomplished many things being pushed into single parenting and being alone—i.e. advanced degrees, running my own business, etc. Overall, I feel SO BLESSED in life. We have WONDERFUL friends, an active church life. My son is a wonderful, caring, compassionate human being with great grades, many awards for community service, boyscout eagle, etc. accepted early decison to a top 10 university, etc., So, overall, I feel our lives are wonderful and blessed in so many ways.

Now, the problem. Even after all the above, I still feel so much emotional pain over my siblings and their actions. My first nephew is getting married in June, and in December a pre-announcement was mailed specifically to my son, and not to me. In other words, I am not invited to the wedding.I told my son the choice to go or not is his, and I do plan to send a card and monetary gift to my nephew and his wife after the wedding, because I do wish them very well. Even though I went through many years of therapy, I still have times when the emotional pain of it is so overwhelming, that I just spend long periods of time crying.

Please help.

Elder Response

Hi,

You are indeed blessed. Just think you [conceivably] could be just as narrow minded and miserable as your "family." With folks like that, one does not need cancer!!!!

I strongly urge you to—with the exception of your mother—ignore them. Above all, do not let onto them that the situation bothers you.

The forthcoming wedding should not present a problem. You, correctly, told your son the decision is his to make. I am certain that he will do whatever makes him comfortable.

Best wishes,

Arthur

Motherhood

Dear Elders,

I am a stay at home mom. And I feel my husband thinks I am struggling to pull my own weight. I feel he thinks it is a picnic to stay home and take care of our child. Which it is not. I really miss being out in the work field. What can I do to help him realize that I don't just sit at home and do nothing all day. I just don't feel like he thinks I do anything all day. Like I sit around or something. It is just as hard if not harder to be at home all day as it was to go to work. Sure I get to eat whenever I want and I get to take a nap when my daughter does. But other than that I never have any time to myself. I don't think he sees that. Any advice would be helpful. Thank you

Elder Response

Hi. Do what I once did in the same situation: for five days I wrote down everything that I did and the time involved in doing it. At the end of five days I presented it to my husband and suggested (?) he never criticize me again for "not doing anything" during my days at home.

He never raised the question again.

If your husband doesn't get better after you do this, say "I can do a lot less." If he persists in this attitude, then start doing less and less until he realizes how much you really do day after day.

Good luck and best wishes,

Jane

Terrible Two's

Dear Elders,

It seems like today there are the 'politically correct' ways to raise a child. I have two children; my son Thomas who will be three at the end of August and my daughter Emma who is 17 months old. Well, my two and a half year old son is now getting into the 'terrible twos' behavior and is starting to become quite vocal when he doesn't get his way—he screams and cries. I'm looking for some suggestions on how to deal with his fits and hopefully get him to learn the difference between acceptable and unacceptable behavior.

I know that I personally prefer to give my children toys such as pots and pans or blocks instead of the battery-operated toys of today. I also believe in shows such as Sesame Street, but very much limit the amount of time my kids watch tv. I just want to give my kids the best foundation I possibly can so they develop into kind, caring, beautiful people. I know that my grandparents did a wonderful job raising my parents and I would welcome any suggestions/comments as I head into the toddler stages with my two kids. I don't ever want someone to look at my kids, shake their head and say 'kids of today…'.

Elder Response

Hi! Thanks for writing.

Well, today I just finished an afternoon with my 4 yr old grandson. I ended up trying to remember how I managed to raise three pretty good children. I think it was based on "ignoring". What I mean by that is that it is my thinking that the 2-3 yr olds are involved in some sort of "testing" procedure. They are not yet capable of any real coginitive acts but they seem to have the ability to know how to "test" us. I found that to ignore was the best policy. They don't quite have the ability to understand any rational explanations (which frustrates us). They are just testing, and only Gawd knows how they learned that! They have to simply learn what "NO" means without your having to explain. It becomes a matter of understanding that there is nothing you can possibly explain to a 2 or 3 year old. So the word "NO" is given without explanation and tantrums are ignored. IMHO to try otherwise will drive you to the "home for the parentally, pre-maturally aged".

Best regards,

Not Dr. Spock

Living With Parents Again

Dear Elders,

I moved back in with my parents last November to go to school. My mom is the most nosiest person and is the 'queen of gossip.' I can tell she's been in my room when I get home, I have caught her in there, and she will sometimes flat out told me she's been in there. I want to start journaling, but I'm afraid she'll read my stuff. I use to confront her when I was living at home before, but now I know it's no use. 'It's her house.' Any suggestions?

Elder Response

Hi there. Sounds like some changes are in order in your house, eh? Apparently, no amount of honest discussion is possible with her so how about getting a lock put on your bedroom door? Do you pay any "rent"? If not, how about contributing something every month, say $25.00) to both help out and use it as the basis for more privacy? I agree with you that she's read your journal so can you write it on a computer and hide your password for it there? Is it possible for you to room with other students at school and still afford to attend? Ultimately she holds the keys and that's the tradeoff for living at home. Hope some of these suggestions work out. Best of luck,

Laura

Directing My Son

Dear Elders,

My son is 16 and trying to figure out what he wants to do with his life. He loves the drums and can only think about the entertainment industry but we want him to go to college. How do we keep his dreams alive but also steer him into a career suited to him?! Thank you for any help!

Elder Response

Hello,

I was a college professor who saw many students with a dream they couldn't fulfill or try to because parents forced college on them. On the other hand, many young adults aren't very good at assessing their skills accurately. You two could compromise by suggesting he attend a college that has a good music major with performing/musical areas of specialty OR you could wish him well as he pursues his career in the entertainment industry and let him have a go at it. In a short time, he'll know if he's got what it takes. He can still go to college in the future but if he really doesn't have any interest in college why waste your/his money and time? Talk it over with him, try not to panic, and see if you all can come up with something that does justice to his goals for himself.

Best wishes,

David

Bad Relationship

Dear Elders,

my mother and I don't get along very well. We always have different opinions and never agree on anything. What can I do to change this?

Elder Response

Hi. My advice is that you sometimes listen to your mother instead of being so busy disagreeing. You will be surprised that she has something valuable to say. Why should you always agree? That doesn't mean her opinions aren't worthwhile and valid…and she has certainly had more experience with life than you have.

Best wishes, and enjoy life.

Lisa

Money for an Inmate Relative

Dear Elders,

I have a nephew who is incarcerated. I have lent him money to make Christmas presents for his mother and siblings. He has asked again if I would lend him money. I'm torn as to what to do. At times I feel like I am enabling him, but then, at other times, I wonder what Jesus would do in my situation. Would Jesus not lend him the money?

Elder Response

Hello,

It's hard to say what Jesus would do, but I wonder if your nephew did make and send those Christmas presents? Did you find out from his mother/siblings? If so, I'd be more impressed and willing to lend him a bit more money for something you deem appropriate. It's hard to make money in jail and I hope you remind him that these are loans, to be paid back. That could give him a sense that you trust he will straighten out his life once he's out. It's important for you to keep in touch with him, support him emotionally, and if you can afford it, to loan him some money.

Bless you and good luck,

Sam

MotherAdvice

Dear Elders,

My mother has suffered chronic migraines for about 10 years. She has since grown into a deep depression that antidepressants haven't helped. She's seen every spcialist there is for her migraines, and nothing seems to help. My feeling is that once she gets over her depression, she would better be able to control her migraines. But she's VERY unapproachable to this subject. I was wondering if you had any ideas on how I might be able to help her. Thank you!

Elder Response

Hi! Thanks for writing.

It has been our experience that dealing with the very elderly is often no easy job. It seems to take a lot of small suggestions, delicately given. A demonstration of constant concern for her well being. Be a nag without showing it. It sounds like Mom could well benefit from some professional advice. But it's hard for some elderly to admit they might need help. If you give her examples of how you seek help and others you know seek help, maybe she will "come around" and realize she would not only be helping herself but making you happy in the process. It's a "win-win" process but it will take some work. Don't give up! Listen carefully to her, asking, "why is she reluctant", and "read" between the lines.

Good Luck,

Jane

Stepmom

Dear Elders,

I am married to a wonderful man. He is highly loved by his children and mine.

Background...I have been divorced for several years with a messy divorce. My kids wanted the stability of a family.

His side...He has joint physical custody, the kids never knew there were problems with the marriage. It was an amiable divorce. The parents have great communication with the kids concerns.

I met my husband 2 months before the divorce was final and met the children right after the divorce. The first year we dated, it was like the Brady Bunch, no arguments and always the best times. Six months after the wedding trouble starts, I had never felt it was my place to discipline them until then and enforce the 'chores'. My husband and I started having marital problems that caused us to seriously talk divorce. Kids were taking sides, his kids thought this was reunion time between their parents and pushed the stressful situation. My husband told them it would not happen.

Well, that was a year and a half ago and we are much closer because of working through it. It wasn't counselors that helped, it was my husband coming to the lord and us as a couple following the scripture. God's word is truly a handbook for life.

The kids love their dad dearly but I am not included in the I love you's unless they are told. Many times, I want to give them the same treatment back. I feel it is because I myself backslide in hurt and anger. My kids resent his now because of their indifferent attitude towards me. The children are the ones really that suffered from the breakup. Do you have any advice?

Elder Response

Hi,

You are 90% home!!!! Your husband's children are venting their emotions, and by your own admission you often take the bait.

My advice: don't let them "get to you," and above all, do not give them opportunity to feel that they do. Take heart!!!!!! They will grow up and will be out of the house before you know it.

Best regards,

Sherry

Unhappy Husband Since 9-11

Dear Elders,

I love my husband. We have been married for 6 years in July. Though we have had ups and downs, mostly we get along well. We do not have children—by choice. We do have 2 cats we adore.

Ever since 9/11, my husband has been depressed and moody. He snaps out of it but then gets right back in it. Sometimes he is angry at the world. I can understand his feelings but am having a hard time living with them.

What would be the best thing I can do to support him?

Thanks for any advice.

Elder Response

Hello and thanks for writing...

Many of us have had a very hard time getting through 9/11 and I know from my own experience that it hit me much harder than many of my family and friends so I, too, can emphasize with you and your husband. Many of us are very angry, hurt, frustrated, fearful about both the events themselves and the issues it raises about our own mortality, vulnerability and the lives we are leading. Each person responds to this crisis differently, of course, but it might be useful for you to talk with your husband about his responses in more depth. Maybe it will help him to clarify his reactions and to see how they impinge on your relationship. His anger and moods do affect you and he might be able to notice that and help you to not take them personally. Often, we lash out at those closest to us, not fully appreciating how it affects them.

Sometimes, a person's depression might be helped by getting more exercise, eating more healthily, doing meditation/praying, getting some counseling. If your husband's depression gets worse it might help for him to see a physician.

Generally, time will help to heal and you need to take care of yourself emotionally so as not to be harmed by his lashing out.

Best Regards,

Cindy

Uncomfortable And Feeling Guilty About It

Dear Elders,

My mother was diagnosed with schizophrenia when I was in grade school, and as I grew older, she became more unstable. Now that I live on my own, my mom has moved into a group home type of living facility. I call and send her mail frequently, but have only gone to visit her twice. Visiting her makes me feel very uncomfortable because she's very 'out there' due to her medication. I'm reaching a point in my life where I am contemplating moving out of state where things are less expensive, but I feel like she's going to think I am abandoning her. I feel badly about it on one hand, and that I shouldn't leave her. On the other hand, I wonder if I should have to put my life on hold for her. Ack what a muddle! What do you think?

Elder Response

Hello,

Sorry to hear about your mother's condition, which is very stressful for her and the family. Without knowing too much more about your situation, I'd be sure that my mother's living arrangements are safe and secure. Since you don't visit her much, leaving her would not be as hard for her as if you were closely involved in her life. I assume you'd continue your calls and letters/cards as you've been doing? Would you be able to be reached in an emergency should you move away? If so, I'd say you sound like you really don't want or can't have more of a relationship with her than you've already chosen to have. The move seems to be making you feel guilty, but if you've really done all you could, given the circumstances, then work through the guilt and I'd suggest making the move.

Best regards,

Julia

Family

Dear Elders,

I feel like my husband is cutting himself off from our children. Our son is 22 and living at home and going to college. Our daughter 19 and away at college. I think because my husband has had employment problems and made some poor life choices, he's afraid our children will do the same, so he nags them to do things and is very critical of them. His mother is also very critical of him. Our kids are typical good kids—get average grades, stay out late, but don't get into trouble. They turn to me for everything because they don't want to deal with their dad. I feel like I have to be a buffer between them. My husband thinks I should be on his side, but I not going to spend my life nagging our kids. I very proud of them. I love talking to my kids and spending time with them. Do you have and ideas about how I can show my husband what he's missing out on? Thanks for any help you can give me.

Elder Response

Hi! Thanks for writing :-)

Well, I've (excuse me, "we've") got three children, now 35, 33 and 30. Been there and done that. I have this theory. It says that Mom handles a lot of things up to the age of 18. Then Dad kicks in with "life experi-ence lectures". By this time he mistakenly thinks they will listen. Unfortunately, he already had his chance and now they want to find out on their own.

It's too late for you to "take sides"….LOL! the kids are on their own and your conversations between each other should involve discussing (over candle light dinner) how you will both let them "fly" and just be there to listen and respond when they come back. (They will come back.) But they will only come back to you for advice if you do not chase or hound them. A bird cannot fly for its offspring. The new must learn to fly on its own. It cannot do this until it falls out of the nest. We don't want them to fall, but, my friend, IT'S LIFE!!!!!!!!

Tell your husband he is missing out on the adventure of actually "letting go" and watching his children learn to fly on their own. It's a wondrous adventure....trust me!

God Bless.

Treefrog

My Brother's Controlling Girlfriend

Dear Elders,

Hi. My brother and I are very close (both in our mid-20s) and he had a son about 1 year ago with his girlfriend of 2 years. Even though my family is gentle and accepting, none of us feel comfortable with his girlfriend as she is rude and abusive to my brother. One evening before she got pregnant, I talked to her about it very gently and really tried to be her friend. Unfortunately, my brother later paid the price for my attempts after I left. He is deeply in love with her and has a very good heart that is forgiving, so he accepts everything about her, even her verbal abuse of my family.

Since their child was born, she now has power over us and him, not even allowing my mom, the child's grandmas to see him but about 5 times in the last year. I have seen the baby twice when she was not around. After my last visit with the child, she found out and verbally abused my brother for weeks. I have talked to my brother about my sadness in not knowing and being a part of my nephew's life, but he simply shrugs his shoulders sadly and says that his girlfriend has a grudge against me.

I can't retaliate against her as my brother pays the price and attempts to befriend her do not work either. I have bought her gifts and always been polite but she doesn't care. I really want to see more of my nephew but I don't know what to do. Can you offer any advice?

Elder Response

There is an old saying that goes like this "A daughter is a daughter all of her life, a son is a son til he takes a wife". I know you brother is not married but he might as well be.

His girlfriend is very controlling and does not want anyone to stand in the way of her controlling your brother, so she sees his family as a major threat.

You have only two chances in my opinion, one is to win her over (not likely) or two is to have your brother stand up to her (also not too likely). Usually relationships that you have described don't last forever so it's important to stay as close to your brother as possible, stay in contact and take whatever contact you can with your nephew.

If you start to see a change in your brother where he doesn't seem quite as happy in the relationship you might bring up the subject again, if not keep quiet, if he is that blinded by love he may push you away.

Best Regards,

Mary

Nervous That I Won't Succeed

Dear Elders,

I am in my freshman year of college. During my first semester, I did very well and am now in an honors society. My family is excited and pleased that I am getting such good grades. However, I fear that, in the coming semester, I may not do as well. If I don't do well, I feel as though my family would be disappointed and this troubles me greatly.

Elder Response,

Hi!

Well, I vaguely remember my freshman year, it was back in the dark ages (1960). "Free, free at last!" But the ties to the family, they do not just disappear, especially if you come from a loving and caring family…you know, the kind that took everything you brought home from grade school and pasted it on the refrigerator . It's a tough act to follow. But you've grown and the frig is an imaginary one now. Believe me, your family understands this (although they may not want to admit it). It's a little difficult but if you can convince yourself that you are now required to please yourself, to set your goals (not the goals of others) and to stay focused on them. Your future depends not on others being disappointed but on your satisfaction with what you do and achieve. Take one semester at a time. Congratulations……you are very much an adult. Post your successes on your own frig.

Best Regards,

Treefrog

4

Relationships

Reality In Relationship Issues

Dear Elders,

I recently moved away from home to go to graduate school. My parents were very strict, and I didn't start dating until I moved away at the age of 23. I had my first boyfriend for only three months, although we were great friends three months before that. After we broke up, and after I got over the attachement I had to him, I found that I started 'looking'. I never was 'looking' before. So I started hanging out with someone else, just as friends, and we started fooling around after about two months. I don't think it will turn into anything serious. The thing is, I didn't really like the current guy as anything more than friends (as was the case with my first boyfriend) until we started getting physical; but i'm developing an attachement that is backed up by my insecurities when he doesn't call. So a few questions......

Why am I pursuing (or accepting) relationships that I'm not really initially into; lack of experience, desire to be wanted, attention, being a away from home (friends/family)?

Am I fooling myself by thinking that I could be just friends with men? There is only one male friend I have now, and he is my best, that I'm sure we are only friends....and there was never an awkwardness there. We just had that understanding. And the he and I get such satisfaction out of interacting with each other with no sexual undertones. It's great, but am wondering if relationships where there might not necessarily be that understanding of nothing physical could ever turn into great friendships like that.

Thanks.

Elder Response

Thank goodness you're still young, so you have plenty of time to change before it's too late. Do NOT demean yourself by accepting whatever is available; particularly do NOT accept a relationship based on sexual activity—it is a real bummer after a short while, and you will end up feeling used and discarded.

You are probably latching onto this relationship to make up for having lost the first one you had, but this is not good, because you are now defining yourself as someone who is nothing without a boyfriend, regardless of the quality of the relationship. That's called WANTING, and most people stay away from a wanting person.

Throughout my life I have constantly had male friends, all through my marriage. I have great, supportive and terrific male friends who have added a dimension to my life I would otherwise have missed. Certainly it's possible—why in the world would it not be, unless you can't stop jumping into bed with every guy who shows you some attention!

You in large part control what type of relationships you have, and who you have them with. I think you need to do a little soul-searching to find out:

1. Who you are.

2. What you are.

3. What you want.

4. What traits you need to develop to truly like and love yourself; i.e., self-respect, self-love, self-control, pride, logic, and so forth. I know you can straighten this out with yourself without too much trouble, and believe me, your life will be so much happier and you will be so much more content when you truly know and appreciate yourself. You are a fully independent woman; you don't NEED a man; you might WANT one, and that's to be expected, mostly. But you cannot live

your life searching for a man to make you happy. You can be happy with many people, but you must be happy with yourself first.

Best regards,

Sharon

My Girlfriend's Pregnant

Dear Elders,

I will really appreciate your time and advice. My girlfriend just told me she's pregnant. I love her very much but she believes she's not ready to have this baby. She is absolutely sure she will not have an abortion, but she is very confused. I've have tried to convince her in many ways (with words and actions) that I will be always there for her and the baby (She and I have been going out together for about a month and we have experienced many wonderful things during this time). I have been married in the past and I know what implies to be a responsible person. I don't have any children with my ex-wife. I know I care dearly for my girlfriend, and I am really willing to do anything for her and our baby. My question is: What could I possibly say or do to make her feel more secure? (We are both graduating in May from the University-SDSU-and she just signed a contract to work in a school...I just got approved to work part time at the university for next semester while I earn my Master's Degree, so I don't think money is an important issue here). Thanks again...

Elder Response

Hello,

You can show your love by being loving in small and big ways. This is a difficult time for your girlfriend and she has lots of choices to make. She needs extra care, attention and support right now and you seem willing to give it. If she really doesn't want the baby and abortion is not an option, has she considered giving the baby up for adoption? This is a very hard decision, as are all her other choices. She'll need time to think about her options and, with your support shown in your behavior and words, she'll hopefully be able to make the right decision for herself and the baby.

Best wishes…

Sam

Is This Normal?

Dear Elders,

I'm twenty one years old and have been with my steady boyfriend for four years. I love him very much but sometimes, especially being at college with many attractive men (we dont attend the same college), I wish I was single. He is the man I see myself marrying when I graduate but sometimes I wish I could act on my desires and date other men. We almost took a break a while back to explore these feelings but I changed my mind. I did so because I thought 'Why break off something so wonderful for something else that might not be out there?' I'm scared if I break up with him he might find someone else. He treats me like a queen and I really do love him but is this me just being young or is there something wrong with our relationship? I've always been the kind of girl who didn't randomly make out with various guys and I know I don't want to be 'used and abused' by guys who only want me for one reason. I think personally that part of me wishes I could be in the married, settled down part of my life and the other wishes to stay young and do crazy things. So is our relationship in a rut or what is wrong with me?

Thanks!

P.S. I think this is the most amazing service online and a great way to connect with older people with so much life experience!! Keep the good work up! You all are awesome and do a great service to society!

Elder Response

Hi, thanks for writing. I strongly recommend that you do NOT take this relationship any further without taking the time to resolve your feelings. You have desires to date other men, and you should not ignore those feelings, especially if you are thinking of marriage with someone else.

Now is the time for you to determine exactly what you really want, and not what you think will be the best you can ever have. That's no way to choose a husband—you must want to be married to that man beyond anything else, with no questions in your mind about whether you should or not.

Until you have come to a complete decision about this being the man you will love the rest of your life, please don't make half-hearted promises. Find out for sure, and if you do lose him, then it wasn't meant to be the two of you.

Best regards,

Claudia

Affairs

Dear Elders,

I am on my second marriage, 12 years + 4 dating, after an abusive 9 year first marriage. We are empty nesters and my children (by first husband) are no longer in the home and self sufficient. Problem: I have known a man at my office for seven years. We have a great time together and I totally enjoy his company. We actually find things to talk about. I feel that I am missing something very special in my life and would like to pursue a more significant relationship. My husband is sweet, quiet and an introvert. I am an extrovert. This is the first time in my life that I am totally financially self-sufficient and we have a 'new age' relationship where we split the bills and keep our money separate. Based on your life experience do you settle or take relationship risks. I would appreciate your advice since I cannot talk to anyone about this matter.

Elder Response

Hi,

Rule #1: Don't go "potty" where you earn your bread and butter.

Rule #2: Once you have "crossed the line" your relationship with the man will not be the same as it was before.

Rule #3: Knowing that you have hurt your husband—by your own words "a sweet guy"—you will experience difficulty in living with yourself, not to speak of looking in a mirror.

Rule #4: If you think that you might enjoy throwing lit matches into a gasoline can and have no fear of the consequences: "Go for the man."

Good luck, you may need it!!!!!!

Philip

Keeping The Spark Alive In Marriage

Dear Elders,

I was wondering what advice you would give on staying happily married. My husband is the most wonderful man in the world. We have been married for 5 years and have known each other for 13. We are still very much in love and enjoy our time together. What are some ways I can keep that flame alive for years to come? I love to do little things for him as he does me. Thought you may have some tid-bits that I haven't done for him yet. Thank you for your time. Have a blessed day.

Elder Response

I often hear that communication is the key to a successful marriage. That is partly true, but it must be a positive way of communicating. I feel it's more important to respect and love the other person at least as much as you love and respect yourself. This means you don't demean each other, you don't cruelly argue, you don't try to pass off blame to the other, you don't hold a grudge or think of "getting even". You never, never talk disparaging about your partner to others.

You think of your partner with love, liking, fondness, kindness, gratitude, eagerness, thoughtfulness, anticipation. You plan special treats, special acts, special gifts.

In short, you relate to each other with the best in both of you, and you always remember that you married because of a deep love, and every day you both encourage and feed that love. With all these feelings, communications will be easy, good, and positive.

Best regards,

Carol

Boys That Like Me & Shouldn't

Dear Elders,

Hi, I have this friend who has a really big crush on me. Ok, basically he wants to marry me. I really do not want him for a boyfriend at all, but I want to be friends with him still. I feel that his feelings for me are really getting in the way of that though. He is depressed about it. I think that he really really wants to have a girlfriend in general and has gone through some tough relationships in the past. I feel horrible for rejecting him as it is. I want to be there for him because he is depressed and needs a positive friend. But I don't know how to be his friend with the way he feels about me.

Thanks for your help

Elder Response

Please—give me a break! Having a crush and talking of marriage have absolutely no connection with each other—or shouldn't have, in a realistic world. So stop!

This is a problem most of us face, especially when we are young. If you don't want to have a more serious relationship with ANYONE, you be a friend and tell him so, kindly and gently, but with absolute certainty.

To do anything else is both cruel and dumb, because the problem will not go away until you confront it and lay it to rest.

You can be his friend without talking nonsense about marriage. If he can't, then he can't be your friend. You have no other obligation if he cannot be your friend under the conditions you wish. Nor should you feel any regret or guilt if it cannot be worked out to the comfort of both of you. Some relationships, no matter how involved, are not meant to be, and a quick ending is the kindest way to close it.

Best regards,

Julia

Older Man/Younger Woman

Dear Elders,

I am a 48 year old man, in very good health, financially stable. I never married, mainly because I never met anyone I wanted to stay with for my entire life.

I have now met a lovely woman whose company I enjoy immensely. She has let me know that the feeling is mutual.

The problem is, she is 29. I am 18-1/2 years her elder. She and I don't have much of a problem with the age difference (although it is in the backs of our minds). But both her parents and my family are besides themselves over our budding relationship. Her father and mother like me on a personal basis, but do not approve of the relationship. My brothers and my sister think I have lost my mind, although they too like her very much.

What I'm wondering is, what are the chances of our relationship working out? We are seriously talking of marriage and children, and if we go ahead, it will be sooner rather than later.

Thanks for any advice. As you can imagine, the advice I've been receiving from my loved ones is less than objective.

Elder Response

Hi,

Who is contemplating marriage? You and the lady, or various and assorted relatives and the lady?

If I were you, I'd tell them to sweep in their own front yards.

As for the age difference: Nothing in life is certain other than death and taxes.

Enjoy!!!!

WO Owl

Love's Labour Lost?

Dear Elders,

I have been in a relationship with a guy for about a year. We are both mid to late 20's. I love him deeply, but am worried about our future. First of all he has a son with a woman whom he detests. But he does everything he can to make it peaceful for his boy. Secondly, he has a habit of drinking that worries me…he doesn't around his child, but I see it a lot. He drinks to cope with things, i feel. All my friends say, What's wrong with a little drink? But I think they are also borderline alcoholics aswell. He has a tendancy to let things build and build until they become so overwhelming that he doesn't know how to fix it, b/c he doesn't know where to start. I've been patient because I love him so much. It really hurts to think of a life without him—but sometimes I get sad b/c we have so little time together (he works as a waiter aswell, so his schedule is very inconsistent) and I share this with his 'other family' and the bar. I think that his son should come first, but I also worry that in 2 years from now I 'm going to resent it—and feel left out. He hasn't introduced me to his ex-girlfriend, though he says she knows. I understand he does this since she is a very malicious person who would do anything to keep his son from him…but I'm at the point where I feel that if things don't change, I 'll become a person who I don'tr like anymore. There are other little things, personality traits, like his unreliability, his lack of money (constantly) that also worry me. But he's looking to become a law enforcement agency so that should solve a couple of those things…

I apologise for rambling, but I feel a little torn. I've been toying with the idea of breaking up, because I would rather be unhappy for a few months than resentful and depressed for a lifetime being with someone who doesn't care enough about himself to care about others.

Many thanks for the advice.

Elder Response

Hi, thanks for writing. Things will not get better for this relationship; there are too many problems. Do you really want to have to handle all this stress?

You have a boyfriend who "has a son with a woman whom he detests." Was he forced to have UNPROTECTED sex with a woman he DETESTS????? Poor, sweet, little guy!

He DRINKS A LOT!! To cope? Sure! How about his growing up so he can cope??

He lets "things build and build until they become so overwhelming that he doesn't know how to fix it, b/c (does this mean 'because'?) he doesn't know where to start." Hey! How about growing up?? How about accepting responsibility??

And you think his ex-girlfriend "is a very malicious person who would do anything to keep his son from him…"?? Maybe that's a good thing, and you know nothing about her except what he says, this guy who willingly had unprotected sex with her.

How about his making sure you know she is a really malicious woman, instead of her being so concerned about their son being with an irresponsible, alcoholic father??

And then there are his "personality traits, like his unreliability, his lack of money." But—you say all this will be okay, because "he's looking to become a law enforcement agency" (huh?). Yes, we all want police officers who are irresponsible and alcoholic.

I have just returned your thoughts to you. Do they sound like a future you really want? My advice to you is to run-run-run, as fast as you can, the other way. Give it up; this is not a man to create a life around. You deserve much better, and better you leave him now than have children

(such as his so malicious poor ex-girlfriend) and then have him abandon you, too.

Best wishes, and good luck.

Arianne

Love Life

Dear Elders,

Hello and thank you for your advice. I am a 20 year old female. My fiance and I have been engaged for a year now and I love him so much, but the problem is that I miss my single life. I don't want to be with another guy or anything, I just miss living on my own with my friends, being able to worry about me only. I know that's selfish but that's how I feel. I don't want to lose him because I love him and I know he's the man I'm suppose to spend the rest of my life with, but I don't want to resent him twenty years down the road because I missed out on part of my life. What do I do?

Elder Response

Hi. Well, the problem is yours, not his. I mean, you're the one who has made the move to being so emotionally dependent on him. There is nothing stopping you from being with your friends or living on your own or worrying about only yourself (which is a little selfish, considering that you're engaged). If you've completely given up having a separate life from him, it is a sad mistake!

Now, before you are married or even more deeply together, is the time you should be getting on with doing what you want to do as a single person. I do not include in this dating other men, but continuing to have a life that is all your own.

I found in my own life that I had to have this separation from my husband; it works well because I have interests he doesn't and I can indulge myself with them without him, as he can also do. Then we have our mutual interests, friends, activities, family and social life.

I believe remaining individuals strengthens a marriage. In the end, you will find a much greater happiness if you can still be your own self, which is essential.

Best wishes, good luck, and go slowly.

Jane

What Is Love?

Dear Elders,

There are many people in my grade (10th) who claim to be in love. I don't understand love. I have always thought that true love was once in a lifetime; that it was something you only felt for your soul mate. Is it possible for these people in my grade to be in love? Those relationships most likely won't last long, and I don't understand how you could love some one and then not love them. Maybe they are just infatuated. In that case, what's the difference between love and infatuation? I understand that love is a complicated issue, that no one really knows the answer, and that it's not the same for everyone. Despite this, could you please offer me your opinion on the issue? Thank you for your time.

Elder Response

Hi, and thanks for writing. You might have gotten another answer from someone else, but this is my view of love. We have an unlimited capacity for love (well, most of us), it is a renewable feeling brought about and created by many different things. All love is related but different, similar but not the same. It is all very precious and fulfilling—IF it is love.

I do not believe that love is a once-in-a-lifetime emotion; I wouldn't like love to be so limited. I also believe there are many who can be our soulmate, that it is not a question of finding one person in the billons of the world or live forever alone and sad with love never prevailing. No, that cannot be true.

Infatuation is a selfish feeling, and one that does not usually include trust. It is a highly emotional state incorporating strong sexual feeling. It is also volatile, jealous, demanding, limiting, controlling and selfish. I know it can turn into true love, but most often it doesn't because each partner does not know and see the other realistically.

Love does not try to change or control a partner. This is why true love must be based on realism and truly seeing each other as they are, not what one would like the other to be. This is infatuation, when we are so blinded by our feelings for another that we refuse to see clearly who, what and how they are; we lie to ourselves and make them into an unreal person so we can be pleased.

Love is not limiting, it allows growth and individuality. Mature love is freedom to ask honestly for what is wanted, and the willingness to accept 'no' sometimes. It is giving and receiving the same way, to give and receive pleasure.

Love encourages each to have strong self-esteem and well-being, trusts each other, and loves unconditionally without guilt or dependency.

Love also is capable of accepting the limitations of each partner, adjusting to reality. It does not demand unconditional love, but allows it.

True love brings out the best in partners, not envy, jealousy, fear, hatred, distrust, control, fighting. It encourages respect, self-discipline, commitment, cooperation, generosity, humility. It is flexible and powerful, but never obsessive. It is commitment without resistance, total trust without fear, closeness, vulnerability, equality of partners, and a mutual dream of the future.

Love also means being able to let go and say goodbye if it is best for one of the partners, but this is very hard to do.

I could go on and on, but that one small base on which true love is built.

Part of 'The Prophet' by Kahlil Gibran has always been invocative of true love to me:

'Love one another but make not a bond of love:/

Let it rather be a moving sea between the shores of your souls./ Fill one another's cup but drink not from one cup./ Give one another of your bread but eat not from the same loaf./ Sing and dance together and be joyous, but let each one of you be alone,/ Even as the strings of a lute are alone though they quiver with the same music./

Give your hearts, but not into each other's keeping./ For only the hand of Life can contain your hearts./ And stand together yet not too near together:/ For the pillars of the temples stand apart,/ And the oak tree and the cypress grow not in each other's shadow.'

Best wishes, and enjoy your life,

Arianne

Problems Of The Heart

Dear Elders,

Hello, I'm 24 years old and a bit confused. I am currently involved in a relationship that has been going on for a little over a year. I have noticed, of course, that it's not quite as exciting as it once was, and it's much harder work than it used to be. I guess what I'm wondering is how much work is too much? is this just the way it's going to be in a long-term, serious adult relationship, or should it feel a little easier? Thanks!

Elder Response

There is a lot of work in maintaining a healthy and loving relationship, but it shouldn't seem like hard work. If it is that you must constantly "work" at the relationship, then my advice would be that it isn't "working" and why are you still in it?

Love is not a chore, it is a joy and pleasure, no matter how much effort is involved. If you don't have a large portion of this from the relationship, then leave, go away, abandon it, say goodbye, start anew. Life is too short to waste time with a relationship that is really a burden without the rewards or mutual love and respect.

Only you can answer this question, but I urge you to consider the truth of the matter, and not necessarily what you perceive it to be; be careful, be clear, be honest and be brave.

Best regards,

Julia

How to Get Over Someone

Dear Elders,

Back several months ago, I broke up with a boyfriend of about two years for various reasons. I loved him *very* much, but it was abundantly clear that we could never work things out in the long term—he was simply unwilling to compromise on several important life issues, and I also didn't think it fair for me to give in on everything for the sake of saving the relationship.

Otherwise, he was the most wonderful man I'd ever dated, albeit I do realize that anyone who isn't willing to compromise probably doesn't love you as much as he says he does. I'm not a doormat, so when I realized how things were going, and that my feelings and what I needed for my own life weren't being considered at all, I broke it off, even though we got along extremely well. His response to my breaking things off was to grow immediately cold and distant. In anger, he said he never loved me, and it just broke my heart. We were inseperable nearly every day of the two years we were together, and once the break-up occurred, all contact stopped.

It's several months later now, and I feel as though I'm still broken-hearted. I have a very busy and full life, so distracting myself and letting things process subconsciously just isn't working. I have other men pursuing me now, but I just can't seem to give my heart away to anyone else, so evidently dating someone else isn't the solution to the problem. I don't feel as though my ex is worth this hassle and all of this torch-carrying, but I just can't seem to get my heart to heal and move on.

I feel rather silly and pathetic about all of this—I'm usually the one counseling *my* younger friends in their 20s about not wasting time on men who don't really love them! But can anyone offer advice on healing a long-broken heart?

Elder Response

Hello. You can't get over someone until you have chosen to do so. You're wallowing in self-abuse right now by remembering him as something he was not. Like this:

'he was simply unwilling to compromise on several important life issues'—'Otherwise, he was the most wonderful man I'd ever dated'. Contradictory! Both cannot be true; a man who is simply unwilling to compromise with someone he supposedly loves is not a wonderful man, no matter what your definition is.

'my feelings and what I needed for my own life weren't being considered at all'—'even though we got along extremely well'. You got along extremely well because you had no say in the relationship, you gave in every time, you lived and acted as he chose. Is that extremely well for you?

'His response to my breaking things off was to grow immediately cold and distant. In anger, he said he never loved me'. This is what you should have expected from someone who had no consideration for you at any time. I could believe he never loved you because of the manner in which he acted during your relationship; I wonder why you never considered that.

Truly I don't understand how you can spend another minute regretting the breakup. Nor do I understand why you feel so hurt by his last words; he is not worthy of your feelings for him.

You're right, it isn't the time for you to begin dating again. First, you might make the same mistake in your sorrow. Second, you need time to heal, and this is what you must do. You can do it (we all have) if you remember him as he was, and not try to downplay his horrendous selfishness and inconsideration. He is not a very nice person, and you were not treated well, no matter that you thought you were. In the end, he proved it by his attitude, behavior and words that he meant to hurt you.

The only way to get over this is to want to, to put him away, stop idealizing the relationship, and get on with life, in all its aspects. Don't look for another man to heal you—this you must do yourself, in your own time. But....do not let this guy know by any way that he has caused you pain and hurt, because he also doesn't deserve the satisfaction of knowing that.

Good luck,

Linda

Dating

Dear Elders,

I have to do a paper on interracial relationships. I was wondering what your views on the matter are? Thank you.

Elder Response

Hi. My personal opinion is that it's no one's business except the couple involved as to who dates whom. It is also my personal opinion that there are people who will always be rude and nasty and create problems for interracial couples, and that is an unfortunate fact. I suspect it's envy.

Best wishes.

John

Friendship

Dear Elders,

I recently broke off a relationship with a man I really adored when I found out that he was married on my own (He didn't tell me). We went a few months without me contacting him and when he would call I would basically keep the conversations short and not friendly. He claims that he enjoyed my friendship most of all during our relationship and wants to continue as friends. I would like to be his friend, but don't see how that's possible since he lied from the beginning and he and i were intimate. His wife does not want us to have contact obviously and I don't blame her and feel that I should honor her wishes. I told him that I don't like the idea of him being friends with me against her wishes but he still continues to call and talk to me as a friend ie: trading ideas, advice, general conversation. I feel I am strong enough to be only a friend now, but am confused as to if it's morally right after all we've been through. If it is okay how do you handle a relationship of this type. It seems odd.

Elder Response

Oh, come on. Why do you want to be friends with a guy who you know not only cheated on his wife, but cheated on you at the same time by lying to you!

You really think he wants to be friends and nothing more? You have to be desperate to accept him at his word after this. His wife has the right to expect him to have nothing to do with you, and his not honoring her request shows you he is not a good person.

None of your relationship with this man has been morally right, nor will it ever be. I wouldn't trust him if he divorced his wife and married you.

You handle a relationship like this by getting as far away from it as possible, as soon as possible, and stop being a victim of a manipulative and self-centered man!

Best wishes and enjoy your life with someone who respects you and his marriage vows.

Claudia

Friends Make Bad Decisions

Dear Elders,

A very close friend of mine has been doing some inappropriate sexual things with her boyfriend of nearly 2 years. My best friend found this out in confidence and was worried so she asked me for advice. Last night we confronted her and tried to get her to come back to church because we are all Christians. She wasn't exactly angry or upset she just sat and stared and we didnt seem to reach her later that night when my friend called her, she said that the only way she would stop would be if she wanted to not if we wanted her to. I'm worried about her because i've known her for a long time and know that before her boyfriend came along she felt very strongly against everything that she is now doing. she this is just what her 'relationship has come to' but i just know things are going to progress and she will end up doing something she will seriously regret. We want to approach her again but she feels betrayed by our other friend. What should i do?

Elder Response

Thanks for writing.

Your friend has every right to feel betrayed by your other friend, whose disclosure of confidential information is grounds for terminating a friendship.

You have neither the right nor privilege to interfere with her choices. Nor is it your duty to judge; in fact that judgement is far less Christian than her behavior. Also, your lack of faith in her ability to manage her life is unflattering.

I suggest that you mind your own business until she asks for your help or for your opinion.

Best regards,

the un-Heloise

When To Say When

Dear Elders,

I've known my sons father for 7 years. I met him when I was 16yrs and he was 25yrs. My son was born 1 month after our 1 year anniversary. The past 7 yrs have been full of ups and downs. I know everyone has ups and downs but our downs include lying, stealing and a lot of drugs. My sons father and I started our relationship by getting high and drunk together and always having a party. When I became pregnant I sobered up and have remained sober. But my sons father has continued his drug use and drinking. He's never done any of this in front of our son. But he's lied to me, stolen money from me, not come home and he's been physically and verbally abusive toward me. I've been verbally abusive toward him as well. We have not lived together for the past 2 years but have continued the relationship. He finally says he's done with the drugs. I am reluctant to believe him. But I stay because he rubs my face in the fact that we use to party together and I feel like a hypocrite. I do would like to work things out but I am very confused. I know that I the answer is as plain as day but I am confused none the less.

Elder Response

If you USED to party with him, but don't now and have given up drugs, then you have no reason to feel like a hypocrite. You need to congratulate yourself every single day!

As for him, for your own sake and the sake of your child, my suggestion is to tell this guy that if he really intends to clean up his act, he needs to stay away from you for ONE YEAR, no phone calls, no contact, no drugs. After that time, you will reconsider your relationship. This is important and I think you know it. Get him away from you and your son and keep him away until he has had at least that year of being drug free. Don't be his crutch, don't make excuses for him, don't enable him. You know what I'm talking about. You had the courage to quit, now have the courage to protect yourself and your child. You owe this man nothing.

Take care—come back and tell us how you are doing. Do it as often as you wish.

Cheryl

Wedding Planning Stress

Dear Elders,

I will start at the beginning to give a clear picture of my problem. My parents were unhappily married for many years, however, they decided to stay together until I was 18 so that I wouldn't get caught up in custody battles. I am very close with my father and love him very much!! My mother became a religious fanatic (in every sense of the word) several years after they had married and it has only become worse as the years go on. I am not very close with my mother but I'm not sure she even understands why. She was always jealous of my relationship with my father which just doesn't seem typical behavior of a mother. My father named the family boat after me and World War III broke out in the house.

Now to get to the point. In July I got engaged to who I consider my soul mate. We wanted a small wedding on an island somewhere and when I mentioned it to my mother she huffed that her and my Grandmother would not travel. To accommodate them we decided to have a larger wedding here with the understanding that she would help us pay for it. Needless to say the wedding is four months away and we haven't seen a dime. Everytime it's a different excuse. She has literally been through 7 jobs in the last 6 months. She never offers to help with anything and I've done the entire planning on my own. How can I explain to her that her actions affect other people without her getting defensive (which happens quite often)?

Elder Response

Hello,

It's impossible to control other people's reactions, so you can tell your mother calmly, firmly and with respect that her actions do affect others, but don't expect that she won't become defensive. As long as YOU don't become defensive, just share your feelings with her. It sounds like your mother is having a difficult time with you and the wedding. In order to have a HAPPY wedding, try to just accept the fact that you can't change your mother. Continue your plans, stop arguing with her, and enjoy the joyful event that's coming up!

best....

Sherry

Will It Ever Be More?

Dear Elders,

I have something on my mind that has been bothering me for a long time. I've asked my friends about it, but I feel like they have been giving me the response I want to hear instead of the truth. I figure that you have been in a similar situation in the past and I am hoping that you will be able to provide me with some assistance. I like this one guy a lot. I think about him all the time, and I can't imagine him ever not being in my life. We are very good friends, and we always talk a few times each week. I really do want to date him and I have hinted that I like him in a 'more than friends' way, but I am not sure he feels the same way. He doesn't seem like he is looking for a girlfriend at the moment. My friends keep telling me that if he was going to date anyone, it would definitely be me. Anyway, I know it shouldn't be a big deal and that I should just look for another guy if he doesn't seem interested in me as more than a friend. However, I have liked him for 4 years now…I can't seem to get over him. I have dated other guys, but my mind keeps going back to him. I'm not exactly sure what I am asking you for…maybe just some reassurance that it is possible that him and I might date. Or maybe a way to let me know how to tell when a guy is truly looking for a relationship and not looking simply to get laid. I feel as if that is all the guys I have been dating have been after. He has tried, but when I tell him no he continues to stick around. I am not sure if it is because he likes me or he is just sticking with me as a friend. Why do guys seem interested in just sex and what do I do?

Elder Response

The easiest way to find out is to ask—"I'd like to take this relationship to the next level—how about you?" You have absolutely nothing to lose—he may be feeling the same way.

And one additional word about sex—here's something MY grand-mother told me forty years ago and HER mother told it to her "imagine yourself finding the most perfect shoes in the store—next door they are giving them away, not here. Where would you get your shoes?"

In my mind, that makes the whole male/female/sex thing come right into focus. Why put any effort into attaining something worthwhile if it is handed to you on a silver platter? And how much is it really worth if you can get it on any corner for nothing. Comes down to how much you value yourself as well as your relationships....Sex has two levels—they both feel good at the moment—"getting laid" always seems to work out better for the male—he really hasn't invested any emotion, even though he probably says so. "Making love" is where you feel valued before, during and after because it's just one part of the good feelings you have about one another. You'll know it when it arrives....

Take care and good luck always,

Linda

Needy Friend

Dear Elders,

My closest friend is very needy. More often than not when we talk she dominates the conversations about her problems. I admit, she has lots of problems, but most are her own making. Sometimes it gets very annoying listening to her go on and on about something we have already discussed. She rarely takes the advise she asks for.

My husband doesn't like her much. He says she is a whining pain in the neck. She is also a hypochondriac, which is true.

I have known her for quite some time and she is also my daughter's godmother. I don't know what to do about her. Should I just sit her down and tell her how I feel? If I do that, I will hurt her feeling. I do care about, but sometimes she drives me nuts.

I'd appreciate some input.

Elder Response

Hi,

As I see it, you have three choices.

1. Not seeing her any longer.

2. Telling her that you don't want to hear her whining and complaining any longer.

3. Maintaining the status quo, and thereby laying your sanity on the line.

I realize that none are pleasant, but there comes a time when most people have to "bite the bullet."

Best regards,

WO Owl

Racist Relatives

Dear Elders,

I recently had a conversation with an uncle and aunt, during which they both made racist remarks. I was shocked and speechless. I didn't know how to handle the situation tactfully. I wanted to tell them how appalling I found their remarks but did not want to be disrespectful to my elders. Yet I feel that not saying anything was/is tacit agreement and a betrayal of myself and my friends of various ethnic backgrounds.

Thank you for any advice you may be able to offer me.

Elder Response

Hello,

I've had similar experiences with my relatives and found that firmly but respectfully confronting them is the best way to go. Of course, this should be done in private and at a time when they aren't harried/hurried. Just tell them that while you care for them and don't wish to hurt them, that you're very disturbed by their comments/remarks. I wouldn't argue with them, be defensive or lecture them....just tell them how their remarks make you feel and why you believe otherwise.

You will be doing yourself, your friends and your relatives much by standing up for your beliefs. If more folks actually did this, the world might be a better place!

Best regards,

Cindy

My Best Friend Walks All Over Me

Dear Elders,

I have been friends with a girl for over 17 years and we are still really good friends, when it is just her and I we get along fine but when we are in a group she either makes fun of me or tries to make me look like a bad person. If I defend myself she says I am being too sensitive and If I say something to her the next day she gets mad at me for being mad at her. I wish I was big enough to just let it be but I hate being walked all over. Is there something I can do?

Elder Response

Hi there. Are you still "really good friends" if she is mean to you in front of other people?

Then you rightfully defend yourself and she tries to make you feel bad and that it's your fault by saying you're "being too sensitive"? Then she gets mad at you "for being mad at her", as you are rightfully so again?

Allowing yourself to be "walked all over" is not being "big", it is not liking yourself enough to defend yourself in a wrong situation.

I think the only recourse left for you is to sometime while you're alone, tell her how really bad she makes you feel when she insults you (yes, that's what she's doing), and ask her why she feels it makes her look better to make you look bad. Ask her if she still wants to be friends. If she says yes, then tell her you can't be friends with her alone if she's going to attack you in front of other people. Tell her friends don't do that, friends respect each other. If she then tells you you're too sensitive, tell her she has no sensitivity, and unless she develops some, goodbye, sweet cakes.

You must respect yourself or others will not. Never in your lifetime allow people to insult you, and then laugh it off. You are too important to yourself not to defend yourself, in a meaningful manner, calmly but definitely.

Good luck, and keep telling yourself what she is doing is not your fault; it's her shortcoming.

Best regards,

Cynthia

Foolish Lady

Dear Elders,

Hello. How are you. I recently met a man 11 years my junior online for dinner. I felt an immediate attraction to him. I sensed he felt the same way about me. As we were talking, I mentioned that my family wouldn't be too thrilled at our age difference. He agreed and said his parents wouldn't as well. We spent many hours enjoying each others company and watching a movie. As the evening ended, I gave him a hug and a peck on his face. All he said was, "I'll definitely be calling you." Well it's been several days and he has not phoned. I feel foolish because I have been thinking alot about him, and I think this was his polite way of not wanting to see me. It's been a couple of years since I've had a date, and I guess the thrill of meeting someone over took me. I don't want to contact him because I don't want to appear desperate. Your insight in this situation would be appreciated. Thanks.

Elder Response

Hi,

First of all, I don't think that you are foolish -and you shouldn't think so either. From what I gathered from your email, I think "brave" is a much more fitting title. You took a big chance by (safely) exploring the real life potential of your online relationship—there are many that wouldn't and don't take that risk. Dating is not easy and it takes guts. So give your self a pat on the back!

However, it definitely takes two to make a relationship, and no matter what your feelings are for him, you cannot dictate what his feeling for you will be in return. Perhaps he hasn't contacted you because he is not ready for a relationship that is "age-challenged" or perhaps there are other reasons why he has not conacted you...Either way, you need to let him make up his own mind about whether this realtionship is for him. Belive me, you don't want to be involved with someone who is not interested in the relationship enough to call you back. Can you imagine who much work that would be on your part?

Relationships are a two person affair—you have indicated how you feel, and "stepped into the circle" and now he needs to decide (for whatever good or bad reasons) if he wants to join you there.

So, get back out there and meet some more new people!

Best regards,

Pat

Living With Someone

Dear Elders,

My fiance & I just moved in together. I imagine we will soon come across the difficulties of adjusting to living with each other. Any advice to make this process easier?

Elder Response

Absolutely! Sign an agreement detailing the exact way expenses are going to be handled, with a mutual household account and a separate, personal account for each of you. Decide exactly how much each of you will contribute toward the household and deposit that into he household account. Keep every deposit slip, bank statement and check written.

Then decide who will be responsible for what, such as cleaning, cooking, dry cleaners, and so forth. Write it down, then sign it! Pick up after yourselves!

The second advice is to respect yourself and respect the other person equally. No one should be #1 or #2. Be fair. Don't be rude.

And if it doesn't work out, leave each other peacefully and kindly. If you've done all of the above, it will easier to do this.

Above all, best of luck and best wishes for your happiness together.

Margaret

A New Marriage In Tough Times

Dear Elders,

My husband and I have been married just a year and a half, and I'm afraid that we don't have what it takes to make it through the difficulties that have come our way. In this past year, both of my parents became so ill that they needed to be placed in nursing facilities (at least for a few months). Since they both lived far away, arranging to have them both admitted to places close to us was extremely difficult. Unfortunately, neither of my parents rallied for very long. My father died in April (one month before we had the "official" wedding celebration with the white dress etc) and my mom, who had been doing well in her battle with cancer, died six months after in November. Now, in the midst of grief, I get the very strong sense that my husband is rather sick of the whole business. He was supportive during the process, but now he seems very impatient that I get back to normal. He seems deeply uncomfortable when I am sad, and finds ways to be out of the house pretty often. I find myself feeling angry and abandoned. I just don't have the emotional energy to explain to him why he should be kind to me. Why should I have to explain? It's not that I haven't mentioned how I feel—I've been fairly specific. It's just that he doesn't seem to be listening.

Thank you in advance for your help!

Elder Response

I'm very sorry to hear that you're going through such a rough time of your life; regrettably, all of us go through such phases, it's all a part of life.

I also understand your husband's feelings right now. Many men try to deny bad emotions, even those understandable. It's simply that they have difficulty dealing with them, and often think that if those feelings are ignored, they will go away of their own volition. We know better.

Since he feels this way, you would be wise to find someone else to talk with and help you with your grief. It is important that you do have someone. I suggest you seek out a grief support group or therapist. You will be greatly helped with this support, and you will also be helping other people deal with the same problem.

Since you know your husband has a problem dealing with your grief, it would be useless and probably harmful if you continue to expect him to be your support. I know you are disappointed, but sometimes people simply cannot change their basic feelings and fears.

Give him a break, too, by finding support that will help you, not make you feel more lonely and alone. Surely you are feeling very alone right now with the loss of both your parents and now your husband's turning away from you, as it seems to you.

If this is the whole problem in your marriage, it is far too early to start thinking that you and he cannot handle marriage. Actually, it's too soon no matter what. This is an episode in your marriage that is troubling, and it is to be dealt with, not used as an excuse to destroy your marriage. You don't want to get in the habit of being angry with him and thinking this means your marriage is a failure.

This is one of the major reasons more than half the marriages in our country fail—because when some difficulty occurs, the first thought of many people is "Well, if he makes me angry and makes me unhappy, then what's the point of continuing in this marriage? I'm better off without him."

You must understand that marriage, just like life, is full of bad times, terrible times, lonely times, unhappy times; frankly, you cannot escape these times. None of us is promised a life with uninterrupted happiness.

What each of us has to do is to learn to deal, cope with these bad times when they come. We cannot always escape by blaming the other person, because we have a hand in creating the bad situations, sometimes.

Instead of thinking your marriage is doomed, you must start thinking how you can get the support you need while relieving him of the stress he apparently cannot handle. Both of you will be helped by this action instead of being hurt by doing nothing positive about it.

The fact that you married means there are very strong feelings between you. What a waste it would be to let the first serious problem destroy a valuable relationship.

But first, you must find support for yourself, and realize that one person cannot be all things to us, even though we might wish it. That's why we have friends, and supporters, and other help available to us when we need it. Go find a compatible group or person who knows how to help you get through this terrible grief. You will find it a helpful and maturing process. Do remember, marriage is a very valuable relationship, but it does require a great deal of work every single day, and well worth it. It truly is a work in progress, and always will be.

I wish you the best of luck, and will think of you from time to time, hoping you are getting better.

Best regards,

Julia

Letting Go Of An Issue

Dear Elders,

I have been married for a year and a half to a wonderful man. He is everything I wanted, and I married him just the way he is, with no intentions of changing him. I have one problem. When we were dating at the end of college, he made three times my salary. I guess I assumed life would always be like this. Once we graduated from college (1997), I've always made more than him. While I do enjoy making a decent living, I didn't think that I'd always have to be the breadwinner. I feel like I can't make a change without drastically affecting our lives. I have stayed in my current job primarily for the salary, as it is not very fullfilling. Inside, I blame him for not being more agressive and getting a better paying job, but that is completely unfair. He is a very hard worker and found a good job just a month after being laid-off as an effect from Sept. 11. It is a great job, but is still paying a great deal less than my position. This attitude is starting to affect the way I view him, and I don't want it to. We have open communication, but I feel like I can't tell him about my feelings on this issue because it would hurt his feelings and it is something I need to work out. I just don't know how to work it out! Any wisdom would be much appreciated.

Thank you.

Elder Response

You need to share this with your husband before it undermines your marriage. The two of you working things out together may very quickly find a solution. For example, you and your husband might decide to live within a tighter budget for a time to allow you to find a more rewarding job. I don't think you are being fair to you husband by hiding your feelings. You are not giving him an opportunity to contribute to the growth of your marrage by working out problems together.

You might start by telling him how unhappy you are in your present job and that you want to start looking around for something else. Tell him what it is that you want to do and why it would be better for you than your present position. Also admit to him your fear that you might have to sacrifice som salary in order to accomplish your goals. I'm willing to bet that if the two of you really love each other, you will work out the income issue together.

Best regards,

Sam

Moving In Together v. Marriage

Dear Elders,

My boyfriend and I are in a very serious relationship and have discussed the possibilities of marriage within 2 years. However, as we live in New York City, economics figure more prominently in our relationship than for couples in other regions.

I renewed the lease on my 2-bedroom apartment last month and he is in the midst of searching for a condo or house. He has suggested that we move in together to reduce expenses—half of each of our take home pay goes to rent and utilities. I agree that consolidating households would help both of our financial situations immensely, but I am concerned about the so-called "milk for free" syndrome.

Advice? Thanks!

Elder Response

Hi there. You're facing a decision that many young people face today because the fallout of a living-together-unmarried relationship all too often is very negative to both parties.

However, there is some help around. There are several books out about making and signing an agreement to cover many of the troubled areas, especially the financial setup necessary.

Both my daughter and my son used the agreements and had no problem. Of course, they both married their co-dweller within a year, so perhaps that isn't a good example.

Nevertheless, I highly recommend having an agreement. It saves all that arguing about who pays for what and how much and when and I did, no you didn't, yes I did. To start, I hope that since both of you will be putting in half your income, that your incomes are essentially the same; otherwise, that's not fair. I strongly suggest you have a household account in both your names for expenses (and for heaven's sake, keep your receipts, deposit slips and checks) and then each of you have your own bank account with only your name on it.

Finally, beforehand, settle all the "who does what" questions. Are you going to do all the laundry and dishes and cooking and cleaning, or is he to share equally? Make a list of anything you think might become a problem, discuss it, write it down and sign it! Both of you.

Lastly, studies have shown that the divorce rate is much higher for couples who live together before marriage. I don't know why, but my opinion is that either the couple or one of the couple is not interested in marriage to begin with, but feels obligated to marry because of the living together. OR couples living together and not married feel less dedicated to each other and perhaps don't act as well toward each other. These are only my opinions, of course.

If you go into this arrangement with your eyes fully open to the points of difficulty, I think you have a much better chance of happiness. At any rate, I wish you all the best, and tell you that it is important that you respect yourself in all you do, as well as respect the other person just as much. Good luck.

Best regards,

Linda

The Third Wheel

Dear Elders,

Hello and Happy New Year to you! Thank you for taking time to provide advice to others. My situation is the following:

My husband and I have been planning for some time now to take a trip to Punta Cana, Dominican Republic. This summer we traveled with another couple who are our very good friends and we had a blast. This year, we want to go to Dominican Republic with a big group or just the two of us. My husband and I are very close friends with my brother's girlfriend Patty. My brother has decided to go to Dominican Republic this February with all of his guy friends. As a revenge, his girlfriend Patty said to him that she was going with me and my husband. My brother and my mom got very upset and told her you can't go with them, they don't want you to tag along with them. Now, I am waiting for her to call me and say something like "you wouldn't mind me going with you guys on your trip to Dominican Republic would you?". I have repeatedly told her straight out that I would not want her to come along by herself, she would have to bring a friend or else she's not coming with us but apparently she has not gotten my point. In the past, my brother has been jealous of my husband and her because of their friendship; they love spending time with each other. My husband and I have discussed this matter over and over and althought we do not argue much, I know that it would bother me big time if she was to come along. How do I make it clear to her that I do not want her as a third wheel without sounding jealous or being rude?

Elder Response

Hi there. Frankly, my dear, I don't understand why you have a problem with this. Just "my brother has been jealous of my husband and her…" is enough for me. Surely you don't need another warning flare, it fairly screams. Why do you care about sounding jealous or being rude? Tell her, darn it, she CANNOT GO with you two. Wake up…I can find nothing that would make me believe this is a good idea, having your husband's very good friend on a vacation with the two of you!!

Well, you always have the option of letting her go with you two and then spending a lot of years regretting the opening you offered to her. Frankly, I think your brother is a lot smarter than you in this situation.

You have an extraordinarily perfect right to tell her she is not welcome, and not be a party to the pay-him-back she is trying with your brother. Who does she think she is, anyhow, inviting herself on your vacation with your husband? For heavens sake, stand up for yourself, woman. You're not a doormat, don't act like one. Best of luck with this—be strong and protect your marriage.

Best regards,

Claudia

Family? Or Career?

Dear Elders,

6 years ago, I moved to Seattle—away from all my family in LA—to express my independence, satisfy my curiosity about life, and to prove to myself that I have what it takes to build a successful life.

Now, I'm 31 years old, thinking about marriage with someone special, and planting our own roots, having a family, buying a home, etc. I'd like to be close to my family again, but the problem is I've found exactly what I was looking for: I've made a successful life here in Seattle, and it's very hard for me to give up.

I want my own kids to be raised near and among my larger family so they have aunts, uncles, cousins and grandparents. And yet, I love my job, I love the pace and lifestyle of Seattle.

When & how do I make the move? or, do I?

Elder Response

Hi,

The issue here is not where you want to raise your yet unborn children; but the wisdom in walking away from all you have built, and the satisfaction and happiness it is bringing you.

Moreover, what are your friend's thoughts and wishes?

I'd say: "Don't rock the boat."

Best regards,

WO Owl

Help....I Feel Inadequate

Dear Elders,

I'm 29 years old. I am divorced. My current girlfriend is 23 and we both just graduated from the university. She just got a good paying job at a school (29k a year) and I'm still continuing my studies (M.A.) and working part time at a not-so-good paying job (We don't live together). I am in a lot of debt and money is hard to get. I don't have time to get another job. Now that she's earning good money she wants to get out more, and I don't feel too good when she pays...How can I overcome this feeling? Any type of advise? Thank You.

Elder Response

Hi! Thanks for writing :-)

Well, congrats to you. I enjoy knowing that there are still a few Martians out there who get embarrassed when their "main squeeze" picks up the tab. I know and can appreciate the male pride. I think it's inborn and may take another few centuries to overcome, LOL!

So you have had a setback but are working on an M.A. Wow! Don't you feel that's putting some money in the bank, so to speak? Supposedly that M.A. will bring enough rewards to cover all the debt. Maybe your girlfriend understands this?

Open your heart to her. Tell her how your pride makes it hard for you to accept her generousity. Allow her to show her love by taking you out to dinner or a movie now and then....you show her your love by making an "in house" homemade pizza, light a candle and watch "Shrek" or something .

Above all, in the future, remember well her love and understanding when times were hard for you. You want to overcome "not feeling too good"? Just ask her how to, you might be surprised :-)

Best regards,

Treefrog

Where Is "The One"?

Dear Elders,

I am 24 years old and am waiting for the right guy to come into my life. It seems everyone around me is married or engaged, and my heart's desire is to find the man God created for me and to begin my life with him. What should I do to find him? Should I just wait for him to show up, or should I be out somewhere looking for him? How do I know if he'll ever come?

Elder Response

Why do you think God is so thoughtless that he created only one man for you? I believe in a generous God, and that means there are many men out there for you. Your job is to find one of them.

You change from year to year, so expect the man who suits you to be different from year to year. None of us remain the same, so the same type of person would not interest us at different times of our lives.

Of course, once you find the one who suits you—and who you suit—it should be forever. Many of us have managed to make marriage our forever, and we are the lucky ones (who did our best to make it good).

This means after you find the "one" you have to work with the one to become and stay the "two". A big problem today is that everyone thinks just finding your mate is the entire job—ha. Marriage is a continual growing, changing, adjusting and caring as much for your mate as for yourself. You can't just find him and then retire from the field. Neither of you.

If you're in such a hurry (as all seem to be now), then go out there and look; there's plenty of places and opportunities to meet people, but you have to do a little planning and preparation.

You're very young to be worrying about "ever", as in "if he'll ever come." What are you doing now with your life other than waiting for the future? Don't waste your life waiting for anything. Live now!

Get busy, get involved with life, enjoy life, enjoy every day, learn something every day.

Best wishes and good luck,

Skye

Ended Engagement

Dear Elders,

A year ago I met a man and instantly fell in love. We were engaged five months later and he moved in with me. I am 27 and have had many serious relationships in the past, but never lived with anyone. I didn't want to until I knew I knew I would be marrying that person. So i was pretty sure about this guy to make such a move. Anyway, as we got to know each other more, I saw that this man didn't have much motivation or sense of responsibility in him. somehow he had lived his 29 years with people doing things for him and picking up the pieces. I felt as though he lived in his dreams and had little sense of reality. For example: we both want to perform for a living, however, I know it doesn't happen to many people that they ever 'get discovered'; therefore, I am in school to have a 'normal' job so that I can make money while trying to perform for money. He, however, did not have a job until I told him he needed to get one. after all, I was working and going to school, and although his doing the dishes and laundry was nice, we needed more money coming into the house. He got a job, but i saw he called in quite a bit and hated it. Long story short, I decided i was frustrated by his lack of motivation and told him we needed to break up. he moved out a month ago and is still in slight contact with me, hoping we can work things out. I know he is looking into computer schools and going on interviews for jobs, but i feel like it's too late. he waited until after i threatened him to do these things. i feel a lot of guilt because i made a commitment to him and i feel like i quit. he says he feels like i lied to him, that i must not have loved him as i said i did or i would have been more patient with him and waited for him to get his act together.

my question (after this huge story!!) is: when is it ok to give up?? should i have waited for him to straighten out his life?? he is at heart a decent, loving and caring human being who just never had to do things for himself. is it wrong of me to have not wanted to teach him responsibility?? i feel like that is a parents job, not a lovers....

thanks for any response you have!

Elder Response

Hi. When he throws charges at you about your lying to him, or not being patient with him, or makes you feel guilty about him, think: "Do I want to raise him as a child?" "Do I want to be constantly telling him what he needs to do to be a responsible adult?" "Do I want to stay with this man with whom I obviously have almost no common ground relating to what we each consider important in life?" "Especially when I feel that in several years, after we're married and maybe have children, and have started building a life together, we can no longer stand each other or stay together?" "Because we have no respect for each other's needs and desires or characters?"

"Is this really what I want to spend the next several years of my life doing??"

Please, be logical, clear, intelligent, and put a firm and final end to it now. You are not suited for each other, it will never work. This is not to say either of you is wrong, but to say that together you will not build happiness. Don't waste your life on regrets and guilt, life is too short. You have the right idea. Make it final, not "So long", but "Goodbye".

Best wishes and good luck; enjoy your life.

With hope.

Sherry

Sort Of Friendship

Dear Elders,

Hello, elder. Well there is this guy and we used to go out a couple of months ago. I have been having trouble dealing with this and am out of answers. We only went out for about 2 months, but to me it was speshul and we broke up for reasons beyond his control. But now we hardly talk. It hurts because we were friends before we started going out and now it seems like the friendship doesn't matter to him anymore. At first I thought that maybe he was just acting like that because it was weird, and I guess in the beginning that was the case, but it's been so long that I think maybe something is up. I duno what it is, I've tried to talk to him about it, cuz I hate dealing with wierdness with a guy becuase I just think that's dumb. So yea, I am not sure what to do about it now. I am not much of a confrontal person so when I did try to talk about it I didnt get much of a response from him, which didn't help much. He said we would be friends, and I know that's a cliched thing, but I really do wanna be friends cuz I care about the friendship alot. I thought maybe if I gave him enough time and didn't talk to each other for awhile, then things would kind of smooth itself over, but I don't think it did because we still don't talk. Whenever we do talk, it seems one-sided. My friends tell me that maybe he still isn't over me, but I disagree because it's been a couples months and he likes somebody else now so yea. I am out of ideas…how do you think I should approach this? Thanks

Elder Response

Hi, thanks for writing. I had this experience once, and it hurt a great deal. Regrettably, he was never able to go back to the friendship afterward, so I lost a wonderful friend and I have been sorry ever since.

I don't know what I could have done differently, and I don't understand why he was unable to go back and reaffirm our friendship. He said he would, but he never could, nor could he explain to me why he couldn't.

It appears you are in the same situation, and I fear you will have to simply accept it. As he has already moved on and likes someone else, I think for your own self-respect and well-being you have to give up hopes of going back to your old easy friendship. If you persist in trying to talk him into it again, you face the great possibility of destroying any good memories for him that he has of your relationship.

Try to forget him and put it behind you, get onto another path, and remember him kindly.

Best regards,

Laura

Two True Loves?

Dear Elders,

I've been married for 10 years. We have two small children, and are great friends, as well as husband and wife. I love him very much. Problem is, over the course of the last two years, I've discovered that I also have deep love for another man, a man I've known off and on for most of my marriage. I don't want to be unfaithful, and since realizing my feelings I've avoided any prolonged time alone with him. But my feelings continue to haunt me. I'm not going to act on them externally, but I don't know what to 'do' with them internally, if that makes sense. What does it mean about my feelings for my husband that I can feel so strongly about another man? I think about him all the time, and often wish I could know what the life we could have had together would be like, under other circumstances. He challenges me and energizes me in ways my husband doesn't, while my husband is wonderful and completely supportive. I'm deeply confused.

Elder Response

Hi. We all love many people, so why is it odd that we can have two men in our lives that we love the same way? We can often not control our emotions, but we can absolutely control our actions.

It appears you have already decided to do something about your situation, because you are now questioning your feelings about your husband. You "think about (the other man) all the time," you want to know "what the life we could have had together would be like," and your "feelings continue to haunt me." That's because you're dwelling on them, you're enjoying them, you're wondering, you're thinking…maybe…

It is sad but true that the grass is always greener. I suspect you've become a little bored, a little lax about your marriage, and you're attempting to put a little pep back into your sexuality. Hey, I've got an idea! Make your husband the recipient! Improve your marriage. Find a new hobby to energize and challenge you, not a new man. Grow up a little, and STOP INVENTING AN IMAGINARY MAN WHO YOU HAVE TAILORED TO YOUR LIKES, because, and I say this as a good friend, YOU'RE MARRIED!!!!

What all this mean, my dear, is that you're normal, you have responsibilities, and it is quite possible to control, to ignore, to put away that great love for another man. When you have succeeded in that, you will find that a great, special friendship with that man which has absolutely no fantasies of a life with him, will be deeply rewarding to you.

Good luck and have a good life.

Arianne

What To Do?

Dear Elders,

I separated from my husband almost 1 year ago. My divorce will be final in next month. Since we separated I began seeing a nice man at work. We have been dating for 7 months. I really enjoy spending time with but there are times when I become very emotional. Especially around my period, at these times I really need some extra attention. Unfortunately my 'boyfriend' has a difficult time giving me the attention I long for. And it is at these times that I call my ex-husband. He obviously knows me well and knows how to comfort me. Last weekend I broke up with my boyfriend and found myself with my ex-husband. We spent a day and night together. I truly miss him at times and I know he really wants me back. But after a few hours together I begin to think about my boyfriend and look forward to seeing him and reconciling (obviously this sinario has been repeated more that once). I know that spending time with my ex-husband gives him unrealistic expectations for getting back together, but there are times when I really miss and need him.

Am I just completely selfish? What the heck is wrong with me? I have a great boyfriend that just hasn't known me long enough to deal with my moods and an ex-husband that sometimes I want back but then change my mind again, what is my problem? What should I do?

Elder Response

Hi. Yes, you're being completely selfish, and something is wrong with your self respect, too. Not only that, you are a liar, a cheater, an adulterer and a user.

I think you should give up your husband so he can find happiness with someone else. I think you should give up your boyfriend so he can find happiness with someone else. I think you should start going to a thera-pist and find out why you're in such a mess.

By the way, the mess will only get worse, and then you will be the one hurting and suffering and regretting. Stop it all now.

Best wishes.

Elizabeth

Long Distance

Dear Elders,

Hi, I was wondering if you have any suggestions on maintaining a long distance relationship? Thanks

Elder Response

Hi! Thanks for writing.

My friend you sure don't give much info to go by!In any case distance always challenges any relationship, something I guess you've already discovered. "That 'ol pal of mine in high school, such a good friend" slips into the night. College buddies, friends and loves strangely are relegated to yearbook pictures. The immediacy of life and its problems around us diminishes our ability to remain connected to those who are distant and remote. It's a frustrating situation, one that demands a serious and constant effort on the part of both sides to maintain communication. It's an uphill struggle, no matter what.

No amount of e-mail, snail mail or phone conversation can replace a sincere hug, kiss or handshake, nor a look into the eyes or a pat on the back. We're human and that's the way it is and there are some things modern technology cannot really make easier.

Take Care,

Julia

Should I Be Looking For A Lid?

Dear Elders,

Do you think that old saying that every pot has a lid is true? I'll be 34 in April and I'm still single.

Elder Response

Some pots are not intended to have lids, but if they would like to have one, then it is best to cease searching—the lid will find you. For some odd reason the universe prefers that one be actively engaged in life and other pursuits before it sneaks up and zaps you with the love of your life.

The condition of "single" is whole and complete. It needs no other part. Sensing that completeness attracts the desired component to construct a marriage that is also whole and complete.

Best regards,

Tom

Marriage Wisdom

Dear Elders,

On Friday, my fiancee and I will get married—a small ceremony for now w/just us & a weekend away together. He is Canadian, so we want to get the legalities going so that he can garner permanent residency status.

I know he loves me & I love him dearly. We're both very comfortable with each other, and we share similar values. For instance, it was of no question to either of us to not spend a fortune on rings/ceremony—the meaning is what's key—and to instead save for a home, travels, kids, etc.

I guess I'm wondering what advice anyone might have for a long & happy marriage. It seems that many 'older generation' marriages lasted longer than do those now. He is 35 & I am 32; neither of us has been married, and we want a marriage to be forever. I'm a sociologist, so I can list many reasons as to why marriages are less long-lasting these days, but I'd really like some advice from folks who had long & generally happy/successful marriages as to what worked for them.

My biggest insecurity is that he'll be faithful/stay in love w/me. I guess this is many folks' deep fear. I do trust him; I know he loves me dearly, more than he ever has anyone. But, I'm, for a variety of reasons, a very insecure person. My shrink says I likely always will be…:) That said, how do I best deflect my anxieties so as not to keep bothering him with them? He already gets a bit frustrated that I don't trust him. The truth is that I trust him more than I have anyone ever—as much as I seemingly can. Truth is rather a catch-22 situation, I think. Still, he feels like I don't trust him at all because I am so generally insecure (though he's remarkably understanding about all this and has stayed true to me despite some rough emotional times/outbursts—he has a very balanced, mature understanding of people, that there are good and bad times & that he is willing to stick out the tough patches if it means being with me).

Any advice?

Elder Response

Hi! Thanks for writing :-)

Advice for a long & happy marriage? Well, for one thing it's got to involve the "trust" in each other's love. You've got to overcome that insecurity of which you speak, otherwise it may always be a tripping block. You are both old enough to have made a mature decision and commitment that will work if you allow the love for each other to grow and flourish. It surprises me that you are a social worker and feel so insecure in your relationship. You mentioned how "very balanced" he is. Take that observation, learn from it and give it back to him in return.

Your love will not grow and flourish if you depend on his "mature understanding" to overcome your insecurity. It's a two way street wherein love makes a leap of faith and presumes only that it returns, each minute, hour, day, year.

Been married for 37 years. Each day one of us silently forgives the other for mostly small things. We've come to recognize our love in this way. We find time each day to sit and talk. "How was your day?" And we DO listen to each other. We sit in the garden room, glass of wine and eat pistachio(sp?) nuts and talk...(rituals are important, LOL!)

Anyway, good luck in your marriage. If you both set your mind to it and keep trying to surprise and excite each other....it CAN LAST!

Best regards,

Treefrog

Only Attract Married Men

Dear Elders,

I am in my late twenties, and I have not been in a committed relationship in over 5 years. I have lots of friends (both male and female), but the only guys that are ever interested in me are either married or have serious girlfriends. I am a friendly and outgoing person, but single guys always seem to want to be my friend. On the contrary, married guys I meet through work or mutual friends are constantly hitting on me. I'm not really sure if there is some 'vibe' that I project that married guys seem to respond to, but if so I would like to get rid of it! I make it VERY clear to these men that I do not get involved with married men (or men with girlfriends), yet they persist. My married male friends say things like "If I were single, you are exactly the kind of girl I would date. I can't believe you don't have a boyfriend!" Yet single guys never approach me, and the ones that I have approached are just not interested.

Any advice?

Elder Response

I believe you probably are giving off vibes and it might be interesting to you to explore this a little and really be honest with yourself as to why you might be doing it….I'm sure it is totally unconscious but people always respond to us in the way we respond to them—often while unaware we are doing so. In the case of unavailable men, are you subconsciously competing with the other females in their lives? Unsure of your attraction to the opposite sex? In constant need of approval? Titillated by forbidden fruit? Unable to form committed relationships of your own? (A married man would, in some respects, be a *safe* relationship—there is no real commitment).

One thing, if men are coming on to you at work, married or not, its against the law and if you truly don't like it, just mention "sexual harassment" to them one time—I guarantee it'll stop.

Married men are testing you with statements like "if I were single...blah blah blah"—it's one of the biggest come-ons in the world—cool their jets—make NO response at all—turn around and walk away. Maybe you could be a little less friendly and outgoing with married men, especially at work; work is not a social activity, work is about competence.

You deserve happiness in this life and part of that might be finding someone of your own to share it with—I know you can and will.

Take care and good luck!!

Pat

Don't Know How To Handle Men

Dear Elders,

ok, well, for the past two years i've been in a serious relationship with 2 different guys, with one for a year and a half, and then with another for 3 months, and for the past month, i've been just dating around. i found a guy i like and we started dating. then he told me that he didn't want a serious relationship right now. is it possible to remain in a dating relationship without getting serious? thank ya so much!

Elder Response

Good heavens, I certainly hope so!! Where did the idea come from that you couldn't simply enjoy dating various people, but had to be in a "serious" and lifetime relationship with each person? How silly!

Frankly, an awful lot of relationships I hear about today would have been far better if each party had not tried to make it into something it was never destined to be.

Life is too short to be continually rushing forward into unhappiness because of unrealistic expectations. Relax, enjoy each person and each day as it comes, and all will come to you in its own time without your forcing it too fast.

Best wishes, and enjoy your life.

Arianne

Is It Love?

Dear Elders,

First: Thank you for taking the time to read this email, and I look forward to your response.

Yes I am in need of advice on my relationship. Please Help.:-)

Almost three years ago to this very day I left my husband of 4 years. We married young, right out of high school actually, which I know now was a big mistake. I left my husband because his anger went completely out of control one morning when he punched me in the back and kicked me, as I lay curled up on the floor.

That very day I called my brother in Florida from a phone booth surrounded in the Indiana snow. I brother made me realize that I needed to make a choice, stay or leave.

Three years I have been in Florida now, three years that I have done a whole lot of growing up, even though I am still at the young age of 25.

A year and 1/2 ago a man with quite a bit of persistence and charm finally got me to let me wall down just a enough to get to know him. Well once I really got to know him, months later after dating, I realized I was falling in love with him. I was honest with him, I told him where my feelings where going, and I asked if I should feel this way.

He told me that he did not yet feel love but he saw this relationship long and lasting. He too is divorced, has been for almost 3 years, and it seems his ex-wife hurt him pretty bad. From all I know she had done to him I understood his reasons for not feeling so strongly for me, or at least not openly sharing it.

A year & 1/2 later and he still can not say he loves me. I have never pressed the issue though I admit there are times where I am driven to tears to know I feel so much for this man and he possibly does not feel the same. Are relationship is awesome, we even live together now in his home.

My friends warn me that if he cant say he loves me then something is wrong, but there is so many times he does the sweetest things that seem to whisper just how much he cares. Am I being played for a fool, chasing a dream that will never be real? Or is he just unable to say he loves me, to afraid to be hurt again.

Just so you know, and he knows too, I am not looking to marry, once honestly seems enough, and I think he feels the same. But what I do want is to be with someone who I love and who loves me.

I appologize for the long email. Please if you have any advice......, thank you.

Elder Response

Hello. Congratulations on having the courage to leave that lousy first husband; it sounds as though you should have left earlier! But, put it behind you now, and feel good about yourself.

My first comment is to never regret that you have loved, for this is a wonderful gift. My next comment is don't listen to other people regarding how you feel, and if you want, include me in that group. Your friends are wrong: not being able to say I love you does not mean he doesn't feel love. It is not uncommon for people, especially men, to have difficulty speaking the words. You need to be sensitive to how he treats you, how he makes you feel, what he does for you,...AND...how you feel about him. It is much easier to speak a lie than to act out a lie.

If you are content with him, love him, and are treated very well by him, if you are happy and he is happy, then you have no problem. Either he eventually will learn to say I love you, or he won't.

But…would you want to give up the happiness you feel with him now just because your friends say you should?

Might he leave you? Yes, he might; he also might not, and we cannot protect ourselves against all that "might" happen to us. If we are lucky, we find love and we enjoy it, and we allow it to transform our lives into something special—even if it eventually ends.

I wish you the very best, and hope you will enjoy all your life and loves.

Margaret

My Friend That Really Isn't...Is Copying Me

Dear Elders,

Hello. I used to have a really great friend. She was my best friend, and we would do everything together. Just recently, my friend got a boyfriend. Since then, she has had a complete attitude change, change of friends, and even tries to take my other best friend away from me. Also, have you ever had a friend in your life that copied every little thing you do? This girl does the same thing. Clothes, hair, words, all kinds of things. I mean, I am actually afraid to tell her what music i am listening to because every time that i do that, the next day she goes out and buys it! I really like to be an individual, and its real nice that she copies me...('copying is the highest form of flattery'), but I feel so uncomfortable because I can't have my special things that I like. I also feel like soon this girl will take over my life, and be the new me...,As I said before, she is already trying to take my other best friend away from me, and I really don't like her boyfriend (and I tried, oh I tried)...any advice? Thanks :-)

Elder Response

Hello. You're letting this friend disturb your life much more than is necessary or wise. I would assume she is a former friend by now, and I would stay away from her. What do you now have that keeps you friends? From your letter, I don't see any liking of each other.

You are also allowing her copying you (which would have to stop if you no longer see her) to be too important. So what? She just doesn't have any new ideas of her own, so she has to use yours. Stop hanging around with someone who irritates you to this degree.

Best regards,

Carol

To Have And To Hold

Dear Elders,

My ex-spouse divorced me a 1 year ago and he never explained to me why he wanted to divorce besides that he did not want any more responsibility. We have one son together who 15 years old. Now that we are divorced and I decided to move to another state, I found out that my ex-spouse has another son that is a year older than our son which my ex-spouse had kept a secret for the entire 15 years of our marriage. I am unable to speak to him because he refuses to speak to me with respect and an argument will arise, I choose not to argue because what is done has been done. The problem is his son that he has never told me about want to interact with my son. I don't have a problem with that but that child is a complete stranger to me and his mother or his father need to clear things up with me. I feel this child just cannot enter into our lifes especially mine when I don't know anything about him. I feel that my ex-spouse or the child's mother need to come forward and we work something out. In the meantime, I told my son that he cannot hang out with the other child. At this point this child is a stranger to me and I don't let my child hang out with someone that I don't know or trust. I carefully tried to explain this to my son and I don't think that he is understanding. I am wrong for telling him that he cannot hang out with his half brother for now? What am I suppose to do? I do have bitter feelings because my ex-spouse introduced me the mother years ago during our marriage and he introduced her as being a high school friend. They knew the truth then and felt that they should keep it away from me. My ex-spouse and myself were both in the military and we traveled around alot. He is from one city and I from another. There had been alot of deceit in our marriage and refuses to talk about it. His family also knew about the child and refuses to talk also. I feel like I am being forced to have other people in my life when I am so desperately trying to move on.

Elder Response

Hi

"I am so desperately trying to move on". Move on to what? Move on to avoiding all the consequences of your past decisions? My dear friend, it just doesn't work like that. Whatever the situation is, and as complicated as it may be, you are most likely 50% involved. It sounds like some communication is in order on the part of all concerned. You mention that "all concerned" refuse to talk. That is not acceptable. Talk is MOST necessary, talk without malice, without recrimination, just talk in behalf of two young half-brothers that had no choice in their situation. Their future relationship can be one of love or one of hate. You have much to do in this regard. They can only succeed if they see something of love. It is possible for two divorced people to individually and together still demonstrate love and guidance to their offspring. Gotta' COMMUNICATE!

Best regards,

Jack

Faithless Grandfather

Dear Elders,

Hi, I have a very strong faith in Jesus; I love him with all of heart and I want to share his love with everyone! But I just found out my grandfather doesn't even know if he believes in God let alone Jesus. What is a unique way I could minister to him because its not that he hasn't thought about it, he has. He has done a lot of reading on different religions and such but has decided to be content with undecided! I love Jesus and I want my Grandfather to know his love to.

Any Ideas?

Much love through Christ.

Elder Response

Be like Jesus and love your grandfather for who he is and what he believes in. Love is what it is ALL about! That is the essence of what He taught. Love yourself and love others equally. Your grandfather can know the love of Jesus through you.

I hope this helps. Best regards,

Liz

Marriage

Dear Elders,

How will my marriage be?

Elder Response

It's like putting money in the bank. The more you put in, the more you are able to draw out.

Best regards,

Lisa

To Marry Or Not To Marry?

Dear Elders,

I have been dating a young man 4 years younger than I for almost two years. I care about him greatly, but I don't feel that I love him. We disagree on religion, how to raise a family and children, and money. I know these are key issues. He has proposed marriage and I told him that I would think about it. I don't feel that I can continue in this relationship because I feel as if I'm living a lie and am being selfish. At the same time I don't want to end it because we've spent a lot of time together, I enjoy his company and I care for him a great deal. I would appreciate any advice that you could offer. Thank you!

Elder Response

Hello. You don't need advice, you know how you feel. But perhaps you need someone to agree with you. Okay, I agree you should break up.

I never ever advise anyone to get married to a person they don't love! I absolutely never advise anyone to marry someone with whom they disagree about religion, family, children and money.

You feel you are living a lie—stop it; being selfish—stop it. You are certainly being unfair to him, keeping him dangling instead of freeing him to go look for a compatible woman.

I suggest you tell him gently and kindly—and truthfully—how you feel, and then attempt to keep him as a platonic friend, if you can.

Best wishes and good luck.

Arianne

When To Tell A Date That I Have Children

Dear Elders,

I have been single for almost a year now and accepted an invitation to dinner. I have children, but did not tell him. When would it be appropriate to tell him? Is it wrong that I didn't tell him when I accepted to go out to dinner with him?

Thank you

Elder Response

No, it isn't wrong—it isn't as though you haven't told him about a terrible crime, or moral issues, or bad ethics…it's your child, for heaven's sake!

I would bring up the subject only after several dates when I realize I might become seriously interested in this person. Sooner than that is not necessary, assuming he has ethics, too. You don't have to WARN men that you have a child, it's a beautiful thing that you do.

Good luck, and enjoy your life.

Arianne

Confused

Dear Elders,

I posted this same topic about a month ago, and thinking about it more, I thought I would repost and maybe get some different advice. I am a 20-year-old college woman. I have not had any romantic relationship for over 3 years and no romantic contact, physically, with anyone in about 2 and a half years. Most of me not being interested in a romantic relationship was due to low self-esteem due to me being overweight.

Now, I am starting to think about wanting to be in a relationship with someone, and here's the problem. I do not find myself attracted to men, but to women. I have sexual fantasies about women, I feel closer and more connected to women, and I feel physically more attracted to a woman's body than a man's. However, I have never had a relationship with a woman, on a romantic level. Could all this mean I am gay? I am very confused, mostly because these feelings are not new, I have had these feelings on and off for the past year.

Any sound advice would be greatly appreciated. The last time I posted something along these lines, I was basically told to see a therapist, and though that may be a good idea, in the long run, I want to try to figure this out on my own and not feel like I am being told what to do, at the same time I feel like I cannot talk to anyone close to me, because if I'm not gay, I don't want them to treat me differently because of these feelings. Thank you.

Elder Response

Dear Confused,

I don't know what advice you received previously, so I may say the same. I want to first correct your thinking that a therapist tells you what to do. Absolutely not! Therapy is for you to find out what YOU want to do with your life, not what someone else thinks you should. A good therapist will never tell you what to do.

Therapy was suggested to you because you are so uncertain about your life, and at this point, it still seems like good advice to me.

Now, if you are being attracted to women because you've been unable to have a romantic relationship with a man in the last few years, that's a very bad reason. One does not substitute for the other, either way.

You may very well be gay, or you may not be; that's where a therapist can help you, but since you seem unwilling to do that for yourself, then I'll give you some more advice.

If you think you may be gay but "cannot talk to anyone close to me, because if I'm not gay, I don't want them to treat me differently because of these feelings", then you're in serious trouble. If gay, you will have to get used to having people treat you differently; that is a sad and awful fact, but true. This you will have to live with all your life. It isn't right and it isn't fair, but it's reality.

Exactly how do you intend to "figure this out" by yourself? Trial and error? I think you cannot figure this out without talking with someone, or you will be very, very lonely. Do you have any gay friends you can talk with? Family members? I do not envy your choice to try this path without someone supporting you, and I think you are unwilling to open yourself to someone helping you.

All I can say now is that I wish you all the best in life, and good luck.

Julia

Is There Only One?

Dear Elders,

I feel that there is ONE very special person out there who was meant to be with me forever. I keep getting out of relationships because I feel that something is missing, but I'm just not quite sure what it is, even if the man is very special. Am I fooling myself to believe that there will be one perfect person for me or should I continue to wait until I meet 'The One'?

Elder Response

Hi, I'm happy you've written. This gives me the opportunity to tell you I believe there is no such thing as "ONE very special person…." I believe there are numerous very special persons throughout our lives. It all depends upon when we meet them, the circumstances of the time, our ability to recognize them, and on and on.

I would hate the thought that I had only one chance in my lifetime to be happy, and if I missed it, I was doomed to sorrow forever. I often wonder why people want to believe in "the ONE" person, "the soul-mate", the "one perfect person," the "meant to be with me forever" person. That you feel something is missing from your relationships means only that you have not yet had a relationship with a person who suits you and who you suit well. Don't start narrowing your chances by thinking you have to search for the ONE.

I do wonder if you feel "the man is very special" but you are disappointed, whether you have realistic expectations of life and love? You will never find the perfect person, since there is no such thing. The perfect person will someday do something you don't like, will be messy, will be rude, will be mean, will be lost, and your "perfect person" has suddenly disappeared. You're looking for failure.

I'm not saying there shouldn't be a special feeling between the two of you, for you must want to be with that person before all others, like and respect that person, care for that person as you do yourself, allow that person to be absent and still have trust in him, and on and on. All this is possible without perfection.

I have been married for over 40 years; we were married so young it created problems with us when we matured in varying ways, and our marriage has always had disagreements. I still think we both made the right choice, and by heavens, we're going to stay married and loving it, until one of us dies. Yes, we both had other opportunities and willing people, so it wasn't a "settle for" relationship. In fact, it created quite a bit of trouble for us. You see, for love to be true it doesn't have to be perfect, in fact, cannot be. Relax a little, be a little more adjustable, and all will work out in the end.

Best wishes, and I send my hopes that your life will be fulfilling and happy.

Claudia

Him & His Kids

Dear Elders,

I am involved with a man who has three children, from two different women. I have been divorced and have no children. I love him and his children very much, but am feeling some disapproval from my immediate family. We have been together for almost 2 years. How should I tell my family that this is a choice that I am happy and confident with?

Elder Response

Are you? I might support your decision if:

1) He pays support for all his children;

2) He had married at least one of the women;

3) He sees all his children on a regular basis and has a good relationship with them.

Otherwise, all I can say is best wishes and good luck. He has a lousy track record. Someday you will be very grateful that your family cares a great deal for you.

Best regards,

Margaret

Am I A Shrew?

Dear Elders,

I have always been a 'women's libber'. I am 23 and I don't agree with most of what the media defines a woman as. Sometimes I ask myself if I am insecure. I really don't feel that I am. I consider myself an attractive and intelligent woman. My problem is that I am dating a man that is scared of my reaction to anything he may experience involving women. He delivers beer and the distributor is always having events where Playboy centerfolds visit his work to give autographs. He doesn't go, but I'm afraid he is only doing that because he is wanting to avoid a battle with me. I want him to not go because he respects me and loves me enough to not want to be in that type of environment. I can't eat or sleep sometimes because I am so scared that our relationship is going to be torn apart because I'm so radical in my beliefs. He says he agrees with me about the role of women in society. I wonder if he patronizes me because he loves me. I should probably trust him more than that as he is a very opinionated man as well and also very smart. But he has lied to me in the past in order to attract me to him initially. (He told me he owned a vehicle that he had borrowed on our first date, and I've second guessed him a lot because of it). My own mother says I'm a little nuts because I don't want to be with a man who takes part in the objectification of women (ie. reading pornograpy, going to nude bars and etc). I feel she comes from a time when women had to accept this behavior from males because it was the norm. I don't want to settle for less than I deserve, I feel I deserve respect and I have obviously determined by definition of that respect. Reading this, do you see major wholes in my thought process? Can you offer anything to put my mind at ease? And do you think that I am robbing my beau of the respect he deserves by not placing 100% of my faith in what he says? Thanks so much.

Elder Response

Dear am-I-a-shrew? worrier:

What a turmoil you have gotten yourself in, so sit back, relax, and let's talk.

I am one of many unknown fighters for women's rights, starting when I was 16 in 1956 and thrown out of college for protesting unequal treatment and privileges of men and women students. I've suffered through serious sexual harassment on jobs, been denied credit except in my husband's name, been paid less than men, and a myriad of other inequities. That's all behind me, because I've always known who I am, and have the courage of that conviction.

You are not quite certain about either yourself or what a "women's lib-ber" is. You are quick to dismiss women who might be Playboy center-folds, and don't want your boyfriend "in that type of environment"; you have him "scared of my reaction to anything he may experience involving women;" and you feel your mother comes from a time "when women had to accept his behavior (reading pornography, going to nude bars and etc) because it was the norm." This has never been "the norm" for men, nor would most women have accepted it as such.

I don't see a lot of respect for women—or men—in your words, and don't like your putting it under the heading of being a "women's lib-ber." You are contributing to the wide-spread ignorance of exactly what women's liberation is. Simply reading your own words, it sounds to me like confusion, insecurity, jealousy and probably low self-esteem.

You are making a serious mistake in attempting to control your boy-friend; this is a dangerous attitude toward someone who, I assume, you love. It is the opposite of love, because it shows great distrust, another no in a loving relationship. Your problem is that you don't trust him at all and are afraid of being abandoned by him. Why would you create a relationship with someone you love in which he is "scared of my reaction;" "he is only doing that because he is wanting to avoid a battle with me;" "he patronizes me because he loves me." Wow! This is a serious relationship problem.

You are going to have to think harder about why you have these attitudes, and stop making such rash judgments of other people, including your boyfriend and your mother.

The ideas behind liberation for women is that all of us be accorded respect, given equal rights, and have the right to choose how we live our lives, without the overwhelming control of society, men, the law, and often, other women. I think a Playboy centerfold has the right to live as she chooses, and if you fear your boyfriend's meeting them, then that's your problem, not one of her making. Being beautiful does not mean she is a predator.

If your boyfriend just lied to you once about the rather boastful but hardly harmful lie of owning a car and hasn't lied since, I don't understand your tremendous distrust of him. Was it so important to you that he owned that particular make of car? Does he actually read porn and go to nude bars? If so, then you have another area of dissent with him that might be of importance, depending on how he treats you in this area.

Truly I don't think you are giving your beau any respect at all, if he feels as you say about your relationship. Certainly you are giving him no trust, nor many of the other aspects of love that are so important: equality with you, individuality, acceptance without control, self-sufficiency, true intimacy, encouragement of personal growth, and self-esteem. I don't have any quick and easy advice for you, because I think you're dealing with several issues, all complicated. I do think you should back off and give him a little peace while you think about what you can do to change, if not your attitudes, at least your behavior. I'm very sorry you're so unhappy, but I do believe if you are truly honest with yourself and work to make this relationship better, you can come out of it with something good and kind.

I wish you the best and hope that you will take the time to enjoy your life and your interactions with other people.

Arianne

What Kind Of Man Is My Husband?

Dear Elders,

I am married to a wonderful man for 6 years now. We have two beautiful children and he is a wonderful father, not to mention we are best friends. However in the last few months, I have realized that he lacks compassion for others. If something happens that doesn't affect him, it doesn't concern him. This has really hit me and really bothers me. I will talk about something horrible that has happened and his response is 'oh well'. I don't like to think that the man I married can be so insensitive to others. September 11th didn't really bother him. He may have said once that it was too bad, but no emotion. Now my stepfather's brother has died and my husband (who isn't fond of my step father) said 'do I really have to go to the funeral'. And this was said completely selfishly. How can I help him to be more compassionate? I am scared that he will never feel for someone other than himself. I think that in the 7 years I have known him, I just didn't want to see it?

Elder Response

Hi,

You are married to a wonderful man, wonderful father, and you and he are best of friends. In the scheme of things, you won big in the lottery.

Yet, there are the following truisms: By and large and generally speaking, men rule with their heads, while women do so with their hearts.

Consequently, women are prone to be more compassionate then men.

If I were you, I'd not be concerned, and highly recommend that you not let his presumptive "lack of compassion" become an issue.

Best wishes, and enjoy your husband's good qualities.

Sherry

An Unusual Situation...

Dear Elders,

Thank you in advance for your advice. I am a 34 year old non-custodial mother of two beautiful children. I became a non-custodial mother because I became clinically depressed after the birth of my second child and got sucked into the big black hole of depression. I was convinced that going out into the world and finding something else would make me happy. After almost two years of medication and therapy, it was like I had emerged from a long, dark tunnel and when I re-entered the world I realized the unimaginable mistake I had made by leaving my family. My husband and I were divorced in January of 2001, and he treats me like the devil incarnate. My children are conflicted because they love me, their mother, but feel guilty for loving me because their father hates me so. I guess the reason for my letter is that I would like advice about how to rid myself of the guilt I feel for having left my family, and how to move on with my life and pick up the pieces that are left while enduring the hatred that my ex husband feels for me and demonstrates whenever we interact (which is weekly since I pick up the children from his house.) I am with an extremely loving, caring, understanding and patient man now, but my guilt and inability to enjoy life to any degree is destroying the relationship I have now. I don't want to lose the relationship I have and make another mistake, but I live life every day with guilt and sadness. Although there may not be anyone in your wisdom circle who has ever experienced losing custody of your children, I'm hoping that someone might have done something they regretted and learned how to deal with the past and live for the future. Thank you for listening.

Elder Response

Hello, and thank you for writing. I understand much of what you feel, as I was seriously depressed for several years after the birth of a child. I am concerned about your "guilt and inability to enjoy life to any degree". This is also depression.

Certainly there are reasons for you to be sad and regretful, but guilt is a useless emotion. It does no good and does great harm, to both you and others around you—you say your children "feel guilty for loving me…." You must attempt to ease that guilt.

You need to go to your doctor and talk about your inability to enjoy life, and about the situation you are in. I think a mild antidepressant will help you cope right now.

Since it is unlikely your former husband will change his attitude and feelings toward you, you must teach yourself to ignore his feelings and STOP feeling guilty! I suspect he has much to do with this heavy load of guilt you carry.

You must also work on your reaction to his hatred of you. Start ignoring what he says, then start pretending you can't hear him, and finally, get to the point where you truly don't care what he says or how he acts. You are allowing his hatred to ruin your life.

Most of all, do not allow yourself to speak badly of him to the children, never. If you remain kind, the children will eventually understand that he is very hurt and striking out to hurt you. Then they will no longer feel guilty of loving you.

You are not being loving to yourself, and this is the tragedy. You must love, respect and care for yourself before you can protect yourself from others who would harm you; don't allow your former husband to destroy you, fight for yourself, emotionally.

When you recover your equilibrium, you will then be able to adjust to life as it is, and find pleasure in it again. You might consider going into therapy for a while. Perhaps you might become strong enough and emotionally stable enough, that you might try for more time with your children.

I give you my best wishes and hopes for a successful and happy life, and courage for the battle ahead of you in regaining some of what you have lost.

Pat

Do I Wait For Him?

Dear Elders,

I am a 39 year old female and have been having a wonderful relationship with a great man. We have problems, as many couples do, ours is mainly in our communication style. He has given me the 'I need to get on my ship and sail away for awhile...but all ships need to come back home...' speech. And the ever popular, 'If you love something, set it free...' Of course, I love him dearly and understand his need to take care of his life agenda(he is 6 years younger than me), school, music, career...Our relationship hasn't been the best lately, it has put a strain on our friendship. Perhaps it would be wise to take a break. I'm willing to do it and feel it's important that I not make the mistake again of making a man the most important thing in my life. I just went back to school and have a decent job. I had been married for 10 years prior to this relationship. I don't mind waiting and I realize we are both taking the chance of 'losing' each other, but we are still the very best of friends. What do you think?

thank you for your time...

Elder Response

Hello. He's talking but you're not hearing. He has said he wants to be free, so where is the question?

The greatest mistake a woman can make is to believe that a man is the most important thing in life. Phooey! And I say that after being happily married over 40 years. You cannot keep this man with you unless he wants to stay, no matter what you do. Let him go graciously and you get on with living another, happier life.

You know the only person who will always be with you and be for you, is you. Love you first, then you can love without fear another person.

Best wishes, and good luck.

Linda

Affairs Of The Heart

Dear Elders,

I've met a gal, she's 24 and I'm 47. We are deeply in love, and she asked me to marry her. I surprised myself by saying yes, because I never thought I'd marry again. The problem is her mom. She thinks I'm 37, and that I've never been in trouble. I'm an ex-convict and a recovering drug addict. I tired of people wanting to judge me and not even know the man I am now. That's what her mom is doing, judging me before she even knows me. I refuse to prove myself to future family, I did that once before and I tried for 8 years to prove that I was a decent man. Am I wrong to refuse proving myself?? How can I show her mom I'm really a good person??

Elder Response

Hi,

You do not have to prove yourself to anyone other than the lady you intend to marry, much less do you have to show her mother that you are a good person.

A word of caution: the mother appears to be an opinionated, meddling fool who may well seek to drive a wedge between you and her daughter. I strongly urge you to fully discuss all aspects, present and future influence of the mother i.e. how will each of jointly and severally deal with her. BOTTOM LINE: If push comes to shove, is the daughter willing to cut the mother adrift?

Best wishes and good luck,

Frank

Popping The Question

Dear Elders,

I have a boyfriend of almost four years and we live together. He Still hasn't 'popped the question', even though we both have discussed getting married. (Right down to the details, where we want it, who will be there…etc.) How do I let him know in a nice way that I'm READY!?

Elder Response

Hi,

Ask him whether he wants to get married in August or September. In so doing you will be giving him a choice of month, rather than facing the issue of whether or not he wants to get married.

Best wishes,

Karen

Girl Problems

Dear Elders,

There is this girl i used to date, for about almost a year and we have ha all kinds of problems…i broke up with her, she broke up with me but when she did she left me for another man for about 3 months then she says she "realized" what she lost etc…i am really in love with this girl anfd it's been well over 4 months since we broke up anfd i cant stop thinking about her…i dont know wether i should try to talk to her again or just keep the silence how it is…i wanna talk to her really bad but the fact of the matter is she s hard to understadn and changes states of mind real quick….like she cares then she doesnt….what should i do…?

Elder Response

Hi there. I wonder how old you are; you are probably quite young. Four months is not an unusually long time to grieve the loss of a relationship with a person you love. It is important, however, that you make up your mind that it is over (it is), and turn your thoughts and actions toward your future.

I have two comments you might not like, but you asked for advice: It sounds to me as though she is keeping hold over you, just in case you come in handy in the future. She is promising you nothing, yet telling you she "realized what she lost etc." Obviously, she doesn't want back what she lost, whatever she means by that. But it's keeping you hoping, isn't it?

The fact that you are really in love with this girl might be true, but if she loved you, she'd be with you and not hurt you as she has and is doing. What can you say to her that would make her love you again? What do you think you will accomplish (except perhaps embarrass yourself and hear more empty words from her) by talking to her?

If someone loves you, she does not hurt you, or be hard to understand, or change her state of mind so quickly. She would be steady and stalward, and very mindful of your feelings. It is a difficult task to put into its proper place a love you have lost, but it is possible—and necessary. Otherwise, you go through life just a little crippled, a little lost, disappointed with yourself and your life. No former love is worth your life, because it will forever be unappreciated by the person you most want to please. Do your necessary grieving, d not hold hopes of rekindling that love, and start thinking of other matters in life to fill the void that will exist for a while. You have so many years ahead to enjoy life, to love and to appreciate. Take that first step away now. I wish you the best of luck.

Best regards,

Paul

Boys

Dear Elders,

ok i know this guy and he really likes me but i don't feel the same towards him. I don't want to be mean and tell him that i don't like him like that. i don't know what to do can you help?

Elder Response

Hi. There are times when only the truth will do, and this is one of them. Mistake me not, there is only one way to handle this situation—tell him. Be kind, be truthful, don't hold out any false hope to him, and be a friend by being honest with him.

Any other course of action will lead to displeasure, disagreement and annoyance. Trust me, I speak from years of experience.

Best regards,

Cynthia

Hot And Cold

Dear Elders,

Hello. I have a guy friend who I care for very much, but I get mixed messages about him everytime we get to talking about our feelings for each other. Basically, he is hot one day and cold the next, and it frustrates me very much. One day he'll email me, call me, talk to me for literally hours about everything, and the next day he is exactly the opposite. He doesn't call or even email, until I do, and then he seems too busy for me. I've known him for two years and he's like this a lot, especially lately. I don't exactly have an exact question, but I would like to ask you advice. I care for him a lot, and despite everything, I do know that he cares for me and does see me as more than a friend(don't ask how I know, I just do!=). He is the kind of guy that gets bored of people quickly (annoying!), and changes friends and girlfriends very quickly, expcept for me. Like I said, we've been friends for two years, and that's the longest female friend relationship he's really had. I'm getting sick of this whole situation, though! He's a typical thickheaded, egotistical male pig (with everyone, not just me!), but he's still irresistable! Our relationship is always either freezing cold or boiling hot,and almost never in between. I'm frustrated! =) So thanks for any advice you can give in advance…thanks! Bye!

Elder Response

Hi,

If you believe that you can change the spots on a leopard, go for the "guy." If you can't [change the spots] drop him like you would [drop] a hot potato.

Best wishes,

Julia

Torn Between Two Guys

Dear Elders,

Recently there is this guy, who is sweet and funny, who asked me out. Sure there are some problems with him, in fact almost everything…but I am tired of waiting for my prince to come. But there is this other guy, who I am crazy about, but I don't know how he feels about me…He is my dream guy, the most perfect in all the world…I am afraid to ask him though because while he is perfect in almost every way, I am not. I don't look perfect and I don't know if he will shoot me down before he knows me at all. The first guy is a sure thing, even though he is wrong and bad for me in almost every way possible. The second guy I don't know…any advice?

Elder Response

Hi. I can't imagine my eating something that I didn't really like just because it was put in front of me, especially if it is "wrong and bad for me in almost every way possible." I can't imagine settling for a man just because he's there. What are you thinking?

Why don't you just ask the guy you really like and get it over with? What do you have to lose that you have now if he says no?

Stop using the other guy, and tell him goodbye, since you think almost everything is bad about him.

What are you, 125 years old, that you're tired of waiting for your "prince" to come??? Get real.

Arianne

Long Distance Marriage

Dear Elders,

My boyfriend and I have been dating since summer of '99, and friends 3 years prior to our dating relationship. Unfortunately, we are in two different areas of the country. He is in Virginia, and I am in Texas.

We've always decided to do what's best for each other on an individual basis so there would be no regrets regarding our life goals. Now we want to get married and we are not sure how to go about it. How do we determine who moves where, and when?

We are both raised old fashioned so living together prior to marriage isn't something we particularly want to do. How can we make a smooth transition without wasting a lot of money on rent? Currently, he still lives at home, and I own a townhouse outright. It is paid for. Should he go ahead with his plans to buy a house, then have me move in for a short period prior to marriage? Or should the person who moves, just rent an apartment instead?

I'd really like your advice on this issue. How do we make a smooth transition with this long distance relationship?

Elder Response

Hi! Thanks for writing :-)

First, congratulations on your effort to think things out. That's a good start. Distance does indeed make things a bit more difficult. I'm a bit old fashioned too! Never did think living together before making a permanent commitment really helped much. Texas is nice, so is Virginia. From reading your letter I surmise that it doesn't matter where you live as long as you are together?

Actually I think you both have to bring it down to asking some very practical questions. Are you both working, who might stand to lose more by moving? Who might be able to find a job easier? Who is more attached to immediate family and friends? In other words, who stands to lose or gain more than the other. In any case someone will be making a sacrifice for sure. But, then again, love makes it all possible.

If you decide to move to Virginia, you would sell your townhouse. Could you not move into a home purchased in Virginia and he stays in his home until marriage? If you stay in Texas it's no problem. He simply arrives for the wedding.

I lived in Michigan, my wife was from Ohio. When she came up to visit she actually stayed in my parent's home (had a spare bedroom). It wasn't easy but we did it! Got married in Ohio and felt that there were more opportunities available for us in Michigan. So here we are 36 years later.

The more you honestly communicate with each other the better chance you have that you will work things out just fine! Love has a way :-)

Good Luck and Best Wishes!

treefrog

Try To Get Him Back?

Dear Elders,

I have been with this guy for almost 2 years. We've had our hard times even taken brakes. A couple of weeks ago he broke up with me. I love him very much. I don't know if I should try to work things out or just let things work them self out. Is it worth all this emotional stress just to try to get him back? Thanks for your opinion; it matters very much to me.

Elder Response

Hi! Thanks for writing :-)

Stress is not a good thing. It can affect you both physically and mentally. You know that old cliche about loving someone and then letting them go? If they return, then the love is real (or something like that). You know that love is a mutual thing. When one lets go, the other suffers hurt and frustration. You can't "make" love return. It has to of its own. Distract yourself for awhile and leave the "door open". Chasing a departed love depletes you, your self esteem, and self worth. There is much life to live....be "inner directed" and not "other directed".

Keep Yourself Well!

Treefrog

Afraid of Life

Dear Elders,

I feel "self-improvement" to be the best title for this query, as I can tell you at this very moment what the problem is. Simply put, I do not feel good about myself and am afraid to believe anyone could care about me.

I just graduated college and moved across the country, and this has been an incredibly stressful period in my life. I have been thus far unsuccessful in seeking employment, my mother did not and does not support my choice of majors, insisting I return to college—which I do not think I wish to do—I only have a couple friends in the area, whom I do not see often, and to my horror, things with my boyfriend are, after almost two years, finally working out. To my horror, you ask? I am someone who does not meet people easily, and although today I am told how beautiful (When I went into New York City the other day, I was whistled at and talked to many times. How annoying!) and intelligent I am, such was not always the case. As a child, I was constantly informed of my ugliness and stupidity, remarks that imbedded themselves deeply in my consciousness, and unfortunately, my warring parents did little to reassure me that the opposite was true. I rarely had friends through the course of my first twenty-one years—usually when I met someone, something would eventually bring he or she to leave—and no men seemed interested in me. When I made overtures of any sort, they were always rejected. Naturally I believed that I was not worth loving or even admiring.

Today I am twenty-three. I have found a few friends, and I met the boyfriend mentioned above. I was open and ready to show him how much I cared when our long-distance relationship began. Yet he did not respond in the same manner, remaining distant and closed. This began to wear on me, although I did not want to give up. At long last, in April of this year, we broke up. I was in Europe, studying for the year, and this broke my heart. However, after returning to the States at the end of the summer, I saw my ex-boyfriend again, having moved to the same state as he. For the first time in our relationship, we were actually in close enough proximity to be able theoretically to see each other every day, if we so chose. That seems to have made all the difference. From the cold and mysterious person that he was, my boyfriend has become warm, affectionate, and open, and he has even told me the three magic words. That all sounds lovely, right?

That begs the question of why I am afraid now to accept this. Sometimes when we are together, I can relax and be myself—just allow myself to enjoy the realization of my heart's wish. Other times, however, I panic and do everything I can to push my boyfriend away, jumping on innocent remarks he drops, getting angry or sad, and telling him he should find someone who does not have my emotional baggage. Logically, our relationship makes sense, and my heart is delighted to have him, yet there is a large part of me—the child hurt all those years ago, I suppose—who cannot accept his love. "One day, he will see the truth about me and leave, just like everyone else has always done," it tells me.

It must be clear to you by now that I have very low self-esteem. I am attempting to seek counseling, but free services are a bit harder to find. Do you have any other advice for me before I ruin the beautiful thing I have, my gift from the Goddess? I have already discussed this with my boyfriend, and he says he sees the beauty in me, that I am a lotus, a very special woman who does not blend in with the rest, and he thinks that, in the end, I am fine, not confused and crazy as I feel. Why is this not enough? Why do I not see my own shakti (goddess power) in myself? What can I do to learn to love myself and, in turn, allow myself to be loved?

Elder Response

Hello,

You sound like a very bright & emotionally deep woman. You are so wise to already determine the issue(s) of low self-esteem & abandonment, that is 1/2 the battle in moving forward.

As much as we'd like to write you a few magic sentences to fix everything we can't. Your issues have come from years of programming and may take some time to work out. We suggest several sessions of professional counseling. Every state or county has a mental health agency and you pay as you can on a sliding scale. If you are affiliated with any religious organizations many offer counseling also, again you'll need to check it out.

Be cautious about pushing away your boyfriend, make sure the lines of communication are open and ask for his support in your journey. Learning to love yourself can be a process that requires years, be patient and don't get so wrapped up that you miss out on the fun & beauty life has to offer as you learn.

Best regards,

Joan

My Boyfriend & My Daughter

Dear Elders,

my boyfriend of nine years is so jealous of my daughter mostly because he wants all of my attention, but another factor is that he always wanted his own children, which I would not give him. He still takes her places with us and treats her to diner out, but he just can't bring himself to love her. She is now 13. Any suggestions?? He is Very good to me. Thanks,

Elder Response

Hi,

You won big in the lottery but seem to be unaware of the magnitude of the prize.

Your boy friend of nine years is "very" good to you, takes your 13 year old daughter places and out to dinner, but "doesn't love her enough." Yet, he would like to have a child of his own—WHICH YOU WILL NOT GIVE HIM.

You ask for suggestions: "Count your blessings, and love, honor and cherish the gentleman."

Should you desire further assistance, please do feel free to contact us again.

Best wishes,

Chuck

Friends' Bad Marriage

Dear Elders,

I have this friend—yes, it really is for a friend.

His wife, we are sure, is manic-depressive, but she refuses to hear it. The couple is already in marriage counseling. They also go to therapy for their 7 year old daughter. When his wife is in a downswing, she is intolerable and says the meanest things to him, threatens divorce, etc.

He does not want a divorce because he loves his two daughters. Without them, he would clearly choose divorce. He wants to let the girls continue to live in the house they now have.

What advice can you give him? Thanks.

Elder Response

Hi,

As I see it, the issue here is: "The effect on the daughters and what is best for them!!!!"

Since a therapist already is in the loop, I suggest that Ted PRIVIATELY consult the therapist.

Best wishes to all concerned,

Frank

Scared Not To Be with Him

Dear Elders,

I am 22 years old and have been in a relationship for 3 years. He is 27 and tells me that he knows for sure that i am the one for him. I, on the other hand, feel like i need more experience, although i am so (and let me emphasize SO) scared to not be with him. I really don't know what i would do without him, but at the same time, i feel trapped. If it were up to me, we would open up the relationship to the status of "seeing other people" too, but i know he would not be okay with that. I feel like i have to make an either-or decision and i don't want to. I would be miserable without him, but i feel trapped with him. I have talked to him about this, and it breaks his heart everytime i bring it up. We talk for hours and i come to the conclusion that what i have is too special to give up. But then a few days later i feel the anxiety set in again. i don't know what to do.

thank you so much for any advice you can give me.

Elder Response

Hello, and thanks for writing.

You are speaking of very serious doubts, too many to allow this relationship to go on without some action.

You feel trapped (twice), want to experience life without him, want to see other people, feel anxiety about this situation. Good for you. It is time for a decision from you.

On the other hand, you are dependent emotionally on him. You are so scared not to be with him, you don't know what you'd do without him, would be miserable without him, and you then conclude this means that what you have is too special to give up...but you feel trapped! What this means is you have already become too dependent, and are looking for him (or someone else) to assure your happiness. This is wrong. Only you can do that.

With this amount of doubts, I think you should try for the see-other-people status. If he still is too heartbroken to open up to this, then I think it is necessary for you to follow your own heart and break up with him.

You need to see the world from another point of view, grow a little, learn a lot, experience more. Don't accept what isn't right for you. If he cares for you, he will not want to use guilt to keep you with him, but will want what is best for you—and himself.

How can it be good if you marry him with these doubts unresolved, have children and in a few years decide he really wasn't the one for you? What a tragedy that would be. NOW is the time to find out what is right for you, not after you've made many more mistakes and will hurt more people.

You are being manipulated by him, with your opinions and feelings being ignored or dismissed as not as important as his heart being broken by your attempts to talk with him. You're going to have to be stronger and more resolute. Do what is best for both of you now.

I wish you the best, and urge you to enjoy your life. Be kind.

Best regards,

Joanna

Am I Normal?

Dear Elders,

hi. I hope your having a wonderful day today! My question is very very random and maybe a bit personal, so I hope I don't embarrass you. I wondered your opinion on my life. haha, really, keep reading!

I am a junior in college and I have never had a boyfriend. And I am not unattractive, I just seem to always either push guys away or ignore them…even if I think I might like them.

In a few words or less: When I was growing up, my parents were divorced and neither of them ever dated after that, so I was never really exposed to boy-girl affection when I was young. I think that kind of effected me somehow. In middle school and high school, when other girls were ambushing grocery store check-out lines for the latest teen magazine, I was doing my homework, rearranging my room, and writing. I never had (and still do not have) pictures of male models or celebrities on my dorm room walls.

I have even begun questioning my sexuality, perhaps I'm gay? I think I'm attracted to guys though…actually I think I must be asexual. Honestly, I'm not particularly attracted to either sex. Does everyone go through a period like this, have you known anyone who has, or am I just really weird? haha. Anyway, I'd appreciate your opinion, even if it has no real basis in anything. Thanks again in advance.

Elder Response

Hello,

Sexuality differs greatly among people, and I've known quite a few people with a fairly low sex drive, both straight and gay. Also, one's sex drive may also vary during the course of one's life. Are you worried that you might have something physically wrong? If so, then go to a doctor for a checkup. From your note, it doesn't sound like you're unhappy, but perhaps just worried a bit? Maybe you fear getting close to someone, a common trait among some children of divorced parents, who feel they won't be able to make a marriage last. Why not just continue being friendly, warm and fun-loving and continue to meet people. When and if the right person comes along you might get that feeling of intimacy. It's also possible to have a wonderful life without sexual intimacy—lots of people find work, sports, hobbies and good friends give them a full, complete sense of closeness. Try not to worry too much and get on with your life!

best of luck,

Julia

Go To The Next Step?

Dear Elders,

About four months ago, I met someone during my school play. Well, after practicing with each other for so long, we became really good friends. Roughly a week ago, he said that he had feelings for me that were stronger than just friendship. I told him that I wasn't ready for a relationship, but I really am. I mean, I like him, but I'm not sure if I do in that manner. He is really sweet, smart, talented, and so forth. He is the perfect gentleman, always cares for others, and so much more.

He sounds like the perfect person, and it would be easy to have a relationship with him. However, I don't want to ruin our friendship. I have been in relationships before that just end horribly. I don't want that to happen here. What if I don't really like him the way he likes me? What if we just end up in quarrels after each conversation? Please help me over this asinine 'problem'.

Elder Response

Hello,

In response to your inquiry:

A possible method would be to sit together and make some boundaries and ground rules for a friendship. Explain that you want to know him better socially before you start any other kind of relationship. Also, remember that this is a new person and not one of the ones you had a bitter relationship with. Do not bring the old "garbage" into any new relationship, either with this person or anyone else. If you do then the relationship will end just like the others.

Good luck.

Carol

What Did I Do?

Dear Elders,

This may sound stupid to you, but right now I need someone to talk to. There is a man I like very much and we seemed to be on the right path to getting to know each other and then all of a sudden I find out he has a girlfriend. I wrote him a letter and left it on his car windshield and I got no response from him. What will help me mend my broken heart? Thanks for being around I appreciate it very much. :-)

Elder Response

Dear :-)

It never pays to rush a relationship. Because you "seemed" to be on the right path, you ran ahead when you shouldn't have. You didn't know him well enough, since you didn't know he had a girlfriend...unless he deliberately misled you; in which case, you didn't know him at all.

After learning of the girlfriend, I don't understand your next move in leaving a letter on his windshield. What did you expect to gain from that? Did you tell him how sad you were? Why didn't you simply ask him if he did have a girl friend, and if his response was "Yes," then you should have said, "Fine," and walked away. If he said "Yes, but we're not getting along and I'm not happy with her," then you should have said, "I'm sorry to hear that. If it doesn't work out, give me a call."

Why do you have a broken heart? You like a man very much, you're getting to know each other, he has a girl friend, you have no claim on him. This sounds like a girlfriend-boyfriend relationship that never get started. That's no reason to be brokenhearted. That's a good reason to sigh and say, "Too bad; it might have been nice." Next time, be more careful in letting your heart rule your common sense and look more thoroughly before you leap. Don't sit around and feel sad about this and sorry for yourself. Get out there and mingle, have fun, enjoy yourself, and find a guy who's not already attached to another person—there's plenty of them.

I wish you the very best of luck and hope you enjoy your life.

Best regards,

Joanna

This Summer Apart

Dear Elders,

i was in a relationship with a good friend for bout a year, and after we broke up,which was really ugly, i didn go out with anyone till about a little over 4 months. Well this guy is sweet, nice, a gentlemen, and really in touch with his religion. and well see thats the problem,he is so great, but i dont get to see him. I was afraid this would happen after school let out, but it felt right to be his girlfriend. the problem is that, he seems satisfied with not getting to talk, and i dont mean i want to talk to him everynight, i mean at least once a week, and that doesnt even happen. Can you imagine how much we actually get to see each other? Well I love that he is getting everything setup for next school year, and we are both busy doing that. thats what i want, but when we do get the chance to talk or go do something, he backs out one way or another, i know it always isnt his fault, but, it just sucks sometimes. help, i would talk to hiim, but he nver calls, and i cant call him cause he is rarley home.

Elder Response

Ok—he is trying to tell you he is not ready for this kind of relationship. He thinks he is saving your feelings by not telling you up front, but in reality, well, you see that is incorrect.

My advice is to back way out of this. Tend to your own life, do not wait by the phone, do not contact him in any way. If he comes back into your life in the future, go real slow.

As you may know already, deep down somewhere, someone who really cares for you does not avoid you. Someone who really cares for you makes excuses to SEE you and talk to you, not avoid you.

This will pass, in the meantime, be good to yourself. Get involved with life, have fun, volunteer, plan your own education. Don't ever wait on a man for any reason, ever. Those are the seconds of YOUR life ticking by.

Take care,

Cheryl

Not Advice...Just Insight

Dear Elders,

Okay, I am not exactly looking for advice, but insight. I am 29, and have been separated for 2 years, with two beautiful daughters, ages 4 and 6. I was with my soon to be ex since I was 14 and he 17! We had a wonderful, perfectly happy marriage for 6 years, and great relationship for the 4 years before that. He made an abrupt change in many ways. I won't go into big detail, but he became angry emotionally abusive, and in the end, wanted an open marriage, with me and the other woman who he decided he wanted to be with also. Believe it or not, I considered it, as I so much loved him and so badly wanted it to work out. However, I couldn't do it, and I left with the girls. He has been in a relationship with this woman, moved in with her after six months, and is also living with her best friend. This has been hard for me, as my girls spend the night there on some weekends.

I guess my question is: Will he one day regret his decision? It seems as if he may be regretting a bit now, but I can't be sure. Do people who choose to leave their families for some other person ever end up being happy in the end? I wouldn't mind if someone told me that they knew of people who did end up with whatever they needed by leaving the first person they were with. I just want perspectives from those who have either been there, or know someone who has. Thanks!

Elder Response

Hi! and thanks for writing :-)

I think it's pretty apparent that things have changed much from when you were 14 and 17. Actually what has changed was marriage and having to share responsibility. Love is supposed to get us through this into old age. I may be going out on a limb here but it seems to me that women seem to be much more attuned to "nurturing" and a "make it work" ethic than are some men. There is no way you can make a relationship work by sharing one you love with whatever escapades that person is involved in beyond YOU and the children.

At this time methinks you have a real loser. From experience I believe that people who leave their family and seek "greener grass" most often come to realize it's not that much greener, and they often "regret". As we mature we change our concepts of what life is all about. We come to understand that seeking self pleasure doesn't really bring happiness. Pleasuring others, being our spouse, our children, our friends, returns us 100 fold. But that takes time.

Yes, sometimes one or other of the relationship does recognize and feel an emptiness, regrets their actions and seeks a reunion. It's a pretty unpredictable thing. If I were you I would not place myself in a situation of "waiting" or "anticipating" some sort of resurrection. I think that is what you are considering. Go on with YOUR life. Apparently he has the right of visitation with your daughters. Restrictions should be placed on these visitations. It is not appropriate for him to share his "fatherhood" with his girlfriend.

Go on, leave the door open as much as you still feel love. Miracles are still happening and it is indeed strange that that happen more often the older we get.

Hope it works out! and Keep Well!

Treefrog

How Many Frogs Must I Kiss?

Dear Elders,

Here is my dilemma. I am a well-educated, attractive, outgoing, interesting, well-traveled, positive, employed, cultured, 31 year old woman who is still single!!! My worst nightmare is getting older and never finding my soulmate. If that isn't bad enough, the statistics are against me; supposedly the more education a woman receives the harder still it is to find someone because her expectations get higher, and I'm on my way to completing a Masters degree! My problem is not that I don't meet men, I do, but no one that lights my fire. I'm looking for someone who loves life as much as I do and has similar ambitions, but that I'm attracted too as well. I don't want to settle with someone just because he is 'nice' or 'would make a great husband/father.' I want to feel passionate about him-intellectually and physically. Is there anything wrong with that? Or, am I just wasting time (I would like a family someday) and perhaps missing out on the 'nice' person who would make a good dad and provide me with the security and love I so wish for?

When I was younger it was fun going out, but I'm at a different place in my life. Many nights I'd rather order in and rent a movie than go out with some of the men I meet. I want someone to share my life with already. I'm tired of being alone, and please don't say I need to keep myself busy because I do; I work out, visit with friends, read, practice playing the piano, etc. But I want to share these things with another human being!

Please help! Your advice would be most helpful. Thank you.

Elder Response

Hi. Looking for passion is fine and never a waste of time. Trust yourself to fulfill your needs in life—forget statistics, alarming notions from others, nagging doubts, etc. They are usually the reason people have problems "finding" each other.

Just go about your life in a positive manner, knowing that you have a strong desire to share your life and love with someone. You are already going through a transition—it used to be fun just to go out, now, however, you only want to go out with someone of substance. That tells me you are narrowing down your focus and have clearer goals—wanting to share your life, tired of being alone, etc. Once that transition happens, success is never far behind. So, relax, keep up your studies (grin) and enjoy that piano—you might be playing a tune for that special someone soon!

All the best.

Frangi

Anger & Pain Over Ex-Husband

Dear Elders,

My ex and I were recently divorced (finalized 2/20/02). He left me and our 2 children for his high school sweetheart. They were engaged to be married a month and a half after the divorce and are set to be married in September. He has visitation with our children, ages 5 1/2 and 1 1/2 years. I have some low points and was hoping for some tricks to keep the blues from playing such a big part in my life. I'm okay for the most part, but every now and then I feel slighted and angry that he seems to be happy when he doesn't deserve to be.

Elder Response

My dear, I understand your hurt and anger. I am sad about it because it is harming only you and your children, not your former husband at all.

It turns out your ex-husband is a scuzzball—or maybe not. Perhaps he is simply a weak man who cared more for himself and what he wanted than he cared for his wife and children. But that's what is. His leaving is no reflection on you, it is strictly his wanting someone he didn't have and being a selfish enough person to go after it by betraying his family. Your marriage might have ended another way at another time, since he seems to have forgotten the pledge of marriage and its meaning.

You must give up these feelings before they really hurt you and the children. You must give to them a feeling of care and safety, and not make them feel that half of themselves (their father) is very, very bad. They must continue to love their father so they can love themselves and you.

I know you'd like to get revenge, but in this case it isn't worth the cost. Please, put your thoughts toward more positive things and turn your life and attention away from him and toward something beneficial to all of you.

I urge you with great seriousness to make absolutely certain that he pays all the child support to you that the court will order. If you haven't filed for this yet, please do so immediately. I also urge you, if you and he just have a personal agreement of what he will be paying, that you go to court to get the amount set. So often the husband negotiates a much too small sum on his own to avoid his rightful responsibility for his children, especially when he immediately gets involved with another woman.

I know how extremely difficult this is, believe me, but I am concerned only about you and your children, and urge you to train yourself to stop thinking AT ALL about what he is doing. I wish you the greatest luck, and want you to find new ways to enjoy this glorious life we have.

Lisa

Virtual Boyfriend?

Dear Elders,

The last time I had a boyfriend was the 8th grade, if you count one school dance and going to see the latest batman movie having a boyfriend. I figured that being in college would help me a long in this area, neglecting to remind myself that I was going to an all women's school.

Somewhere around November I got really lonely. I had made plenty of good friends in school, but that ever pivitol significant other was missing. My friends just seemed to remind me of how painfully single I was, and made valiant attempts to get me to socialize. However they soon came to realize that I was an endless and infinite geek, I really dislike the party scene and didn't think I would ever meet anyone worth knowing over a keg.

So while they were working to 'find me a man' I turned to the internet and posted a personals ad on yahoo.com. I didn't expect anything to come from it, but in February I got an email from a boy in upstate NY. Long story short, we've been trading two or three page long emails every day for four months now. And we both really want to meet. He lives about four hours from where I live and six hours from where I go to school.

The catch is, his parents don't approve of him having met someone online. If I had the guts to tell my parents that I had become...well almost romantically involved over the internet, I can pretty much garuntee that they wouldn't approve either. We're both being really responsible about it, taking things very slowly, and both have violent oppositions to lying to our friends and family. As much as I want to meet this boy and see if there could be something more between us, I don't want to have to go behind my parents back and he doesn't want to have to sneak around his parents either.

What I'm basically asking is…if its worth it. He lives just far enough away to make it very difficult for me to get to see him. And, long distance aside, I'm sort of, well embarassed by the situation. I feel slightly ashamed that I turned to the personals ads to find someone. I haven't even told my friends the truth about how I met my 'mysterious e-boy'. Should I through caution to the wind, and just tell my parents the truth, and hope for the best (even if it means losing some of their respect for me) or should I give up on this boy, and try for something closer, that doesn't make me feel ashamed sometimes?

Thank you so much. I've been torturing myself with this, not very used to have romantic issues, and any advice you can offer would be much appreciated.

Elder Response

Hi. There is nothing wrong with meeting someone over the net. The difficulties begin when we are foolhardy, not careful, and rush into a relationship based upon only what the other person has told us. This is a very dangerous state, and one that must be guarded against.

What you need is some way to verify that what you are being told by this man is correct. Is there a way you can do this?

If he is in fact what he says, then do try to arrange a VERY SAFE meeting with him. My son met his present soon-to-be-wife on the net, so I know it can be successful. Everyone he ever met this way arranged the first meeting with him accompanied by a girlfriend, in a public place. This is a VERY smart procedure.

I believe this relationship should go no further until the two of you have met. Can you talk with your parents and tell them you are interested in this young man and would like to have him visit you—in your home—with them there, for a short time? He could come down and stay in a hotel overnight and meet you and your parents. I think they might not object to this.

On the other hand, if he objects to it being handled this way, be aware that something might not be right about him.

I do wish you the greatest luck, and urge you to proceed with great caution until he has proved to be all that you think he is.

Best wishes, and do involve your parents or other respected adults in this meeting.

Arianne

Living With A Man

Dear Elders,

What are some rules you recall for living successfully with a man? I am in college, and am staying with a guy I used to date but now are just friends, hanging out for the summer before I go to school away next year. He says he forgot how to act when living with a girl (we used to live together about a year ago.) He acts distant and gets annoyed easily. I think it is so easy to hang out and get along. He doesn't. So I figure there are some rules to this game that I haven't experienced yet or enough. What do you think?

Elder Response

Hi,

What do I think? I think that he is not the one for you.

By what rules is the game played? Don't endeavor to cast yourself in a mold. Be natural and normal.

Best regards,

WO Owl

Marriage & Kids??

Dear Elders,

This is my first time visiting, so I don't know exactly how it works, but here it goes…

I've been dating a great gal for almost two years. She has a wonderful upper class family, fantastic friends all doing very well in their lives, and a good job. About a year or so ago, some of the gals in my circle of friends were introduced to her and started talking behind her back. I think this was because they didn't know that our relationship was serious and that some of them were interested in my and were a bit jealous. Regardless, I ended up cutting them out of my life and dedicated all of my time to my girlfriend. I've been miserable ever since, and I realize I need to repair those friendships. Now we're getting to the point where my girlfriend wants to get married and wants a future with children (she would be a great mom), but I'm starting to dig deep inside and have realized that I really don't want kids. I have no desire to be the parent of a child, no desire to watch them grow up, to support them, to be responsible for them. We get along great in every other way, but I know I'd be miserable, regretful, and resentful if I just went along and had kids. She has said that maybe she could get by with just a dog, but I don't believe her. This girl is on this planet to have children—there's no doubt in my mind. So, what do I do? Continue dating her with and let nature take its course, or let her go and look for someone who will give her what she ultimately wants? By the way, she's almost 30 and I'm 31. Thanks.

Elder Response

Hi,

I think that there is a major problem with your relationship. Having agreement about children is a prime necessity in a marriage.

If you get married and have children, you will be resentful and probably show it to your kids and your wife, making everyone miserable. Children can be a wonderful joy if they are wanted, but will be a real pain if you don't want them.

If you don't have children, your wife will be resentful and it will make your marriage unhappy as well.

In either case, it seems to me that the marriage will not last.

I believe that the primary purpose of marriage is to have and raise children. If you really believe what you say about having children, I think you both would be better off moving on and find someone with like preferences.

I have never been divorced, but know many people who are and it is not a happy life. I have been happily married forty years and have two children and two grandchildren which brings us much joy.

I hope that this is helpful. Best regards,

Bob

Time To Move On

Dear Elders,

I am 20 years old and I am in a relationship for over 3 years now. However, I am very unhappy. My mate has cheated on me more than once and recently had a child. The baby is now 3 months old. I love him so much, I continue to forgive him, but I am so hurt so much of the time. I want to leave but I have invested a lot of energy into this relationship. What can I do to help the relationship or is it best to give it up and move on?

Elder Response

Hello. The question you have to answer is: "How much more of my energy and life do I intend to put into this relationship that is hurtful to me, where I am not respected by this man who continues to cheat on me?"

You alone cannot help the relationship, and it is clear that he doesn't intend to help. Why are you wasting more of your life every day you stay?

Pull yourself together, give up all the dreams that will not come true, consider the three years a learning experience, and GET OUT!

I am sorry you have had this experience, but there is absolutely no reason to stay. Please consider not only yourself, but the child, and go find a good life for you both.

Best wishes.

Arianne

How To Deal With Hypocrites

Dear Elders,

Greetings, I have recently been troubled with conflicting thoughts. I recently found that my friend, whom I shall call Karen, is a very big hypocrite. Usually, we often complain about the mass amount of corruption in society and how so many people cheat all the time. However, I realized that she belongs in that group of people. I did not know that she had lied to me numerous times by denying that she cheats on tests. Now, I look at her in a different perspective and it's hard to forgive her. If I simply say that it's ok and I forgive her, then she will continue cheating. However, if I confront her and tell her that I think she's a hypocrite and she should change her ways, our friendship could be in danger. I still want to remain friends but I am very disturbed. What should I do?

Elder Response

First of all, be assured that confronting your friend will not change her habits—it will make her angry that you know and she will most likely get defensive and come up with some kind of justification as to the "degree" of corruption that its ok to have.

The most important clue in your letter is the fact that she has lied to you and you know it. You need to decide if having a friend who lies to you is valuable—is it ok to tacitly approve of her behaviour by not mentioning it? That is what you are doing and it is the message she is getting.

I think you feel very uncomfortable not only with her lying/cheating but also because she has used you. My advice? Tell her your friendship is over and tell her why. She will be angry. However, she will start thinking about what she is doing and whether or not your friendship is important to HER—important enough to walk her talk.

Good luck—take care,

Cheryl

The Number Question

Dear Elders,

In your opinion, do you think it is your right to know how many people your boyfriend or girlfriend has had sex with before you? Why or why not?

Elder Response

Absolutely not. Because it is absolutely none of your business.

No matter what the answer, it will do your relationship only harm.

Best regards,

Arianne

5

Thoughts and Reflections

Choices

Dear Elders,

Hi. I had a questions about your thoughts concerning choice in life. I tend to believe life is what you make of it and that your choices are therefore inumerable, but aren't there other things that limit our options, like family, money, race/ethnicity, etc. Things that we must consider when we are choosing our important avenues in life.

Your thoughts?

Thanks.

Elder Response

Interesting question. I agree with you that life is what we make of it. I think our choices are always influenced and informed by our circumstances but this doesn't mean our options are limited. Often, these "limitations" merely divert us to a different path where many other options open up to us. Or we may continue on with a choice even though our circumstances make it more difficult to pursue this path. I think the major thing is to realize we have many choices before us—any of which can lead to a fulfilling and satisfying life. We are only limited by a lack of imagination.

Thanks for an interesting topic. Best regards,

Frank

Space Cadet

Dear Elders,

hi, i am a freshman in highschool, and i am very ivolved in various things at my church. I am also not the quickest person around I do well in school but when it comes to everyday logic i have very little, in addition i forget just about everything. This causes just about everyone to make fun of me. Weather it be about me being a cheerleader, asking if i was born a blond, or about how i am constanty giggleing about nothing imperticular. i was wondering if there is anyone who can help me get over this spaceyness and on to being a little more normal. Thanx! :)

Elder Response

Hi. Spacey is as spacey does, and you're doing it! You're playing a role that you like, so I'm not sure why you're writing us. It seems to me you're deliberately foolish—giggling about nothing in particular (do you know how irritating that is?), forgetting, being illogical, and enjoying being a cheerleader and blond. Why do you giggle so much?

My daughter was the captain of her cheerleading squad in high school. She was also a scholarship winner, a leader in her class, editor of the yearbook, and on and on. No one ever suggested she was spacey or foolish. She is now the Executive Editor of an extremely successful fashion and beauty magazine in New York, and everyone takes her seriously. She was the youngest woman ever to be an Editor-in-Chief of a national magazine.

The lesson here is not what you do, but the image you project, and that you are doing willingly. When you find that you don't have to project dumb, blond and spacey, you'll be a much happier and fulfilled woman.

Best wishes, and good luck.

Linda

Keeping The Faith

Dear Elders,

In the past few years, I've been struggling with religious faith—whether or not there's a God, the place of organized religion in today's world and in my life, etc. The recent horrible events in the world have only made me question religion more—including it's relationship to violence and hatred.

To make matters more complicated, I lost my father in Nov. of 2001. I am an only child and was very close to both of my parents so this has been a sad and sometimes difficult time for me. My relationship with my Mom is being re-defined and everything seems tumultuous. I've also recently moved and am living with my husband in a part of the country that I'm very unfamiliar with. I have a strong network of friends back in my hometown who are super supportive but I haven't yet made friends here. I've been to church a few times but haven't mustered the faith to go more often.

I realize this is more like 12 issues instead of one but perhaps you have some advice to offer to this 28 year old.

Thank you so much for listening.

Elder Response

Hello. I'm sorry recent events have caused you to question your religion more. It's had the opposite effect on me—I am more deeply dedicated to my religion. The failings of a warped-religion group of men has sharpened the great thankfulness I feel for the good people who have responded with such courage, kindness and compassion in this and other countries. I am reminded yet again that our love for each other is what makes life worthwhile. The hatred we see is of man's making, not God's, and it is a hatred we must counter each moment by being better people ourselves.

I am sorry for the loss of your parents; this is something all of us must suffer, and there is nothing I can say that will make it better. It is a part of life that must be endured, mourned and set aside in a special place in our heart.

You have many friends in your former hometown. This means it will be easier for you to find and enjoy friends where you are now living, because you obviously are also a good friend. It will take a while, though. Get involved in the community; go to the library; read your local paper thoroughly and find some groups you might be interested in joining. Continue to be open to life—it is all we have in this world. Continue to go to church; it will help in time. I think this bad time for you will begin to fade soon.

I wish you the very best, and hope your life is full of happiness and good fortune.

Stan

Why

Dear Elders,

How does this service work? Are you all trained professionals, or just a bunch of old fogies who think you are wise enough to dispense advice?

Elder Response

Thanks for writing.

There are a number of us with this organization, with various forms of training. However, life in itself is a form of education. We answer the questions we most feel comfortable with; and with our wide range of experiences we can find an answer for almost any question.

Old fogie? Well, yes I am, and thanks for noticing :-D

Best regards,

Paul

Current Events

Dear Elders,

Hello, I'm a college student and was interested in your opinions on the current situation in the middle east. It seems as if the whole world is going to explode. I guess I allow myself to become overwhelmed with the state of the world. I was wondering if any of you felt this way when you were growing up. I know that the media tends to distort the truth, and it's hard to separate the truth from lies. I'm interested in your point of view.

Thanks.

Elder Response

Yes, of course we felt this way when we were growing up. For me, my father was a paratrooper in WWII dropping over enemy territory; I was quite young, but I remember the fear of my entire family, as many of my uncles were also fighting.

Later we were very worried about the "Cold War", an undeclared war that threatened to break out every minute of every day, combined with a nuclear threat. Many people built bomb shelters in their backyards in case of an attack.

The history of the world is fraught with conflicts between peoples and nations. It has always been so, and I regrettably suspect that it always will be so unless we can change our nature.

It is our obligation to humankind to make each day of our lives count for something—for us to be happy, to make others happy, to help each other, and to support each other. Our constant complaining and meanness to each other is in a small way what every war is about on a larger scale. Only we as individuals can stop this destructive cycle.

Best wishes, good luck, and enjoy your life.

Arianne

Three Questions

Dear Elders,

1) Why didn't God stop the Sept 11th attack?

2) If you had the choice between staying home for the third summer with your child or going back to work, which would you do? If you stay home, money will be very tight.

3)How do you make an aging dog comfortable?

Elder Response

Hello, thanks for writing.

(2) If I had the choice, even with tight money, I'd stay home with pleasure. It is an important year for a child.

(3) Make sure the dog always has food and lots of water always available. If you can, get a dog bed that has sides to help keep old bones warm. Love the dog a lot and talk kindly to him often.

(1) As for your first question, we are told the ways of God are mysterious, but perhaps time will reveal some reason. We also have to remember that Man was given free choice, and with that many of our mistakes are made. The following is not original to me, but was sent to me by a friend; I don't know the author, but I believe it absolutely.

"I know where my GOD was the morning of September 11, 2001; He was very busy!

He was trying to discourage anyone from taking these flights. Those four flights together held over 1000 passengers and there were only 266 aboard. He was on four commercial flights giving terrified passengers the ability to stay calm. Not one of the family members who were called by a loved one on one of the hijacked planes said that passengers were screaming in the background. On one of the flights he was giving strength to passengers to overtake the hijackers.

He was busy creating obstacles for employees at the World Trade Center. Only around 20,000 were at the towers when the first jet hit. Since the buildings held over 50,000 workers, this is a miracle in itself. Many of the people who were employed at the World Trade Center told the media they were late for work or had traffic delays.

He was holding up two 110-story buildings so that two-thirds of the workers could get out. It is so amazing that the top of the towers didn't topple when the jets impacted. And when they did fall, they fell inward. GOD didn't allow them to topple over, because many more lives would have been lost.

And when the buildings went down, my GOD picked up thousands of his children and carried them home with him, reassuring his frightened children that the worst was over and the best was yet to come. He sent his children who are best trained to save those still alive, and then sent many others to help in any way they could.

He sat down and cried that 19 of his children could have so much hate in their hearts. That they didn't choose him, but another god that doesn't exist, and now they are separated from God forever.

He still isn't finished; he held the loved ones that were left behind in his arms. He comforts them daily. His other children are given the strength to reach out to them and help them in any way they can. He will continue to help us in what is to come. He will give the people in charge of this great nation the strength and the wisdom to do the right thing. He will never leave us in our time of need.

So when anyone asks, "Where was your GOD on September 11", you can say "Everywhere"! And yes, although this is without a doubt the worst thing we have seen, God's miracles are in every bit of it."

Best wishes,

Arianne

Shining On The Football Team

Dear Elders,

I'd like some advice on gaining the respect of my varsity football coaches and teammates to prove to them that I am a great football player, they just don't realize it. It's difficult to gain the respect of immature teammates, which at times can be demotivating. Any replies would be appreciated.

Elder Response

Hello,

From what you have written, it appears that your attitude is in the way of gaining the respect you appear to feel that you deserve. When you refer to the teammates as immature, that is saying that your attitude towards them(which they will sense) keeps them from getting to know who you are and your "greatness" as a football player. Don't judge your teammates as harshly as you appear to be doing and they will sense that you are a serious player, both on the football field and in life.

Best regards,

Tim

What You Know Now

Dear Elders,

What are just a few things that you wish you would of known, as a woman, at the age of 25, that you know now? From your point of view, what are the major differences in being a woman back then, to growing up a woman in this day and age?

Elder Response

Differences in growing up now? not many—the basics are still all the same.

I wish I had known that there was a lot more time than I thought to get married and have children and a lot LESS time to do everything there is to do without the confinement of marriage, etc.

I would have tried everything possible and known better than to think I NEEDED to have another person in my life. I would have been my own person spiritually, financially, career-wise before venturing into any kind of partnership and I would have let no one into my life for any other reason than I wanted them there (not needed—wanted). I would have climbed mountains, explored jungles, danced on bars and gone skinny dipping w/out anyone telling me I shouldn't. I would have made absolutely, positively sure I wanted and was capable of being a GREAT mother before I allowed myself to be one. I would have become a research scientist and a broadway actor and had a house on top of a hill surrounded by secluded acres with a view for forever.

I wish I had known I could have done all this by myself, for myself, and thus have been spectacularly more available to other humans because I would have had true confidence and kindness.

I wish I had known that education is important far beyond its ability to guarantee a good income.

I wish I had paid more attention to my grandmother and less attention to looking sexy.

Take care—good luck in everything you do!

Carol

Old-Fashioned

Dear Elders,

I am 17 years old and feel like the world is moving very quickly to corruption. I don't know what exactly I am asking; I guess some words of
wisdom might help. I want to have a simplistic life-style, and stay
home as a home-maker and to raises children. I don't know that this
lifestyle will be very easy financially! Also, the divorce rate is getting so
high that I am living in fear of marrage. I feel that a lot of our nation's
problems of violence and psychological illnesses would be greatly
reduced if a parent (I am all up for equally opportunity, so either the
mother or the father would do as a domestic caretaker) stayed home to
keep up with the chores and raise their children. Not having to work
all day and then come home to cook and clean would reduce a lot of
our nation's stress! Also, kids are not getting the attention they need to
grow up with confidence and morals, which would be solved by a parent there all the time without having to divide the attention with work.
I guess that what I really need is hope that others are seeing this and
there will be more one-income families with two parents in the future!

Elder Response

Hello. I agree with much of your letter, but not all. I agree that many
children are being ignored by too-busy and too-stressed parents. However, many more are well cared-for and valued. I think a shift in priorities from job to home would be a great improvement.

I don't advocate a parent staying at home in all circumstances. It does
no good to have a resentful parent raising children, when the parent
would be happier at work. What we need instead is parents who take
the time to enjoy, instruct and listen to their children instead of watching television or doing other, less important things. Communication
between parents and children is, I believe, at an all-time low, and this is
causing very serious problems in our society. Working parents can be

in great contact with their children if it is important to them, and it should be.

If you want to be a stay-at-home parent, then make sure you marry someone who can support the lifestyle you desire without your help. Of course it can be done, but I see few people today who want to give up material goods to have more time to give to their children; they think giving children things will make up for giving children attention and respect, and it never does.

I began working when I had three children, the youngest five years old. I had worked before we had children and stopped when the first was born. I hired an older woman to be in my home when I was working, so the children could come home, have their friends over, and still have supervision. I paid my sitter more than half my salary from my first job, because I wanted her to feel valued and good about her job. It was worth every single penny, and I have never regretted paying out that money for my children's routines to be uninterrupted.

I never missed a conference at school, we attended all school functions and knew our children's teachers. We oversaw homework and helped when needed. We had dinner together every night, even though all my children were very active in school and school activities.

During this entire period, we continued to renovate a large Victorian house, to make it the home we all wanted, and we all shared in it. We were never so tired that we didn't do what needed to be done, or what we wanted to do.

Our children are grown now, and all are productive, successful, heathy, and kind people of whom we are very proud. We are still a close family, even though they don't all live close to us.

I tell you this to show that all is not bad, even though it can be improved. There are many, many families that are functioning well and happily. You will have the opportunity to do as well, and I'm sure you will. We can improve our conditions one day at a time, and each of us has the responsibility to do that with our life, and by examply, with the lives of others we touch.

As for divorce, I think the trouble is that everyone wants instant gratification, and no one wants to work for a better marriage. When trouble rears its ugly head, which it will, the first thought is to divorce rather than work on the trouble. You don't have to be like that, and certainly you don't have to fear marriage. Believe me, there are many happy marriage out there, including mine and most of my friends.

Best regards,

Sam

Getting Over Guilt And Remorse

Dear Elders,

Hello. I know this might seem a silly request, and an unanswerable one at that, but still I mention it: My grandfather died 6 years ago, on a Saturday evening. I was supposed to go with my mother that morning to visit him in the hospital, but I refused, sick of spending sad and draining hours by the bedside of a half-sleepy man who didn't recognize me and who didn't match my memories of a strong, smart, vibrant man. In tragically ironic fashion, he died that evening, without me having seen him that day. I know that he wasn't very coherent and so he probably wouldn't have noticed me if I had been there, but I can't forgive myself or reconcile these feelings of guilt, especially since I no longer accept the concept of heaven and reunions with loved ones as easily as I once did. Any advice? Thank you.

Elder Response

Hello. Of all the emotions we have, guilt is the most useless—it does nothing except make us feel bad and inadequate.

Feeling remorse or regret, however, is not the same, and is useful. You have acknowledged that you deeply regret not having visited your grandfather the day he died. I understand that. There is nothing more you can do for him, so why are you punishing yourself?

Do you think you'd do this again? I know you won't. Is your grandfather suffering because you didn't see him? No. Are you suffering? Yes. Does this make sense? No.

Sometimes the greatest difficulty is to forgive ourselves. For some reason, we think we should be perfect. Ha! Who else do you know that is perfect? Why do you think you should be? You learned a lesson from this, but it probably isn't what you think. The lesson you have learned is that life will sometimes unexpectedly come right up and hit you in the nose. That's all. You were not cruel to your grandfather, so don't be cruel to yourself. Forget and forgive.

Best wishes, and do enjoy your life.

Arianne

Continuous Improvement?

Dear Elders,

Perhaps this isn't so much a request for advice as an expression of curiosity and a want to know more. How would you describe the process that we assume occurs which leads to the general acceptance of a site like this? In other words, it is generally accepted that as certain people (majority? most?) age, they become more wise and have a lot of comprehension for the secular and spiritual worlds as they interact. So, looking back over your life, please describe what features most influenced your own progress toward becoming a wise elder. For example, was it trial and error, life experiences, meditation, prayer, self-help tools, counseling (getting or giving), religion, a single, life-altering event? All of the above? What do you think is typical and does this sort of exchange between the elders and youngers fast-track the development or can it? Does it mostly salve the angst over the urgent worries and questions of the youngers, but cannot lead to wisdom before its age? Hopefully, these questions make sense. Thank you.

Elder Response

Good questions!! As a "wise elder" of 61 years, I have asked myself the same as I truly believe there is "wisdom" to exchange between all the generations. Furthermore, I believe that wisdom is not so much a function of chronological age as of soul age.

In explaining this site to friends and family, I have noted what I have long believed and observed…people have a basic need to "touch" with others and share their experiences/problems. At the same time, people of all ages are more and more dissociated. Friends and family move into and out of our life, physically and emotionally, at a greater pace. On the other hand, even if this is not generally true for a given individual, friends and family can be less than objective, may "listen" with preconceived judgments and answers, i.e., may not listen. Note the increased prevalence and use of psychologists/counselor/et al during the 90s and beyond in addressing this situation.

As writing things down often clarifies, this site may, in addition to sharing, also provide the advice seeker this opportunity to make more concrete his/her problem. Getting a reply communicates that someone has heard and taken the time to think through and acknowledge the situation with a response and perhaps some fresh ideas. Is the quality of this response improved with chronological age? My opinion…not necessarily.

In response to your specific question about what feeds "elder wisdom"…for me, it would be the sheer volume and variety of experiences and reflections on same over my lifetime. However, I still ask my daughters, my parents, others what the "wisdom" of their life has been.

I salute the mission of this site as I truly believe our society tends to associate the certain deterioration of the body with a similar deterioration of the mind and life savvy. I would probably expand on this mission to include all generations having the wisdom of given experiences.

Why are you curious?

Pat

How Do You Know When It's Right?

Dear Elders,

Hello, I'm almost 21 years old and I have a lot of concerns. I analyze a lot and am always curious about what the future will bring. I know I'm young, but I can't help but worry about when or if I will find the right person for me. I like to take a lot of time to get to know someone in a relationship. I know that once I start dating someone again I will want to date for a long time before I commit to anything serious like a proposal. Then, I will want to take a great deal more time before having kids. I just want to make sure that everything is right. Being cautious is good, but I wonder if this process will take so long that I will be older than I would like once I start my family. What do you think about this? Also, I know that most people say that the majority of regrets one has in life are the things they didn't do rather than the things they did. What is your take on this? Is there anything you would change about the decisions you've made in life?

Elder Response

Hi. You're in too much of a hurry, and it's confusing you. Why would anyone your age worry about whether you'll EVER find the right person for you? You don't have to search the world through to find "the right person;" there will be more than one in your life, as in everyone's life. The person you believe right at 21 but not marry may not be the same person you believe is right to marry at 30, or 40, or 80. This depends upon how you change, how your wants, desires, goals and life change.

Stop being so darn impatient; impatience does nothing except make life more difficult. Deciding that a person is one you want to marry needn't take 10 years, but about 2 years is a good span, maybe even a year, if you've done well.

There are many things I might have done better in my life, but our most serious mistake was getting married too young. We would unquestionably have gotten married if we had waited, and we would have had a much easier time. We would have known each other better, and have been more mature and understanding about our differences if we had waited. We were TOO YOUNG at 18 and 20! We are also very fortunate, for our marriage has lasted over 40 years. But it was very hard, and it would have been easier later.

There are other things I have regretted that I did, but not seriously. They are minor. My greatest regret is that I didn't learn to enjoy life enough until I was older. Had I been more patient and thoughtful, I would have understood that each day, each week, each month is precious and must be enjoyed as they come. No matter what our life contains, some part of it can be enjoyable and make us happy, if we don't persist in chasing dreams instead of taking action.

Best regards,

Donna

Growing Up

Dear Elders,

Looking back on your teenage years, what is the most significant difference between how you acted then and how you act now? Why did this change come about, and what was the most significant thing you've learned about attitude or how to treat others since your years in high school?

Elder Response

Hello,

This a very profound question which has been discussed by people for many years. Each individual probably has his own answer. Mine is the area of judgment. I have learned from experience, others, and education that if we can refrain from making judgments about others, we can leave ourselves open to accept them as they are. This has allowed me to see many people that I have met as friends, when before I would judge them on some whim and not want to spend time with them. This has been the most difficult area to conquer, as first we have to recognize that we do it and then train ourselves to not do it.

Best regards,

Paul

Getting An Exercise Routine Going

Dear Elders,

Thank you for reading my question. I'm in my mid-twenties and working a full time job. It's a typical 8-5 job and I use public transportation so that's another hour each way from my day. I have tried time and time again to start exercising but I cannot get a handle on my weekdays to do this! Whenever I come home I have to make dinner, wash the dishes, take a few minutes to relax and the next thing know it's time for bed to start the routine again the next morning. I have tried getting up earlier to exercise before work but I am not a morning person at all. I think maybe it may be that I'm not motivated enough to work out because I eat reasonably, have a high metabolism, and well, don't 'look unhealthy'(yet). But I know how important exercise is in our lives especially when you have a sedentary job like mine and I want it to be a part of my daily routine. Do you have any pointers how I can go about scheduling this into my day or how I can motivate myself to actually do it? Thank you.

Elder Response

Hello,

Not being a morning person either I agree with your lack of desire to get moving too early! I've found that joining a gym and/or getting a personal trainer (often at the gym) forces some people to work out after coming back from their job. The key is NOT to go home after work but go directly to the gym! I've tried it and it worked wonders for me. Once you get home, change your clothes and eat/clean up you're too tired to go out again.

Another option that works is to do your exercises at work. Take part of your lunch time, even 20 minutes, and WALK briskly. Leave a pair of running shoes/shorts/top at work. You can eat a healthy breakfast, have healthy food at late morning/afternoon break. Or, you can get off the bus at an earlier stop and again walk briskly home for 20 minutes. If you walk just 20 minutes daily at a good pace (start slowly at first) you'll be surprised how much energy you get, how many pounds you'll lose and how much tension/stress you'll walk away.

There's also isometric exercises you can do while sitting at work. Clench and release your muscles in your arms/stomach/buttocks/legs 8-10 times each and you'll give them a good workout while no one notices. If you make your dinners on the weekends and freeze them you'll find that you're not so tired at night when you have to cook/clean up, should you want to go the gym right after work. Since you only need to go to the gym twice a week this shouldn't be much of a burden.

Hope some of this helps. Best regards,

Cindy

Timing & Priorities

Dear Elders,

Egad! I am desperate for a mentor who can teach me how to prioritize and find time for my responsibilities and my 'Joy' time! My work is stressful, high pace. The older I get, the less energy and motivation I have for other more important things like my friends, family, volunteer work. If I take good care of myself (enough sleep, exercise, right food, time alone), I feel better but there's not enough time then to call, write, support, visit, pray for, help the people in my life who are important to me, some of whom I know well, and some of whom I do not know (such as in helping anonymously). I know that I'm not much use when I'm tired, overwhelmed, cranky, so I know to take care of Joy first, and then give from within. Yet I am tortured when my 'box' is full and there are things I still need/want to do???

Any thoughts/advice would be much appreciated. Thank you!

Elder Response

Hi. You want it all, but you don't want to prioritize as you must to have your "joy" time not be just another stress. Looking back over my life, I would absolutely have put my family and friends before my job earlier than I did, and I know that I would still have done an outstanding job. I had to feel that I was so important at work that it must have my prime time. Baloncy.

I'd like to know more about you: do you carry a cell phone—ON all the time? What do you do or think about when you're waiting in line? Do you listen to music when you drive, or the news? Or, God forbid, talk on the phone? Do you talk business at lunch time? all the time? Do you ever take 15 minutes and sit quietly relaxed during the day? Do you watch television every night? Do you ever go for a meandering walk?

I always carry a cell phone—OFF. It is for MY convenience, and no one has the number. While I'm waiting in line, I plan a night out, or having friends over for dinner, or decide on a movie I want to see, or what to have for dinner, or where to vacation. What a wonderful way to spend waiting time I can't avoid. I always have my mind with me, and I use it for pleasurable thoughts whenever I can.

I once had to carry a beeper—remember those? I carried it—OFF—and never once (I owned and was running a medical company) did an emergency come up that I could have helped just by listening to it. No serious problems were ever not handled even when I wasn't on-line to discuss them.

What I'm saying is that we all essentially form our own lives, and if we want something enough, we find the time to have it or do it. As someone once said to me when I complained about being too tired to do anything, "If this place caught on fire, I guarantee you'll find the energy to run out of here." He was right, of course.

I send you my best wishes, good luck, and enjoy life.

Arianne

Jealousy

Dear Elders,

I am extremely jealous of my best friend. I want her to do well in life but I want to always make sure I have more friends, beter grades, and better clothes. Is there some way i can stop feeling so competitive all the time?

Elder Response

Hi. This type of jealousy, that is actually envy, is caused by your lack of self-esteem and self-worth. For some reason you think you are impor-tant only if you do better than your friend in every aspect.

You're the only one who can find the solution to this serious problem, one that will haunt you all your life unless you find a way to overcome it. It is important that you accept there will always be someone who can own more, do better, live better, and look better than you. What is the point in causing yourself to suffer from this? This acceptance is a large part of gaining some maturity to see life realistically.

Having the most friends, best grades and best clothes are none of the things I would choose to make my life satisfying. To do the best I can myself, to have close and caring friends, and to look the best I can is what I strive for each day. This pleases me and makes me happy.

I wish you good luck, send my best wishes, and hope you come to the time when you enjoy your unique life without measuring it against the lives of others.

Linda

Overweight

Dear Elders,

i am overweight. i have tried different diets atkins, limit calorie intake, taking appetite suppressant, metabolife, exederdrin, but none of those things helped me to lose weight, it seems i am almost always hungry even after i eat a large meal i am hungry later, i have been walking every day yet i am staying the same weight , i realize that most of my depression is coming from me being overweight. i am open to any suggestions, on a diet that i can stick to, on how to lose weight, on what to do.

Elder Response

Hi there and welcome!

Clearly, if I knew the secrets I'd be rich :)but some things have worked for me and friends: don't eat one big meal (it makes you hungry, as you noticed). Try eating 5-6 small meals during the day…eat breakfast, lunch, dinner but also eat something in between each, a small, healthy snack of low calorie foods (i like yogurt, others like a few slices of turkey meat). Then, we must all understand that it's not only fat but also calories that are important so try to lower your calorie intake slowly but steadily. Also, you need to stay active/exercise daily and don't expect to notice any weight loss for at least a few weeks. Losing 1-2 pounds per week is best because it won't come back. I'd get off those medicines, congratulate myself on wanting to try something different, start slowly and learn to love every ounce of yourself! Best of luck…

Downward Spiral

Dear Elders,

This is a bit strange for me as I am sure it is for you as well.

Before I begin with my current situation I think a little background information is necessary: I am a 36 year old white male. I was raised the middle of three children by a single mother working two jobs so that we could exist in low-income housing. My mother had little time to support us financially let alone any emotional or intellectual support. There was no male influence in my life until the age of 14 at which time my mother sent me to live with my father.

A 14 year-old teenager has about as much use for a commanding father as a man does with a son he's never met. We stayed out of each other's way for three years until I graduated high school. One week later I moved out. I got a job and put myself through college.

Growing up I knew my situation was bleak compared to other children. I vowed that when I raised my family, my children would be the most important focus of my life.

Fast forward 18 years. I now own a successful wholesale meat and seafood business in the Pacific Northwest. I have a beautiful wife and two perfect sons (toddler and newborn). I have accumulated all the trappings of a successful businessman, a dream home walking distance from the Puget Sound; new Lexus, LandCruiser, Porsche. Without the advice of anyone; with no role model for how a successful man should conduct himself, I feel as though I've made a good life for myself and my family.

It is at this point I find my wife has been going outside our marriage and is in love with another man. It is now that the wheels fall off of my life:

I kick her out of our home

I stop working

I start drinking excessively

I start using drugs

I lose all desire to live

This downward spiral continues for almost two years. I sell off my business and declare bankruptcy. My cars are sold or repossessed. My physician diagnoses me as clinically depressed and puts me on medication. I start 'feeling' better but still do not have my former drive. Another year passes, my home is in foreclosure and Im being evicted. My credit is ruined. I am out of money and have only sales jobs as work prospects. This brings us up to date on my situation.

Ironically, I feel in control of my life once again. I guess I thought it necessary to completely destroy the life that I had worked so hard to build in order to move on. Now it is time to move on but now I have this ENORMOUS mountain to climb.

Oh, wise elder of our species, WHAT AM I TO DO?

Elder Response

Climb it!!!

There are many ways to be successful in life.

Learn from your past. Don't be afraid to change. Be honest with yourself about decisions you make so that you can spot destructive tendencies. Love yourself. You can become your own "father" and give yourself "fatherly" love and advice. Love yourself.

Good luck

Liz

Responsibilities

Dear Elders,

i have a summer job. not very unusual coming from a teenager, i admit, but i suppose it's not like any normal summer job. i got the opportunity this summer to homeschool a fellow teenager. i love to teach, and i love to help people. but some days, i just don't feel like doing anything. i get very depressed sometimes, and i just feel like laying in bed to cry…or to sleep, or just to breathe and think. i pride myself in being a responsible person, but there are times when i would rather not have any responsability so i could have the time to do as i please. to sit and write poetry, to watch the world go, and not do a darn thing. i feel that this sort of attitude won't be good once i get around to having a real job afer college…. but i ask myself, will it be worth it? do i really want to be chained down to a job for the rest of my life where i have to go in at a certain time of the day or get fired? i like money, i won't lie…but sometimes i really wonder whether after a whole life…i'll regret not doing what i wanted to do…or maybe if i continue living the way i am…i'll regret not living up to what people expected of me, and letting so many people down…i'll regret not doing anything worth doing. what amount of responsability should i have? is it necessarily wrong to feel and act the way i do?

Elder Response

Thanks for writing. None of your feelings or thoughts are unusual or rare, especially for your age and stage of life.

It will be almost impossible to escape responsibility in your life if you want to have a rewarding and fulfilling one. You don't have to get a job that requires structure and stability, but since you like money, you'd better start looking now for that odd job that will allow you to do only what you want to do when you want it, and still make lots of money. When you find it, tell me so I can get one, too.

I never had a job where I felt "chained down"; I enjoyed each job I held, and continued to search for one with more responsibility, diversity and money. I was very happy working.

I was also very happy raising my family, and that is about as responsible a job as anyone will find. It was enormously rewarding, and still is.

BUT…"there are times when i would rather not have any responsability so i could have the time to do as i please. to sit and write poetry, to watch the world go, and not do a darn thing." There are times called "vacations", and "evenings" and "weekends" that are sort of used for these types of activities (although not as much by many people as they should be, through their own fault).

The degree of responsibility you should have is the amount you can handle, or want to handle. It is more important that you live up to what you expect of yourself and don't let yourself down, more than what other people expect of you, unless they're being supported by you.

By the way, if an employer can't depend upon your being at your job when required, why should you even be hired for it? You're being paid to be there and do that job, not given a choice of when you want to be there and do that. This is called reality, and that's the condition we live in.

There's nothing wrong in how you feel, but I am puzzled as to why, at your age, you're already regretting your future life, when you don't seem to have very clear cut ideas of what you want to do, other than not being required to do something.

You should be optimistic and eager to live your life, discovering all the new and wonderous events, people, occasions, love, work, relaxation, fun, hope….

If you have further thoughts you'd like to discuss, please write again; we'd be happy to hear from you.

Best regards,

Carol

Life

Dear Elders,

I want to ask about life. What makes people wake up each morning and go to work or school? What motivates them to go on living their life even though they don't really know what would happen next. These past days I've been wondering what am I working so hard for when I could just die any moment. What would become of the projects and other things that I've started? I have some reasons in my mind, but I'd like to hear some of yours. Why can't we just stay at home and spend our time with our family and friends instead of going to work or school? Wouldn't life be so much more happier if we were all together with our love ones and enjoy each others company?

Elder Response

Hello. Well, yeah, it'd be fun to just hang around and enjoy everything, for a short while. Who do you have in mind to feed and clothe and shelter you and your family and friends?

I don't now have to go to school or work, but I still get up and get busy. Why? Because I feel like being active, involved and accomplishing something. Call me crazy. I enjoy a challenge and I enjoy being busy. I always have at least three projects going at the same time, and one of my greatest pleasures in life is completing them. Then I start others.

It doesn't matter that I don't know what is going to happen next or when I will die. I live each day of my life as if it were the last. I can't understand why anyone wants to sit around, do nothing and worry about whether they're going to die tomorrow. What a waste of a life.

When I worked I worked hard because I wanted to do my best and I wanted to earn a lot of money, so I did. I still study, still take courses, still learn something everyday. I read always.

When I die, someone will finish what I was working on, or someone will discard it. That is not my worry. I live my life so that when I die others can easily clean up my projects and requests. I feel very prepared for whatever comes next, and am in no hurry for it.

Best wishes, good luck, and enjoy life.

Arianne

Anxiety

Dear Elders,

I have been having a hard time sleeping and feel very anxious and nervous. I believe it is due to the fact that I went back to college after 5 years off. I really don't want to take a prescription drug to cure the lack of sleep and anxiety. Does anyone know of a natural or home remedy for either of these? Thanks

Elder Response

Hi! Thanks for writing :-)

I guess we ALL go through some anxiety at one time or another and to different degrees. Otherwise why would there be commercials on the radio to help us solve our problems . Sometimes trying to find out what is REALLY bothering us is very difficult. Professional help should be sought if it really depreciates and inables us mentally/physically.

In my humble opinion distraction through exercise, hobbies, reading, etc. works wonders. Many small things & worries seem to accumulate in the recesses of our brain. Sometimes we can't quite put a finger on what they are. We just feel "anxious" and worried but do not know why. In exercising we can feel good about our body & it's health. An inner feeling of strength develops. In seeking distractions for the mind we give it a chance to think about other things and the mind develops strength. There is no shame in escape now and then, otherwise Hollywood would go bankrupt! And you can find the time!

I know there are many "natural" herbs, etc. touted as solutions to anxiety (e.g. St. John's Wort). Most have been proven to be ineffective.

Find the time to exercise your body and mind in things aside from work and school. It's the best investment you could make toward a good night's sleep!

Dream Well!

Treefrog

Parents Have Problems With My Expression Of Christianity

Dear Elders,

My parents and family are Jewish. I have recently been doing lots of reading into Judiasm, and I realized the truth of Christ's love. My parents have grounded me and restricted me from going to church. I will not give up faith for their sake, but how can I show them that I'm still thier child and that I love them?

Elder Response

Hello, thanks for writing to us. I am a firm believer that every person has the right to choose the religion that is meaningful to them without interference by other people—as long as that religion is not harmful or approves of harming other people.

I can understand why your parents are upset, because they feel you have no regard for the religion that your family has probably had for generations; change is very hard, especially with something so personal and powerful as religion.

Explain to them that your choice of religion is not motivated by a lack of regard for them and their culture, but by your yearning to participate in the religion most meaningful to you. Tell them you have the greatest respect for them and their choice, but you cannot participate in their religion anymore because you are drawn to another.

I think with a few kind and non-hostile discussions of this subject, they may accept your choice as being your own matter. Do not, however, expect them to agree with you or to stop feeling somewhat as if you have rejected all their values.

I admire your steadfastness in the face of this difficulty and punishment, but as time goes by perhaps your parents will realize their punishment of you is only causing the gulf between you to widen, not changing your mind. It is important that they come to understand there is nothing they can do to change your mind, and punishing you is a futile and mean act. This is a difficult situation, and I wish you all the best of luck and send my best wishes.

Bonnie

College

Dear Elders,

I am a junior at high school. This summer I am spending time looking at colleges and such. I am struggling between the majors I desire to pursue in college. I want to be a criminal lawyer, but some members of my family have other ideas about what I should grow up and become. How can I break it to them nicely that I am going to do what I want to do and not hurt their feelings?

Elder Response

Hello there…

As a former college professor I can relate to the difficulties you mention in your email….lots of college students have similar concerns. Regarding choosing a major for law school, any of the liberal arts or social sciences are good majors; generally avoid Criminal Justice which usually isn't recognized as a strong major by most law schools. Take difficult courses, extra courses in writing and communication and you should do fine getting into a good law school (assuming you have high grades :)).

Regarding your family, my students used to tell me that their parents had career goals for them that they didn't share. This is often hard news to break to parents but there's no reason to go into much detail until you're a sophomore in college so you have lots of time. For the first 2 years of college most students will be taking basic core/required courses that give you a general overview of many fields and a core set of skills and values. Tell your parents that you greatly appreciate their concerns for your future and your career. Don't be hostile or defensive. Listen to their position, thank them for caring about you and tell them you'd like to pursue your dream of law but will keep other options open (which, of course, you should anyway; over 30% of majors are different from the ones that were first chosen).

Good luck...

Tim

Letting Go Of Difficult Experiences

Dear Elders,

About a year and a half ago a man on drugs hit our truck and ran my 8 week old daughter and me off the road. Our truck hit a tree, rolled over and ended up upside down in a ditch. Miraculously my daughter had only a small scratch on her head. I had severe injuries to my left forearm (tendons and tissue) and a broken pelvis, not to mention scrapes, cuts and bruises to my entire left side. Driving a safe vehicle and properly installing our daughter's car seat prevented more serious injuries.

I have recovered well from my injuries and can pursue my work and studies well physically. Since the accident I have finished graduate school and started a new job. I will received my Ph.D. this March. My daughter is a beautiful, active, happy 17 month old. In most respects my life is on track and going beautifully. However, I can't let go of the idea that each time I leave the house to drive somewhere that it may be the last time I see my family. I have no control over what I fear the most—crazy and intoxicated drivers. I see erratic, speeding people all the time and it brings a cold feeling into my stomach.

The trial for the accident is coming up soon, the state's case against this man for felony DUI charges. His lack of ability to decide whether to plea guilty or not guilty and procedural events have delayed the trial for quite a while. I am hoping that finally go through the trial and hopefully seeing this man taken to prison will help the healing process for me. But, I'm not sure it will.

For the most part I am an optimistic person and successful at most everything I set my mind to. There are just moments when I am paralyzed by what if questions—What if I had been killed? What if we had lost our daughter? or worse, What if my husband had lost us both? and What if it happens again? Tears come much more easily than they used to—just signs of raw emotions that were not as close to the surface before this event.

Could you offer any words of wisdom for me?

Elder Response

A little over two years ago, on a sunny Sunday afternoon we received a phone call. It was from our eldest son. It was a cell phone call from Moonlight Beach, California. "Mom…Dad please come, Rebecca is dead". The first and only love of his life, his soulmate, his wife of one year was crushed to death by an eroding sandstone cliff on the beach. He saw it all and, with the help of others, dug his wife up. The trauma he and we felt was excrutiating.

The weeks and months that followed were living hell. We read just about every book written on trauma, trying to understand our son's experience and out own suffering. always trying to answer the big question "WHY".

Finally we went to a psychologist counselor, specializing in trauma. It was a good choice. We were becoming dysfunctional, distracted, inoperative and found it difficult to smile in normalcy. Congratulations on you imminent PhD . At that level of accomplishment you must have come to recognize that there is no shame in seeking help and assistance. With a trial coming up it is even more critical that you get balance and perspective back into you life. Please seek it out for your well being and those you love. It may just help you go on with life without having the answer to the question and fear of "why".

Keep Well,

Paul

Find A Professional

Dear Elders,

I have a friend who's really going through a tough time. I've tried to make myself available, listen, and ask him how I can help, but I think it's time for him to talk to a professional therapist. He's open to the idea, but intimidated by the process. The health insurance company provides a few names in his local area…but now what? Does he make an appointment with each one? What are the questions to ask to figure out who the right person is? I'm concerned that he's just stalling and making himself unhappier in the process, and I don't know what to tell him.

Elder Response

Hello,

Thanks for writing. Finding a therapist isn't as easy as finding a doctor for a broken arm, but here's a Web site with good tips:

http://www.psychsite.org/findther.htm

Basically, it's a process of asking a set of questions of each therapist (type of therapy, goals of therapy, therapists' experience and training, etc.) and then making an appointment to actually meet the therapists. It's mainly after a month or so into the therapy that you'll know if you're working well together. On the other hand, it's always better to have a therapist than not in difficult situations, so encourage your friend to go. It would help if the recommendation of a therapist can come from a patient/former patient, but if that's impossible then go with the list provided to him. It's a bit intimidating, but almost all people feel that way at first. He's lucky to have a friend like you!

Best of luck…

Jules

Is There Anything Wrong With That?

Dear Elders,

I tend to jump from activity to activity, having a new idea for something every day. Sometimes I don't follow through as well as I should. I tend to learn about a lots of different things, but never know everything about any one of them. Should I try focusing on things better or am I just a jack of all trades. My friends tell me both.

Thanks!

Elder Response

Hi, and thanks for writing. You obviously don't have a terrible problem. The first thing that springs to my mind is "Jack of all trades, Master of none." So what?

If you enjoy all that you do, I see no reason to change. If you are frustrated that you don't follow through, then make it a habit to focus more on what you're involved in and finish it. It isn't an impossible task.

I am a jump-about person (my husband calls me a dilettante, which is fine with me), but I do mostly finish projects, because that gives me both pleasure and a sense of completion.

I'd say, live your life as you choose, and don't bother with defining yourself.

Best regards,

Linda

Just Talking

Dear Elders,

well I'm 20 years old and as I get older I notice certain things about myself internally. Their are certain things about me that are not that good that I notice, such as being so nonchalant, keeping my inside feelings locked in. when I was a child I was sexually abused by my step-uncle while my aunt sat there and watched I kept my eyes closed the whole time, and never said a word until I was nine and when I did my family did absolutely nothing and we all went on living like everything was a-ok, except I haven't seen my step-uncle since that episode. He and my aunt separated, so now I realize from that that god it has messed me up in such a way. I find my self wanting to talk about everything I feel now, to improve myself, I find my self wanting to do things like talking to people on the subway, I ride the long island railroad and everybody is so damn quiet on the train sometimes I want to stand up and just speak my mind on how my day was, or talk about anything ask the older women for advice, and I realize that this is because I've kept everything in for so long. what would u feel like if you were sitting on the train and all of a sudden someone stood up and just started talking? I feel that this is something I want to do I think about it all the time.

Elder Response

Hello. I'm sorry you are in pain, and I think you truly do need someone to talk with. I quickly recommend professional therapy if you can afford it. If not, then you still must find a way to release the pressure you are feeling inside.

You have had a very bad experience, and one that often haunts someone all their life; that is why I think it is important you get professional help. Is there some way, some program or some way of funding such medical care?

Sexual abuse is a most serious crime, and one that is even worse if the family refuses to acknowledge it or help the victim. Your step uncle did a dreadful thing, and he should have been arrested and tried for it.

Now, however, the important aspect of this situation is that you find some way to lessen the burden that it has become to you. Do you have a very good friend who would be understanding if you talked about it? Have you ever confronted your aunt and asked her why she allowed it? Have you tried talking with other members of your family?

This is very important, and you must spend some time and thought on how you can gain relief from the feelings you have about it. I do not recommend your talking with strangers about it, however. Most people riding the train are grateful for some peace and quiet, and probably would react badly to your disclosures. You don't want that type of response.

I wish you the best of luck, and hope you come to the time when you can enjoy your life without this black cloud over your mind. Continue to occupy yourself with other matters that please you and make you happy.

Best Regards,

Joanne

Pride Goeth Before....

Dear Elders,

Okay, so I don't actually expect you to have the only answer out there, but I'm hoping someone might be able to provide me some insight.

I feel as if I have too much pride in my life. Its almost as if I'm afraid to be humble. I don't even know how to explain it fully, but I'm afraid that I act in certain ways, due to my pride. Is there any way to make myself more conscious of my actions? I don't know if I'm even giving you enough information to run with here, but I'm hoping you get the basic idea.

Thank you for your insight,

Tom

Elder Response

Hi, Tom. I believe you're saying that you think pride gives you the right to not respect others. Wrong!

Pride is how you think about yourself, and what makes you proud. If you are proud of yourself because you are a good friend, a kind person who can be counted on and so forth, that's good. If you have pride that makes you think you're better than others, that you have the right to be rude or mean, that's wrong. In fact, that makes you less and worse than others who are not so prideful.

Self-esteem has to be built on the respect and liking that we and others have for ourselves because of our actions, attitudes and concerns. It is not a totally self-involved emotion, as pride is.

Many writers have concentrated on this pride that you feel, not many judge it well. The bible says, "Pride goeth before destruction, and an haughty spirit before a fall." Note PRIDE will lead to DESTRUC-

TION, not a fall. Alexander Pope wrote, "Pride, the never failing vice of fools." He's right about that.

Self-rightous pride is destructive to you and your involvement with people. Pride is ofen simply arrogance, never a positive habit. Seek instead to develop your self-esteem and self-respect, and there will be no need to rely on pride to make you wrongly feel superior to others. You have my best wishes and hope that you enjoy your life and live it well.

Best regards,

Edward

6

Elders' Favorites

Family Discipline Problems

Dear Elders,

I am a single mother of 2 girls who has recently moved us in with my boyfriend of 3+ years. Things seem to be going fairly well, but we are experiencing problems in the discipline area. My girls are pretty well behaved, but my boyfriend has asked for the authority of disciplining my daughters when they get to fighting, are mouthy or just simply won't do their chores.

I really want a coparenting relationship with this man and this includes my dealings with my children, but I'm having a problem handing over these reins to him. He has never married, no children, never had a live in relationship such as this and has a bit of a short temper sometimes.

I've really been the only parent the girls have known, their father didn't take much of a role in raising them and I guess I'm just apprehensive about sharing some of these parenting responsibilities. How can I get over this and let him take some initiative in raising them?

Elder Response

Firstly, your boyfriend is NOT the parent of your children.

If you were married to this man, things would be much different, but you are not.

I can only advise that YOU be the parent of your kids, and that you not give your boyfriend this responsibility—it will bring about much resentment, and if you are not married, the commitment is probably not there for long term.

Best—

Cherokee

Living With Fear

Dear Elders,

I had breast cancer surgery two years ago. I subsequently had 12 rounds of chemo & 38 radiation treatments. I did not lose my hair. I am 43 years old, happily married, childless and am a pharmaceutical representative. I just wanted to know how to stop worrying about dying young. My health has never been better. I have changed my diet to healthy food only , exercise everyday and don't drink. When I read or hear of someone's cancer or their returning cancer I feel impending doom closing in. Other days I don't think about it. I am going to church more so that my faith will increase and I will have greater faith. It doesn't always work. How did any of you handle this?

Elder Response

Thanks for writing. I understand your feelings, but I have moved past fear into a great thankfulness for each day. I had colon cancer and while I was in the hospital having the operation, a friend of mine was dying from it.

The problem of worry you have to solve yourself. First, you are lessening the value of each day. If you are having regular checkups faithfully (did you have annual checkups before the cancer was discovered?), along with the other changes you have made, I think you're doing all you can to remain healthy. You must stop worrying, because that's a destructive attitude. Your chances of dying in a auto accident or of a heart problem are also very high, but do you worry about that constantly?

Change from worry into thankfulness and get joy from every day. Make a serious effort to put behind you this fear and instead live your life as we all must do, one moment at a time. Fate will determine when and how we die, we are not often in control of that. Do whatever you must to develop the faith you need to live well, now.

Best wishes and enjoy your life.

Arianne

Children...Is There Ever A Right Time?

Dear Elders,

My husband and I feel very strongly that we'd like to have children. When we got married, we decided that we'd wait till our financial situation was such that I could be a stay-at-home mom. That day has arrived, but I'm not ready! Tho I'm 29 and he's 31, neither of us feels ready to start our family quite yet, but let's face it...the window of opportunity won't be open forever.

A lady I work with mentioned that if everyone waited for "the perfect time" to have children, no one ever would. I'm thinking she might be right, but I just don't feel very "maternal" right now and we're enjoying our first taste of financial stability after years of being students and paying off student loans.

My question is, if we go on waiting for the perfect moment to start a family...will it ever come along? Might it be better to jump in with both feet and just get it over with?

Thank you for your thoughts.

Elder Response

Hi! "Is there ever a right time?" Good question! Way back in history (the 60's) we really didn't bother with that question. We just got married and figured part of the package was to have children and it was exciting to think about that. It wasn't a matter of whether we would have children, it was a matter of how many!But the times were different then. It was almost a given that your wife would be a stay at home mom and dad would be able to support the concept. We didn't think too much about financial stability since we were both teachers . But the prospect of having a child and the responsibility to nurture something that resulted from the love we had for each other was exciting. I do remember very well falling asleep and feeling the life within my wife growing. I have to admit the happiest day in my life was the birth of our first child. Three children and two grand children later there is nothing to regret and only the happiest of memories and now things to share.

To tell you the truth, the right time to have a child is the time when you look into each others eyes and decide that the love you have for each other needs some visible expression, one that you want to nurture and grow. One that calls you "Mom" and "Dad".

Best Wishes,

A Treefrog

Death Of Soulmate

Dear Elders,

Hi my name is Billy and I'm 33 years old and on nov 25 2001 my fiancee Angela died of ovarian cancer. She was 30 years old. Being only 33 I don't have any friends that have been through what I'm going through. I don't really have a question, just looking to chat with someone else who has suffered a loss like mine and has survived it.

Angela and I were best friends, we did everything together. I can't imagine every loving someone like that again and that scares me. I know she would want me to go on but I'm not sure how. I still have her closets full of her cloths and shoes, I haven't moved anything. Any advice would be greatly appreciated. thanks

Billy

Elder Response

Sorry for your loss, Billy.

It is always difficult to lose the one you love, and at your age that loss is magnified. You may wish to find a support group in your area to help you through this.

Most experts believe that getting rid of clothes and other items that remind you daily of your loss is imperative. Donating them to a charitable cause in her name would be helpful to them and a nice tribute to Angela.

Make sure you keep photographs, but put them away, and look at them only when you feel the need. If they're sitting in the open all the time, they will only serve as a constant reminder of your loss.

You will never have another relationship exactly like this one...and you don't want to. When you finally get out and begin dating again, the worst thing you can do to your date or yourself is to compare her to Angela. Every person is different; henceforth every relationship is different.

It will take a while until this loss becomes just a dull ache. It may never go away entirely; after all, love doesn't die just because the person you love dies. But it also doesn't mean you can't love someone else just as strongly.

I wish you the best of luck!

Lydia

Life Patterns

Dear Elders,

Do you see any correlation with world events and the pattern/path of your life? If yes, what would you do differently given a second chance?

Elder Response

Hi! Ahhhhhh! A philosophical query! To be honest I believe that there is no direct correlation between world events (good or bad) and the pattern/path of my life. HOWEVER, I do believe there is a correlation between my life and how it might affect the cause of good or bad events, events around me, and in a small but nonetheless significant part, the world. If I did not feel this way I would cease recycling, keep all the fish I catch, sneer at people on the street, and ignore those who need help. Instead, I choose the opposite and trust that it's contagious.

Second chance? Trying to live as if there is no second chance is the secret! But, if given one I would, as the cliche goes, "sing louder" and "dance more lively".

No one's looking, right?

Best regards,

Treefrog

Today's World

Dear Elders,

After 9/11/01, how do you not let the worries of the war overseas and the possibilities of what the terrorists could be planning at home not drive you crazy and effect your daily routine?

Elder Response

Hello, thank you for writing.

I refuse to let evil men control or destroy my life. Insofar as I am able to do so, I will control how I live, how I think, and how I feel. I will continue to believe that most of humankind is good and decent, and be grateful that is who I live among.

I will continue to believe with all my heart that we and our country are the best that has ever existed upon this earth, and believe that we will continue to strive to be better. I will continue to believe that evil cannot be ignored, but must be bested. I believe to the depths of my soul that "All that is needed for Evil to triumph is that good men do nothing."

As everyone else, I worry. I have a daughter going to the Olympics this week; I'm very worried about her safety. I said not a word to her, and I will never attempt to limit her life because of my worry. She lives in New York City, and she saw the despicable sight of religious insanity. My husband and I got on an airplane two weeks after the attacks. What is our life if we live every moment in fear? This I refuse to do, although I am not ignorant of the danger to us. I simply choose to live and enjoy my life as I can, and fight evil wherever I can. I fear, but it does not rule me.

Best wishes, and may you enjoy a long and happy life.

Arianne

Believe the Hype—About God?

Dear Elders,

The strangest thing has happened to me lately. For a while now I have been keeping a list of wrongs that I felt had been committed against me. Of course this puts me in direct conflict with what the bible teaches, but, I figured I could just write it off as sin. I know that sounds flippant, but, I wanted to hold on to my grudges. However, it seems that the Lord may have had other plans. To be honest, he has put it on my heart to do the exact opposite. He revealed to me that he knew that I was not forgiving people, but secretly harboring malicious thoughts in regards to them because I felt it was only fair. But God had put his foot down, and I have found myself reaching out to people in ways I have not done in at least 7 good years. My question is, is it really possible that God knew my secret sin?

Elder Response

Hi!

Many people who believe in God and an afterlife also believe that "Final Judgement" is actually we ourselves reviewing our lives, the good, the bad and the indifferent aspects. The philospher Pascal couldn't decide if there was an afterlife. He decided he didn't want to "take a chance". He reasoned that if he led a life of selfishness, hatred, etc. he would not feel good about himself and possibly not enjoy an afterlife. He then reasoned that if he led a good life, helped others, held no ill will, he would at least have a satisfying life even if there were no reward in the afterlife. In his case he decided not to take a "chance".

We commit wrongs against each other more than we should, for sure! Forgiving each other's "wrongs" is the first step in committing more "rights". Make sense? Sin seems to be a negative thing, I believe. It's just a lack or void where "good" should be.

As far as God is concerned, God would not be if God was not All Knowing. The concept of the Divine is a tough concept to comprehend because we are human and therefore have all sorts of limitations, including trying to understand how there is a Being with absolutely no limitations in time or space. None whatsoever.

I know there are many approaches to this whole question of good, bad and God. My thoughts are just observations that help me muddle through.

Thanks for writing and keep well!

Best regards,

Julia

Fear of Death

Dear Elders,

Hi...I'm 30 years old and for as long as I can remember, I've had a fear of death. Not just my own, but anyone who is close to me. When I was 11, my grandmother died, who I was not close to, but I took it harder than most people in my family. I didn't know anyone personally who died again until a couple of years ago—my friend died and it really freaked me out. I'm so scared wondering what happens to you when you die. What if there's no heaven—what if that's it? I don't let this fear interfere with my life—it doesn't keep me from doing anything or going anywhere, but I think about it a lot. I think about growing old or getting sick, or losing my husband, etc. I wish I could just accept that the afterlife will be wonderful, but something in me is always questioning, and I feel really sad when I think about not being with the people I love on earth, or them not being with me. I worry about growing old too. The logical part of me says to enjoy life now, because 10 years from now I'll say 'If I was only 30 again', and 10 years later 'If I was only 40 again', etc. Some people say I won't be so consumed with this once I have a child of my own. I hope that's true. While I wasn't raised with that much religion (we did have some), I do believe in God, I pray, etc. I tried going back to church to feel uplifted , but that kind of support didn't really work for me—I prefer my personal relationship with God and don't enjoy the politics, etc. of a church. Don't get me wrong, though...I'm not depressed, I do have fun (I led a very exciting life in my twenties), I have a good sense of humor, and no one (other than my husband) even knows this bothers me. What advice can you offer me on coping with this fear? Thanks for your help.

Elder Response

Hi!

Well, it's something we all have in common, isn't it? We're mortal and we will die. I watch my 85 year old mother living life as if it will go far beyond her life. She will join dad, she knows that as she knows her tulips will burst from the ground and bloom. It's not logical to believe that there is something after death. I think about this every time I see a squeeshed squirrel on the roadway. But we are different. We have intelligence and a soul mirrored in God's eye. We are capable of love and hate, joy and sorrow. We can laugh and we can cry. We can dwell on life and we can think of death. And we can make a worthy leap of faith and believe that there is a heaven and the day to day battles we fight about what is right and what is wrong will count. Otherwise why the battle? Make sense?

Keep the Faith and Enjoy Life and What Follows....

Best regards,

Treefrog

A Teen Seeking Advice

Dear Elders,

Hello!

How are you? I would like to begin by saying that my topic is a bit controversial, but I would like your true opinion and advice, even though it may not be pleasant.

I'm an 18-year old male and live in a rural town of around 1,000 people. I am really struggling with who I am on the romantic level. All of my life, I have been drawn to guys more than girls (a little bit more than just an average boy), and now I'm experiencing romantic feelings towards other guys. I would really like to emphasize that I'm not like other gay guys who adopt the label and move on through life with hundreds of promiscuous relationships.

I have talked to many gay people on the Internet, but have found no one to relate to—they all just seem to be looking for sex and drugs. I know that's not me at all. Currently, I relate best to my friends, both male and female, at school, but when it comes to the topic of romance, I really have to shut them out.

I have set up a website on the Internet which allows gay Christian teens like myself to communicate, and it helps around 100 people a day now—they all participate and help it grow. It's great, but it only exists on the computer—there's no one to talk to in real life.

When I think about it, there really is no specific answer that I'm searching for, just advice from wisdom that only an elder could have. How can I deal with this and still be happy with who I am? I am very interested on how things used to be back 50, 60 years ago, and I have found many old movies from the 1940s and 50s which cover topics like hygiene, responsibility, self-reliance, and some covering the facts of life and growing up—I find them fascinating. I understand that back then, homosexuality was considered to be a mental illness. I cannot find peace by seeing myself as mentally ill and on an equal level, I cannot repress my feelings from myself. It is very possible for me to not share these feelings with anyone—I do this every day, but I would like a person in life to be able to share these incredible feelings with.

So I am seeking you for a real person's view on some of the things I am facing. There are many gay guys that I've found on my Christian website who are looking advice on how to deal with their sexuality, I'm not looking for this advice because I don't plan to have any kind of sexual relationship at all in the near future, I just want somebody to feel romantically close to.

Well, I hope I have done an alright job projecting an appropriate question, and I welcome any insight you may have. Thank you so much for your time!

Elder Response

Hello:

Thanks for writing. It's wonderful that you have a web site for gays. I can imagine that it's hard to find other people to share your interests and concerns in a small rural town. There are many gays who, like you, aren't interested in sexual promiscuity and they have formed many clubs and groups to share their interests, from hiking to book clubs to travel clubs. Check out this Web site:

http://dmoz.org/Society/Gay, Lesbian, and Bisexual/

It has lots of information and gives you a wide range of ways to find local groups. Your best bet for finding people is at a local college or church in a small or big city. I don't know where you live, but there must be some larger city near you.

You're correct in noting that many years ago, gay and lesbians had to hide their orientation, but even then, they managed to have some fun, get good jobs and live successful lives. It's easier in many ways to be gay or lesbian today, but for men especially, AIDS is a real problem that must be dealt with by gay men especially those who are sexually active.

When you're young, your sexuality is still forming and it's common for many young people to explore their sexuality. It takes awhile for one's sexuality orientation to take shape and it differs in how long it takes from person to person. In my opinion, the most important thing is to be true to whomever you are, to be honest with yourself and to be proud of whatever decision you make.

Living as a gay person is not much different than for straight people these days. Similar problems, challenges, hopes and needs beset all persons. It's harder for young gays to find people to talk with, and many gay sites on the Internet, but NOT all, are for men looking for sex with other men. Check out the links on the page I gave you and you'll be able to find groups and clubs where gays meet just to enjoy themselves!

best of luck...

Cindy

Sex Education for Kids

Dear Elders,

California just signed into law allowing teachers to teach about homosexual starting from first or second grade, I think. And the law does not allow parents to make the choice of whether or not they want their children to be attending such class.

Based on your experience and your opinion, at what age do you think kids should be exposed to sex education? At such a young age, don't you think children should be learning more about math, science, and other more constructive subjects???

Elder Response

Hello. Children should be learning about sex from their very first question about it, answered truthfully, in a manner they will understand. Don't get technical, don't lie.

It is extremely difficult for me to understand why we want our children to have incorrect or no knowledge about one of the strongest influences in our lives. They cannot handle their sexuality without having the correct information and knowledge.

We would never keep from our children other information that will protect them and give them the ability to make proper choices, so why do we do it with the subject of sex? It's disgraceful.

I think sex education in the lives of young people, given to them before they need it, is MORE important than what you consider "more constructive" subjects. Correct knowledge will help people become more understanding and less judgmental about the various sexual types, and, I surely hope, more tolerant and less prone to hatred caused by differences.

By the way, the schools are HAVING to teach children the correct sexual facts because their parents either CAN'T, WON'T or DON'T KNOW how to teach their children. Be grateful someone is willing to help them.

Arianne

Mortality

Dear Elders,

Sinatra sings:

But now the days are short,

I'm in the autumn of the year.

And now I think of my life

As vintage wine

From fine old kegs.

From the brim to the dregs,

it poured sweet and clear.

It was a very good year!

I wonder if it is genuinely possible to look back so contentedly without regret for opportunities not taken and frustration with the brevity of life.

How will I deal with mortality? How can I enjoy today unless I know what tomorrow will bring?

Elder Response

No-no-no-no! The proper way to live life is to prepare for tomorrow, but live today. Don't miss today because of worry about tomorrow.

I've had a lot of very bad things happen in my life, and there were times I was extremely depressed and wondering if I wanted to continue to live.

Today I am serene, happy, contented, excited about life, and have so many moments of JOY that I feel blessed. I train myself never to worry about the shortness of life, and attempt to enjoy each day as I live it.

I think living life teaches us the value of it, and that's why we should reach out to savor the pleasures and good times. It helps a great deal if you can help someone else with their problems, which is what we hope to do here.

I suppose it's possible my days are short, but I am not in the autumn of my life—I'm still in the excited-with-life stage; I think I'll stay here until my life is over. I don't like that autumn thing. But so far, my life continues to be vintage wine. It doesn't have to deteriorate.

Best wishes, and I hope as each day goes by that you find another wonder in living.

Arianne

Problems with Dad

Dear Elders,

I have never had a close relationship with my dad. we don't have any big fights or anything, we just view everything in a different way. He is very stern and strict. The only time I seem to talk to him is when he is yelling at me. I never get a "good job" or "I'm proud of you" from him. I'm not seeking praise from him just a friendship. recently i did something really bad that deserved his punishment. but it seems like he'll never get over what i did. I'm so sorry for it and he knows it wasn't intentional but its so hard to tell. i appreciate my dad for everything he does because he works really hard for your family but i just wish we could get along better. i have a hard enough time just talking to him let alone telling him how i feel about all this. i don't know what to do. my uncle always tells me you don't appreciate something until its gone. I'm afraid that when I leave for college and don't see my parents that often I'm going to regret not having a closer relationship. what should i do?

Elder Response

First of all you must tell yourself that you are a worthy person. If you did something wrong, you should apologize to those you wronged. This is something you did once and does not make you a "bad" person. You are a unique person, with certain strengths—emphasize those and don't dwell on the few mistakes that you might make. Second, realize that not all daughters and fathers have close relationships. If you take the first step and tell you dad that you think he is a swell guy for working so hard to provide you and your family. This will make you feel good that you took the first step toward building a closer relationship with your father. There will be times when things seem rough but try to set aside a few minutes each day when you can talk with your dad.

Things will improve and you will know that you started working on a better relationship with your father.

Best regards,

Linc

Am I In Love?

Dear Elders,

I dont know what else to call you. I hope that's ok. I want to know how you know you are in love. I think I'm in love. I love this guy. He's sweet and understanding and everything I've ever wanted in a guy. I just don't know if its love. Every time I see him i get weak in the knees. I want to know how you know you are in love. How do you know?

Yours Truly,

Melissa

Elder Response

Hi Melissa,

One measure of love is when there is but one piece of bread between two people and starvation, and one or both insist that the other eat it.

Weakness in the knees has also been known to be a clue.

Enjoy!

WO Owl

Interested in History

Dear Elders,

I want to know what it was like for you when you grew up. What the time period was like, and what restrictions you had as a teen, and what you and your friends did for fun. Did you have to work a lot? Did you or your friends ever do drugs like kids today? What do you regret about your life? I'm so interested in the history of other people, especially people who have been alive much longer than I, but my grandparents are all dead so I can't ask them. I would really love to hear from you! Tell me anything you can.

Thank you.

Elder Response

You have asked the questions that no one asks—bless you.

When I was a teenager many decades ago, things were pretty much the same as they are now insofar as parents complained and kids rebelled. And as a female teenager, it seems very odd today to tell you that girls did not wear pants to school or just about anywhere else—even when it was freezing outside—we couldn't wear them under our dresses! I was never allowed in jeans—in fact I never owned a pair of jeans until well in my thirties, and felt a little risque even then! Of course now I wear them every day.

For fun we listened to music, went dancing, got together at the malt shop (really!) gabbed, gossiped, went to movies together. We had curfews and were generally put on restriction if we were late. If drugs were in use, it was only by the most depraved drug addicts. We thought it was scandalous if someone was known to have had beer at a party. Some kids snuck out to the parking lot for cigarettes but they were the *bad* kids—they skipped school a lot, wore their pants around their ankles and lots of grease in their hair; the girls were automatically "sluts."

I started babysitting around 12, then went to work at the local drive-in theatre at 16. If I wanted anything beyond the necessities, I had to buy it myself and I found nothing odd in that, most of the kids did. We were taught more of a work ethic those days I think, sort of a "you don't work, you don't eat" philosophy. I kind of like that still.

My biggest regret is that I did not go to college. It would have been extremely difficult for me to do so, but I should have and could have fought to make it happen. The lack has made an incalculable difference in my life.

I would like to have been braver, tried more scary things, taken more trips, written in a journal every day. I would have gotten married much later in life—had children much later and then quit working to spend each and every day watching them grow. This is especially poignant to me, as I lost a son and so deeply regret not having had more time with him.

There was a lot less permissiveness in my youth; somehow I think we've lost something: we've gained *rights* and *equality* and our freedom of speech entitles us to damage anyone with words. I'm not sure this is progress. I'm not sure we've increased the possibility of the pursuit of happiness for us all, but rather have made that which is basest about our natures gain ground, while that which is fine, such as character, honesty, integrity, have become almost laughable, or at least, unrecognizable.

Well my dear, I have gone on too long…you have the whole world before you—grab it. Enjoy.

Cheryl

Teenage Daughters

Dear Elders,

Hi! I am the mother of 4 girls. They are 17, 8, and twins who are 3. I am married to a navy man who is gone for six months at a time. My oldest daughter and I have had a love/hate relationship for quite a while which I assume is normal. But now she talks about moving out when she turns 18. I am secretly overjoyed to have her out of the house. I feel guilty about feeling that way but I am tired of the fighting and the example she sets for her younger sisters by her teenage attitude. Is this normal or am I a horrible mother?

Elder Response

Hello and thanks for writing. Sounds like you and your teenage daughter are on the right track. As long as she is mature enough to handle living on her own, I don't see any problem with her moving out. In fact, you both might benefit from the change.

I would tell her that I think it is a good idea for her to be on her own. Then, I would help her get a place and set it up—offer her items from home, shop with her, help her clean, paint etc. This is important, so that she feels supported rather than abandoned as she makes this transition into adulthood. Let her make her own decisions regarding decorating, etc. and give her praise and support whenever you can. Even though she wants to move out quickly, it doesn't mean she no longer needs your love and encouragement.

Most mothers and daughters have a closer relationship when they no longer live together and the daughter is allowed to grow up and pave her own way in the world.

Best of luck to both of you and hope the transition is as smooth as possible.

Frangi

Career Aspirations v. Relationship....

Dear Elders,

I am a young college student, just beginning that struggling search for my first meaningful job. I am very insistent on pursuing my passions, of which I probably have too many. My studies have been centered on non profit management, and I know I have the ability to go really far and do a lot of good for people. I realize this sounds rather idealistic, and perhaps naive, but thats what I figure I'm supposed to do in my twenties...dream a little. On the other hand, I have a wonderful boy-friend...everything I could probably want in someone. We are both graduating college the same day...his studies have been in computer graphics/programming. As most people in this situation, I feel a defi-nite pull between pursuing my passions/career, and continuing with this relationship. I'm not positive that he's the one I want to marry, but maybe I'm just too young to figure that out. (I'm 23 by the way) He and I have had our talks about how we would try to compromise after college, but I don't know how I will actually feel at the time. I also am afraid that if I ended up giving up my relationship, further in my life I might look back and deeply, deeply regret losing that. Maybe I just worry too much, but I think it is sometimes difficult for women to imagine this wonderful career we have spent time preparing for, and then on the other hand want a family and obligations that tie us down at the same time. I feel if I get married, I'll end up having children before I'm ready, making it very difficult to pursue grad school...etc. I just feel very confused right now...I used to feel I really knew what was most important, that the people in your life are more important than anything...but as graduation approaches, I get more and more excited about career opportunities because the sky is the limit to me.

Have any of you gone through this point in your life? How did you make such tough decisions? I know taking risks is part of life...just need a little help with this one.

Elder Response

Hello, and thanks for writing. Women facing relationships, marriage, children and career path do have a handful on their plate! I think it is most important to realize that we need to pursue what is important to us—whether it is primarily family, career or some combination of both. All choices involve both risk and accommodation. In that sense, we have to be willing to make reasonable sacrifices in order to reap the rewards of our choices.

You sound like you want both a family and a satisfying career—if you approach this decision with a sense of balance you will make wise choices along the way. Why give up either of them? Keep in mind that doing both means neither will get your full, undivided attention but both will get whatever they need from you. That, to me, is the key to success.

You already have a wonderful career laid out and are filled with dreams for success—good for you! You also have a good relationship with someone who is everything you could want. Sounds to me like you already are learning how to juggle these two aspects. So, just continue on and let your life evolve in its natural way. As for children, there are disadvantages and advantages to having them right away versus waiting a while—let your heart tell you which is right for you!

Keep us posted as you navigate these exciting waters.

Frangi

Should I stay or should I go?

Dear Elders,

Hi there. I have been a teacher for six years and I absolutely LOVED my job the first four years. But now I am so burned out I don't know what to do. I work every night when I come home for about 3 hours and I work a ton on the weekend too. I am putting in 60—80 hour work weeks and am only making around $35,000. I am so busy that I hardly have time for my social life. I never went in to the profession for the money, but now it is getting hard to accept my unbelievable work-load for such a crummy salary. Plus most members of the community have no respect for teachers or what we do. No one knows how much work a teacher does unless you live with one and witness first hand all the work that goes into being an excellent educator. Parents aren't always supportive and some kids can be so disrespectful and lazy. I really thought I would be a teacher forever and most of the time I really love what I'm doing and I love almost all of my students. They're great. I am good at my job and I have good relationships with my administrators and my students. But I feel that I am at a point in my life where I need to make a life decision of staying in this job or moving on. I have a masters degree so I am sure I could get some other type of job. I'm just nervous about starting over and not sure if it's really what I want. Am I just burned out or are these signs that I am in the wrong profession?

Thanks.

Elder Response

Hi:

First, you are working too long and too hard. Ease up—you CAN be a GOOD TEACHER and in less time than you are putting in, then too, after six years, you have matured as a teacher and maturity in ANY worker means less time on any job.

Enjoy being with the kids you teach. This is more important than correcting papers, etc. The kids will know you are on their side and you will find that THEY are on your side also, so it makes a good learning situation for both you and the kids.

Cut way down on the paperwork—you are there to teach CHILDREN, not PAPERS. Enjoy!!

The worst thing about being a retired teacher is that I miss my students. You are lucky in the sense that you still have your students.

Take the summer off and come back refreshed and rested. Remember, it's the kids, not papers that count.

Fondly,

Coog

Helping a Drug Addict

Dear Elders,

How far should a parent go in helping a drug addicted 18 yr old daughter who won't work but want money, food, etc. to avoid enabling them yet to show them love, too.

What steps would you take to help get them into a rehab if they are unwilling to get help?

Elder Response

Hello and thanks for writing...

I've had 2 relatives whose children were addicted to drugs and have counseled many college students about their drug problems, so I can empathize with this painful and difficult problem somewhat.

Many parents today face this problem, as you know, and there are no easy answers or quick solutions. The good news is that your daughter is young and can still have a good life IF and only if she admits her problem and seeks help. Until she does that, nothing and no one can really help her. Often, an addict must hit rock bottom before asking for help. If and when she does that, I'd be sure to give her all the support and help that I could.

Until she does that, however, you should be careful to not, as you say, enable her addiction by accepting her refusals to work or go to school, etc. She needs to realize that she is in charge of the kind of life she leads and that her choices to do drugs have consequences for her and for her family.

Have you been in touch with Narcotics Anonymous (NA)? Here's their National Web site:

http://www.wsoinc.com/

Like AA, they often have support groups for families with addicted children and I'd strongly suggest you find one and join. Your daughter might be interested in going to a meeting, without you, as former addicts are the BEST source of helping those still addicted, in my opinion. Addicts generally refuse to listen to or believe those not addicted, but may do so coming from former addicts.

Have a talk about drugs with your daughter, telling her that you will not allow her to live off the family as a drug addict. Give her a few several weeks to 2 months to find a job, enter a rehab program (they're often expensive but some public ones are less so),join NA or move out.

Tell her lovingly, calmly, without judgmentalism that you love her, want to help her, but can't support her addiction. This is so hard for you and the family, I'm sure, but if you really want to help her, lay out her options and then let her make her choices. You'll get more tips and information from NA as well.

Bless you in what will be a long, hard struggle but there is no way to cure addiction until and unless addicts admit their problem and seek help.

Best of luck,

Cindy

Raising 2 Boys

Dear Elders,

I would just like to know any words of wisdom! I have 2 boys, 3 1/2 and 1. They are wonderful children, but I feel that anyone who's ALREADY raised boys must have something to pass on to me! Discipline tips, things you wish you had done, things you wish you hadn't, etc. Thanks!

Elder Response

Read to them.

Teach them to say please and thank you.

Do not let them hit anyone.

Don't threaten them if you don't intend to carry out the threat.

Praise them when they do something nice or clever.

Don't scare them.

Celebrate their birthdays and special events.

Play with them regularly.

Don't hit them.

Treat them equally.

When they do something wrong, explain why it is wrong.

Best regards,

Scott

Marriage Assistance

Dear Elders,

My husband and I have been married for four years. We have two boys (ages 3 and 1). I am a stay-at-home mom. My life is great other than I feel like there is something missing. I love spending time with my kids. But, all day/everyday is a bit much. I have no friends close by, just a phone call away......My social life depends on my hubby bringing buddies home to hang out in 'his' garage. Drinking and b-s ing is what goes on. Sometimes, wives are here, sometimes just single men. My trouble started when I stayed up later than my husband. I would continue drinking and socializing with the remainder of guests. I became interested in a guy. We would talk about how controlling my hubby was, etc.... Any how, one night we ended up kissing and my husband walked in and saw us......We don't want a divorce. I feel like I need some 'new' attention though. I did talk to hubby about his controlling me, and he seems to be trying to be more relaxed and understanding. But now, he doesn't trust me (which I understand) But, I miss talking to a man who says all the right things.........

Elder Response

Your first mistake was staying up alone with the guys. The second was the obvious one of kissing a friend of your husband. Now he has no respect for you and will feel free to have affairs with other women. Your only choice is divorce or living together under a strain. Any time you fight, he will bring up the kissing incident. He will assume that you have kissed other men and perhaps have had sex with them. The burden is on your shoulders—you married for better or for worse. And where was your husband and the other guys when you were kissing his friend??????

Best regards,

Scott

Keeping Children Focused

Dear Elders,

I would like the advise of someone who successfully raised children who are productive members of society. In a world entangled with drugs, tragedies, and self-importance, what are the keys in raising kids who remain grounded?

Elder Response

Thanks for writing. You've asked an extremely important question. Our children desperately need help.

1. You must maintain their respect. This means you have to act appropriately and ethically. You must be consistent with discipline and praise. You must be truthful and be a good role model.

2. Discipline, don't punish. If a child continues to do something after a parent has said no, remove the child from the room. DO NOT sit there watching him continue to do what you've told him not to do; you must act promptly. Do this as often as needed. Don't yell.

3. Teach respect for other children and adults. Do not allow over-familiarity, talking back to adults or bad language in your presence or your home. Demand politeness at the very least between all of you.

4. Take time to be with—and talk with—your children EVERY DAY! Have family dinners each day if possible; talk with each child separately about his/her day, pleasures or problems.

5. Be very sure the children understand and obey all rules of the household, and make certain other children also abide by the house rules.

6. Love your children; don't try to pacify them with money or things, LOVE THEM TRULY.

7. As they get older, offer help but not advice, unless asked. Offer knowledge but not orders. Help them become the independent person they must be to cope with this world properly.

8. Under no circumstances allow drugs into your home, or into your children. Be aware of your children so you can pick up the first hint of a drug or alcohol problem. They need you!

9. Take time to have activities with your children, including family vacations, however short. Even a day off together is a vacation.

10. Respect your spouse and children and demand respect yourself. Learn the value of a person, and teach it.

I asked one of my children once why they had not become involved with drugs. The response was, "You told us if we used drugs you would throw us out of the house, and we believed you would."

I asked another who had been a very difficult and troublesome young child, "Why and when did you decide to change your behavior?" He said, "When I realized you weren't going to stop making me behave, and that I would never win against you."

This means tenacity is absolutely, positively REQUIRED to raise a child of whom you are proud. You cannot give up just because the child has become difficult, or has created problems in your life. You CANNOT give up. This brings me to my last advice:

11. YOU are the adult. It is YOUR responsibility to make good rules AND see that they are followed. You CANNOT allow your child to dictate to you what is proper behavior, or how he is going to behave, or treat you and other people. THAT IS YOUR JOB—to teach your children good, not bad; following rules, not breaking them; keeping laws, not getting arrested; teaching kindness and concern for others; love for the world. And a millon more things you will think of during your child raising years.

It can be done, it has been done, it is still being done, but not often enough, nor well enough. Sure, you want to have your own life and live it the way you choose (perhaps you should have considered not having children), but your first priority and responsibility is to the children YOU brought into this world. If you cannot give your children what they need to live a good, healthy, fulfilled, kind life, then you are a sorry specimen. With love and responsibility and a desire to see your children have a good life, any child can be raised to be a happy and secure adult.

Good luck, best wishes, and do enjoy life.

Arianne

Help with Difficult Parent

Dear Elders,

I recently found this site via volunteermatch.com and I think it is truly a wonderful site. Now, I'll get to my question. I am 33 years old and have had a verbally abusive mom for as long as I can remember. she has destroyed all of the good relationships that have ever come her way. She has been depressed for as long as I can remember. I have begged her to get help for her anger/depression since I was a kid. We have had many times when we stopped talking and right now we are not talking. She is not talking to me because she is very demanding and wanted to ask my husband a computer question when he was busy. I told her that my husband was busy and she said thanks for nothing and hung up. she is very controlling and she hates it when she can't control me. I have a child and this is her only grandchild. When is enough enough? Would it be emotionally better for me to discontinue contact or should I keep this emotional roller coaster ride going? Thank you very much for your time and advise.

Elder Response

Hello,

In response to your inquiry:

Decide what kind of relationship you really want with your mother. This is your decision alone. If you decide that you want a good relationship, then meet with your mother face to face (even if it takes some doing on your part) and agree on ground rules between you. This again is an agreement that both of adhere to.Make sure that she understands that you want a good relationship with her. Tell her that the consequences will be what you decide them to be (example: she cannot see her grandchild if she breaks the agreement). If you decide you do not want a good relationship with her then tell her that due to her attitude and actions, you do not wish to see her again.

Good luck!

Robert

College

Dear Elders,

I am a junior at High School. This summer I am spending time look-ing at colleges and such. I am struggling between the majors I desire to pursue in college. I want to be a criminal lawyer, but some members of my family have other ideas about what I should grow up and become. How can I break it to them nicely that I am going to do what I want to do and not hurt their feelings?

Elder Response

Hello there…

As a former college professor I can relate to the difficulties you mention in your email….lots of college students have similar concerns. Regard-ing choosing a major for law school, any of the liberal arts or social sci-ences are good majors; generally avoid Criminal Justice which usually isn't recognized as a strong major by most law schools. Take difficult courses, extra courses in writing and communication and you should do fine getting into a good law school (assuming you have high grades :)).

Regarding your family, my students used to tell me that their parents had career goals for them that they didn't share. This is often hard news to break to parents but there's no reason to go into much detail until you're a sophomore in college so you have lots of time. For the first 2 years of college most students will be taking basic core/required courses that give you a general overview of many fields and a core set of skills and values. Tell your parents that you greatly appreciate their concerns for your future and your career. Don't be hostile or defensive. Listen to their position, thank them for caring about you and tell them you'd like to pursue your dream of law but will keep other options open (which, of course, you should anyway; over 30% of majors are different from the ones that were first chosen).

Good luck...

Cindy

Any Advice For A Jobless College Grad?

Dear Elders,

Hi there. Here's a quick description of my situation and maybe you can help me out with a little advice. I graduated from the University of California Berkeley in June '01. I've been unable to find a long-term full-time job since then. I've held several temporary positions and I went on a study tour overseas for a month and a half. While I'm not strapped for cash since I'm living with my parents, I'd like to find a suitable job soon. I was wondering if you experienced something similar at the corresponding time in your life and what you did in the job search and in the spare time. Thank you for your time.

Elder Response

Read you request for advice with great interest.

The overall tone of the request seems to emanate from an individual who has not yet faced the necessity of having to provide for himself.

As to your specific questions:

1) No, I have not had a similar experience at a corresponding time in my life.

In my early twenties I returned from military service in WW II. My first objective was to get a job—not necessarily a "suitable" job, just one that would enable me to move out of my parents home and establish my own life.

2) My job search consisted of asking relatives and friends for assistance and scanning the "want-ads" in the newspapers. I had a job within a week of arriving home. Not a great job, but it paid the rent and fed me. It required four job changes over the course of five years before I

landed the job that turned out to be "suitable"—where I spent the majority of my career.

3) I had no spare time.

Advice:

1) Find a job, any job that will provide you an income adequate to be on your own—not dependent on your parents for food and housing.

2) Move out of your parents home and establish your own "home."

3) Forget about finding a "suitable" job—you probably wouldn't recognize a job as suitable until you had worked at it for several years. I believe that it takes several years for an individual and his employer to determine if their relationship is mutually advantageous.

4) Forget about finding a "long-term" job—no one will offer you "tenure" from day one.

Conclusion:

Given your educational background you probably have the intelligence to be of value to some organization. What you do over the next five years or so will, in my opinion, be crucial to your long-term success—financially and emotionally.

What you have to do now is prove that you can work at something longer than a few months. Every job has good and bad aspects and you have to prove to some future employer that you have stuck to a job long enough to experience both aspects.

Best regards,

Joe G.

Timing

Dear Elders,

When is the right time to tell someone you love him?

Elder Response

When you're absolutely certain its love and not hormones. How do you know its real love? Here's an old test and it works remarkably well; If that person's happiness means letting them go and you can do that without a word of reproach or a cry of pain. You feel deep inside of you that you want that person to be happy and nothing else matters. And its nice if they feel that way about you too.

Best regards,

Cheryl

Epilogue

Thank you for participating in the Elder Wisdom Circle by reading the book in your hands.

Please visit us at **www.ElderWisdomCircle.org** to become part of the ongoing virtual community by connecting with the Elders and seeking to mine the wealth of experience and wisdom they hold.

Or, visit the website to become an elder, and help guide and advise people with questions, just like all of us, at every point of life. From moments of cheesecake crisis to infidelity to deciding what the next career move is, we all have a definite need for an elder in our lives.

About the Author

Blanche Anderson is a fictional representative of the EWC Elders and serves as the volunteer Cyber-Editor-In-Chief. Blanche is the voice of the Elder Wisdom Circle. She acts as our Virtual Editor and as an icon to our online community.

0-595-24909-4